# THE GOTHAM LIBRARY
## OF THE NEW YORK UNIVERSITY PRESS

The Gotham Library is a series of original works and critical studies, published in paperback primarily for student use. The Gotham hardcover edition is primarily for use by libraries and the general reader. Devoted to significant works and major authors and to literary topics of enduring importance, Gotham Library texts offer the best in literature and criticism.

Comparative and Foreign Language Literature:
Robert J. Clements, Editor
Comparative and English Language Literature:
James W. Tuttleton, Editor

The publications of this book has been aided
by a grant from The Andrew W. Mellon Foundation

Djuna Barnes

# The Art of Djuna Barnes
# Duality and Damnation

Louis F. Kannenstine

New York • NEW YORK UNIVERSITY PRESS • 1977

Copyright ©1977 by New York University

Library of Congress Catalog Card Number: 76–55152

ISBN: 0–8147–4564–4 (cloth)
      0–8147–4565–2 (paperback)



**Library of Congress Cataloging in Publication Data**

Kannenstine, Louis F.    1938–
    The art of Djuna Barnes.


    (The Gotham Library)
    Bibliography:  p.
    Includes index.
    1.  Barnes, Djuna—Criticism and interpretation.
I. Title.
PS3503.A614Z75      818'.5'209      76–55152
ISBN 0–8147–4564–4
ISBN 0–8147–4565–2 pbk.

Manufactured in the United States of America

# Acknowledgments

Primary thanks are due to Djuna Barnes for her cooperation during publication and for her generous permission to quote from her works.

The photograph of Miss Barnes appears through the kind permission of Berenice Abbott.

Dr. Robert L. Beare and his staff, particularly Susan Cardinale, of the McKeldin Library at the University of Maryland, College Park, were extremely helpful and informative while allowing me to examine the Djuna Barnes Papers.

The librarians of the Academic Center Library of the University of Texas kindly permitted me to consult the Djuna Barnes material in the Charles Henri Ford archive.

I am greatly indebted to a number of individuals, and especially John Kuehl, for information, advice, and encouragement. These are: Alice Quinn, Stanley Lewis, James W. Tuttleton, Douglas Messerli, Elyse Bloom, Peter S. Jennison, Bart Auerbach, Frances McCullough, Alex Gildzen, Linda Kuehl, M.L. Rosenthal, David Greene, Kenneth Silverman, Despina Papazoglou, Robert Giroux, and Coburn Britton. I greatly appreciate too the replies to my inquiries from many others who unfortunately were unable to assist.

Special thanks are due to Margaret Lampe, who offered numerous suggestions regarding references, and much more.

# PERMISSIONS

# Contents

# Introduction

Djuna Barnes is generally regarded as a minor American author, and nearly all of her work has been neglected. Only *Nightwood*, her poetic novel of 1936, has found a place, however unstable, in literary history, and one suspects that it survives more on the strength of T.S. Eliot's introduction of 1937 than on its intrinsic merits. Most readers are totally unaware of or unfamiliar with her six other books, partly due to the fact that most of them have been erratically in and out of print since their first publication. In addition, there is a sizeable amount of her work that has remained forgotten since its appearance in various little magazines, popular periodicals, and newspapers of several decades. Interest in rediscovering and preserving the diverse material has been insufficient so far to warrant new collections.

When Hilton Kramer reviewed *The Selected Works of Djuna Barnes* in 1962, he regretted the absence of "a comprehensive essay that would place Miss Barnes's work in the context of those modernist expatriate writers with whom she began publishing in the 1920s," an introduction which "could have done much to clarify her work for a new generation of readers."[1] Similarly, Sylvia Beach had stated that her strange and melancholy work "did not resemble that of any other writer of the time," and that, as one of the most talented and fascinating of the Paris literary figures of the twenties, she "doesn't seem to have been given her due in books on writers of the period."[2] James B. Scott's *Djuna Barnes* of 1976 was a first attempt to fill a gap by providing an insightful introduction to the main body of her work. Although chiefly concerned with the evolution of her language, form, and style, this book-length study aptly deals in its course with Miss Barnes's relationship to the "lost generation." The assumption behind the present study also is that it is indeed time to give Djuna Barnes her due, first by establishing the literary context within which her work belongs, and second by recognizing its formal achievement and thematic consistency, qualities not readily apparent upon a piecemeal examination.

To acknowledge Miss Barnes's place among the literary figures of the twenties, however, is but a first step. It is true that in that decade she first appeared in close association with such independent expatriated women as Margaret Anderson and Natalie Clifford Barney, and shortly thereafter as a disciple of James Joyce and T. S. Eliot, concerned with applying their particular discoveries of the flexibility of the language to areas of her own concern. Later on, *Nightwood* summed up the spirit and the residual despair of the expatriate years, while coming to its own terms with the interest in dreaming and subconscious energy stimulated by the studies of Carl Jung and then applied to literature by Eugene Jolas and the contributors to *transition*. But beyond its relation to the literary attitudes and trends of its time, Miss Barnes's work became progressively involved in assimilating and coordinating itself with literature of past periods. One might justly consider her as one of the "last classicists," as George Steiner calls Eliot and Joyce in a recent estimation, whose "works are crammed with quotations from, allusions to, pastiches and parodies of the best art, music, and literature of the previous two thousand years. They were not destroyers but custodians of tradition,"[3] and their work, once revolutionary, now appears as essentially conservative.

Certainly Miss Barnes's work has come to the attention of later generations of experimental writers. In 1955, Melvin Friedman, speculating upon the progress of fictional techniques beyond the refinement and eventual exhaustion of the stream-of-consciousness method, predicted that *Nightwood* would become a particularly influential book in the second half of the twentieth century, as singular a model for fiction as were the works of Proust and Joyce earlier.[4] Its distinction, he goes on, lies in its stress on pattern and its "devotion to the word," its poetic essence, in short, which differentiates it from action-based narrative or the novelistic dependence upon "the index of thought" in stream-of-consciousness fiction. As examples of works which sustain the tradition of the lyrical novel which, in Friedman's opinion, *Nightwood* exemplifies, he cites Buechner's *A Long Day's Dying*, Styron's *Lie Down in Darkness*, and Lowry's *Under the Volcano*. There are suggestions that Lowry's novel and Durrell's *Alexandria Quartet* may have been influenced to some extent by *Nightwood*.[5] Both are examples of a type of work which depends for its design upon the "intricate cross-reference of image and symbol," a factor which both Friedman and Joseph Frank recognize in *Nightwood*. The point is that, in these several prose works, poetic technique serves not to embellish or flesh out the narrative but to reformulate narrative design in the first place.

Further evidence has accumulated as if in support of Friedman's claim. Since certain practitioners of the "new novel" have begun to undertake an articulate reevaluation of their inherited narrative means of fiction, *Nightwood* has come to appear as a pivotal book, a precursor of the time-liberated interior novel. A recent study by Sharon Spencer,[6] for instance, places it in the broad context of postsurrealist "architectonic" novels which attempt, through a tap on other media and other literary genres, to liberate character and narrative from restrictive traditional unities by means of new structural principles based upon juxtapostion in space. With increasing frequency one finds such experimental writers as Anais Nin stating that her formative roots are in Djuna Barnes, or John Hawkes noting the influence of her "extreme fictive detachment," her "pure and immoral" creation[7] upon his own work.

Miss Barnes, however, has remained aloof from any literary movements. When the final issue of the *Little Review* was being planned in Paris in 1929, Margaret Anderson sent out to all its contributors a questionnaire consisting of ten concise and basic questions about their lives and work. Djuna Barnes's reply was, "I am sorry but the list of questions does not interest me to answer. Nor have I that respect for the public."[8] Since the early 1930s she has held firmly to this attitude, living most of the time in New York as a recluse, "a form of Trappist"[9] by her own definition, radically detached from her readers and critics alike. Consistently maintaining her privacy, she rarely permits interviews, provides no glimpse into autobiography, and has withheld any contribution to a theory of literature. Largely because she has published infrequently and irregularly in later years, Miss Barnes's work has been evaluated only sporadically and its position in contemporary letters remains to be established. Her literary reputation at large reflects her isolation, as in the erroneous statement of a reviewer of *The Selected Works*, "Miss Barnes influenced no one; traces of influence upon her are equally hard to find."[10]

Beyond Miss Barnes's absence from the public eye, there are other obstacles which must be met before any such evaluation can be made. In the first place, Miss Barnes presently carries the reputation, despite actual fact, of being a "one book" author. Since T. S. Eliot aptly classified *Nightwood* as a novel with a primary appeal to readers of poetry, most critics have assumed its special distinction on one basis or another, so that the novel has become inadvertently detached from its literary context and consigned to a kind of vacuum of acclaim in which it appears to be a product of some miraculous origin standing virtually alone. It has thus become ready game for literary cultists, devotees of 1920s expatriate lore or proponents of "camp" culture. On the other hand, critical scholarship has not been unkind to the novel. Essays of such critics as Joseph Frank, Wallace Fowlie, and Kenneth Burke have sustained its critical reputation at least in academic circles. However, the possibility that Miss Barnes's collective works might possess thematic and stylistic connective tissue has been generally overlooked. Despite the highly prismatic nature of her career—she has turned up at various times as a novelist and short story writer, poet, playwright, newspaperwoman and theatrical columnist, frequently as a portrait painter and illustrator of her own works—she remains customarily thought of as the author of a single enduring novel.

Djuna Barnes, moreover, has become a difficult writer to classify because of her fluctuating involvement with diverse genres. She began her career as a poet and evidently intends to end it as one, but might she not be more properly regarded as a novelist on the basis of *Nightwood* (or *Ryder* or *Ladies Almanack*)? Is her achievement to be estimated by the spare naturalistic prose of *Spillway*, or by the ornate blank verse of *The Antiphon*? An author who does not work within the boundaries of conventional categories is apt to irritate readers and critics. But in Miss Barnes's case, her early efforts arose from a clear need to transcend traditional generic limits in order to produce writing marked by a unique architectonic quality. Her finest work incorporates the structural properties of the diverse artistic genres in a way that creates a distinctive and unified effect. After Eliot's introduction to *Nightwood*, its affinities to modern poetry cannot be overlooked, and both musical and dramatic elements have been noted in attempts to schematize its complex structure. Components of rococo and baroque design as well appear in the construction and texture of the mature works, fulfilling patterns of visualization developed in both the illustrations and the descriptive techniques of the earlier prose and poetry. In short, what may have appeared at times as random creativity was actually the gradual maturation of a supple style appropriate to Miss Barnes's thematic concerns.

Finally, her writing has been called obscure often enough to classify her with a reputation that blocks recognition of the manner in which each book extends and elaborates recurrent motifs. Hers are works of an undeniable complexity. This appears to arise from three principal sources: a poetic style that draws heavily upon and modifies traditional literary conventions while making use of image and symbol in a modern way, that is, by multiplication of connotations through contextual variation; an oblique approach to narrative which, distrusting linear progression of action and chronological character development, reveals the timeless undercurrent life of its characters; and a tendency, despite a fondness for aphorisms, to imply rather than directly elaborate the themes. In addition, throughout her career, Miss Barnes has shown a persistent concern with the refractive elements of experience that the naturalistic literature of the last century had bluntly excluded. Djuna Barnes's art is marked by its poetic imagery, by what Natalie Clifford Barney called "bribes de sensations," and by a determined avoidance of abstractions.

The resultant ambiguity, then, is essential. The choice to subordinate plot and its concomitant notion of progressive character evolution to fragments of sensations, to eschew abstractions and base narrative upon impressions, presupposes a view of human existence as unstable and altogether tentative in the face of fundamental problems of a baffling universe. A root theme in Miss Barnes's work involves mystery, or, more precisely, the human condition of nonunderstanding, of onto-logical bewilderment following from the historical loss of the patterns of existence available in the old faiths. As the only irrefutable absolutes, birth and death, are themselves myster-ies, intermediate existence is wholly enigmatic. All of the former certainties have vanished along with the systems of thought and religion that maintained them. Behind an illusion of progress, Western history has been a complex record of dis-unity and disharmony, of dislocation and disassociation, resulting in a dead land of empty forms not unlike the waste-land of Eliot. Miss Barnes's view of modern civilization is accordingly highly skeptical. The more advanced and *figée* Western society becomes, she appears to say, the less resistant is its façade or "massive *chic*"[11] against the basic force of the sub-merged primitive.

The individual who finds that he cannot summon reason or convention to combat inner forces that threaten his sense of order and sanity is a familiar figure in Miss Barnes's short stories. Nearly all of her work conveys the impression that the old Christian dichotomies of body and soul, carnality and spirituality, still persist. In the modern age, however, there is no Church to sustain the quest for spirituality but only residual institutions that console by providing or condoning lies. Also, in the contemporary social order, there is no scope left for the animal or instinctual in human nature. So civilized man is as far from the primitive element within himself as he is from the state of holy grace. Figures of animals and saints proliferate in Miss Barnes's books, but the human creatures are either more or less dog or saint, beast or angel, at any moment tending toward or away from either condition. Their lives are struggles to become one unqualified whole, either one thing or the other, but they are blocked by the recognition of their duality, their inescapably fractured being. A vision of original Edenic unity and completion may dimly persist in the form of dreams, myths, and fragments of historical record and memory, but the post-Edenic state is summed up best in Matthew O'Connor's words in *Nightwood*: " 'Man was born damned and innocent from the start, and wretchedly—as he must—on these two themes—whistles his tune.' "[12]

Mankind, in short, is abandoned to a "middle condition." Like the ladies in *Ryder* who are seen only going to and coming from church, or like Robin in *Nightwood*, described as at once child and desperado, whose incessant wanderings at night signify her nervous identity of beast turning human, one is never at rest but constantly moving to and fro between the elusive ends of experience. To perceive oneself, as in a mirror, caught at any moment in the unstable process of ceaseless becoming, forever half a whole, is to experience terror. So the groom in the story "A Night Among the Horses," suspended between the natural world and the cruel *raffinements* of society, fears becoming like the figures which support the roofs of old buildings, half standing and half crouching in "the halt position of the damned."[13]

Only an effort of literary detachment is able to arrest the flux of experience long enough to capture images of the intermediate state of being on the "grim path of 'We know not' to 'We can't guess why.' "[14] In *Nightwood*, an image is called "a stop the mind makes between uncertainties."[15] The author's detachment is like that of the camera eye, as in the silent moving picture which had found how to pick and isolate significant detail from an ongoing stream of sequential action and, by the technique of montage, transcend the frequently mundane requirements of plot and dramatic structure. But this goes beyond the literary camera eye of, say, a Dos Passos, which selects and records surface phenomena in the interest of panorama. As it is guided by the vision of the poet rather than the hand of the historian or teller of tales, the intent is to rescue illuminating images from transience and hold them in memorable and revealing juxtaposition.

To speak of detachment with regard to Djuna Barnes is to imply her relationship to literary tradition as well. From the following examination of her work in its course of development, it will appear that she is related to the main literary movements of the early twentieth century: Symbolism in its persisting influence, *fin de siècle* decadence, expressionism, imagism, surrealism, stream-of-consciousness, and possibly others. But despite conspicuous affinities, the work cannot be said to belong to or strictly represent any of them. And the same is true with regard to the literature of the past. After *Ryder* and *Ladies Almanack*, in which Miss Barnes's parodies of past and present literary modes are fairly obvious, the late books form a body of work which seems both innovative and traditional, and whose debts and sources are more difficult to confirm. Various critics, working backward from contempoorary references, have called them Gothic, Jacobean, and Elizabethan.

In effect, as the writing transcends limitations of genre or medium, refusing to become confined or delimited by the principles it has mastered, it also reaches beyond the historical literary modes and systems with which it reveals familiarity. This movement outside the literary categories and periods is in perfect accord with the author's philosophy, which seeks to erase the line drawn between past and present by textbook historians. It is in the intricate shaping and phrasing of the work from the 1930s on that the effect of this becomes fully apparent. The diction becomes increasingly filled with archaisms, and contemporary usage becomes recharged with the lost vitality of past forms. Miss Barnes's language develops backward, as it were, gathering up what had been discarded, recovering lost property. Under the conviction that the present is "a dial without hours,"[16] her final achievement is a manner and style of no particular era, and thus of any era.

Passages of *The Antiphon* and all of the few recently published poems seem both in and out of time. They project the modern sense of despair and disillusionment that the 1920s left to successive generations of writers, while they continue to sustain the note of generalized or universal misery of Doctor O'Connor's monologues in *Nightwood*. Their lines are intensely worked and tightly constructed into complex units that stand firmly on their own ground, independent and resistant to ultimate breakdown or exhaustion by analysis. These highly formal late writings are evidence of their author's self-effacement, of a willful depersonalization of voice through which the work stands independent of its creator. In addition, they shun contemporary literary trends to such a degree that they seem at times to exist outside of the modern age. Rather than be seen as a representative author of her time, Miss Barnes would appear to prefer to join those anonymous writers of the past whose often fragmented works survive on the basis of their genius and lasting pertinence. It is not the least of many paradoxes in her work that the act of depersonalization has resulted in a notable particularity.

As Miss Barnes's art can be seen as both related to its time and yet apart from it, it can be concluded that she is a transitional writer whose purpose was to get out of the mainstream and participate in a great tradition, and who now takes a place in her own time between the early innovators of this century and the later generations of experimental writers. She reached her point of full development in *Nightwood*. The early writing, however, set the tone of all subsequent work. From the beginning, the author struggled to reconcile contrary impulses to be in and of the world and to be apart from it. From the tension between these contraries, in turn, there developed parallel conflicts between the rational and irrational, and between light superficial and dark subjective interpretations of experience. The extroverted levity of much of Miss Barnes's journalism gradually gave way to a melancholy that also characterized her early poetry, just as her stories and one-act plays, and her novels of 1928, displayed a mordant wit playing against a deepening pessimism. By *Nightwood*, Doctor O'Connor's soliloquies possess a black, tormented ferocity in equal measure with a comic, histrionic intensity, so that Roger Shattuck's remark that he has long imagined the doctor played by Groucho Marx "in his greatest role—a tragic farce"[17] is less outrageous than it may sound at first. And *The Antiphon*, as it swings between its low and high levels, combines coarse irony with tragic eloquence in a manner recalling the equipollence of the comic and tragic in Elizabethan drama. Ultimately in Miss Barnes's works, laughter and lamentation, the comic and tragic, became distorting mirrors of each other. The distinction is not unlike that in *Nightwood* between light and dark, day and night; they interpenetrate, and as they merge at deeper levels of the subterranean life, the dichotomy is seen to be an illusion of waking rational perception. Such a vision, arrived at through the art of distancing, gives the work its unity and its merit.

The assumption behind this study is that Djuna Barnes's middle vision comes to its fullest expression in *Nightwood*, that that immaculate novel is indeed a masterpiece. To let it stand alone as representative of a full career, however, is to deprive the novel of a good share of its merit. *Spillway* and *The Antiphon*, rather than being blind thrusts in new directions, follow from *Nightwood* in a precise and logical way. It may even be argued that *The Antiphon* is a work of comparable value insofar as it gives final shape to Miss Barnes's central themes. Certainly both companion volumes to *Nightwood* in *The Selected Works* greatly amplify the themes and stylistic attainments of their predecessor. Likewise, the uneven and sometimes flawed work before *Nightwood*, if seen with attention to the emergence of qualities that finally cohere in the novel, may reveal merits that have been overlooked. Even the early popular journalism, seeming hardly to bear upon a cryptic and subjective novel of 1936, may suggest something of what was to follow.

# The Art of Djuna Barnes
# Duality and Damnation

# 1.

## Early Journalism and Essays

The earliest phase of Djuna Barnes's career was a varied and productive one. Following her upbringing and private education, first at Cornwall-on-Hudson, New York, where she was born on June 12, 1892, and then on Long Island, Miss Barnes came to New York City at the age of twenty to study art at Pratt Institute and at the Art Student League. She began to publish poetry as early as 1911, and her small volume of "rhythms" and drawings, *The Book of Repulsive Women*, appeared in 1915 as one of a series of chapbooks issued by Guido Bruno from the Greenwich Village garret where he had exhibited her drawings and pastels. In addition, Miss Barnes was involved simultaneously in theatrical activities with such groups as the Washington Square Players and the Province-town Playhouse, where three of her one-act plays were produced in 1919 and 1920. But it was primarily through the medium of popular journalism that she was able to support herself while allowing her diverse talents to develop.

Bruno, in the columns of his several publications, provides occasional glimpses of Miss Barnes as a creative young woman in Greenwich Village in its heyday of bohemianism at a time when she was unable to decide "whether to become a great artist or a great writer,"[1] doing "her dreaming and planning in a quaint garret in that memorable old house where Jenny Lind used to stop during her visits to New York and where for the first time in America, 'Home, Sweet, Home' was sung."[2] "Djuna Barnes," Bruno wrote in 1915, "is one of the few young Ameri-

1

can artists who walk their own way. Not willing to make conces-
sions to publishers and art editors, she is using her pen to earn
her livelihood as a newspaper woman, and permits herself the
luxury of being an artist just to please herself.' "[3] For nearly a
decade before her departure for Europe in the early 1920s,
Miss Barnes reported and wrote numerous illustrated feature
articles and stories for first the *Brooklyn Eagle* in 1913, the *New
York Press* and *New York Morning Telegraph* between 1914 and
1917, and eventually most of the major New York newspapers.

James Joyce once told Djuna Barnes that "a writer should
never write about the extraordinary, that is for the journalist."[4]
It was a piece of advice that Miss Barnes herself might have
been able to offer. As a newspaperwoman, she had already
begun to discover that success in her medium largely
depended upon an eye for the extraordinary at the heart of
events. Her assignments were highly diversified. In addition to
straightforward reportage of events, her duties involved at one
time or another  interviews, book and drama reviews, and feature articles on a vast range of subjects, even including stunts.
"For the *World*," a *Time* interviewer reported, "she did 'stunt'
stories, including being hugged by a New York gorilla, being
forcibly fed in order to tell what it felt like."[5] A wide variety of
perceptions was also characteristic of her illustrative work.
Many of her drawings appeared independently of her articles,
from early sketches in the *Brooklyn Eagle* of assorted street
types to numerous drawings of literary and artistic figures,
including Robert Frost, Eugene O'Neill, Mina Loy, Marsden
Hartley, and Gertrude Stein, most of which appeared in the
*New York Tribune* in the early 1920s. But apparently Miss
Barnes's most recurrent subject, whatever her approach, was
the theater, and her many articles on the subject, most notably
those in the *Morning Telegraph* and the *Press*, were prepara-
tion for her later, more sophisticated work as a theatrical columnist in *Theatre Guild Magazine*. Far from limited in scope,
her early pieces included not only interviews with great figures
of the day, such as Wilson Mizner and Helen Westley, but also
frequent excursions into vaudeville and the continuously
fascinating world of the circus.

While during these years Miss Barnes was producing poems of a personal sort that were uniformly muted and of a pastoral-lyrical nature, her newspaper writing displayed, above all, high exuberance, an active and colorful response to the active everyday world. This work, moreover, took her regularly to and from opposite ends of the social spectrum: from the headquarters of the IWWs, or the rough world of backstage sports, as when interviewing the heavyweight champion Jess Willard, to theatrical dressing rooms, fashion shows, and the world of titled elegance, as for a *McCall's* interview with the Duchess of Marlborough in her Blenheim Palace. When Natalie Clifford Barney commented upon "l'extraordinaire capacité de l'auteur à saisir des milieux qu'elle avait toutes les raisons d'ignorer,"[6] she was possibly unaware of the actual extent to which the young woman in question had observed and registered her impressions of contrasting milieux and personalities.

Immediately evident in the early newspaper writing is an innate ability to match an appropriate image to a passing impression, in other words, a poetic impulse. Jack Hirschman's observation on a representative essay of the twenties by Miss Barnes, "Vagaries Malicieux," applies to the earlier and hastier journalism as well: "The article is structured something like an American's travelogue of Paris, containing the new cliché café imagery, the adulation of intense literary life. But within the context Miss Barnes writes descriptions of sights which have impressed her more deeply than the mainline attractions, and, when she does, she writes no longer as a journalist but as a literary writer."[7] Although Miss Barnes did continue into the 1930s to furnish on occasion strictly objective reportage on demand (as in a 1934 *Cosmopolitan* article, "Marrying Around the World: Arab-Morocco," a straight description of Mohammedan marriage customs and rites), the inclination of nearly all of her prose apart from fiction was in the direction of the literary essay. This may be seen in examples of reportage from the *New York Press*, in her random creative essays and literary sketches, and finally in Miss Barnes's last and most sustained body of popular journalism, her theatrical columns and articles in *Theatre Guild Magazine* appearing monthly from January 1929 until September 1931.

Miss Barnes's prose essays, then, fall roughly into three categories. The first is the body of daily tabloid journalism, including reportage, with some apparently unsigned, interviews, etc. Certain articles, however, moved beyond the stylistic scope of matter-of-fact reportage to take on "literary" characteristics: use of epigram, metaphor, and various devices of fancy to transform witnessed events into poetic experiences. Such pieces lead to the more purely creative essays that appeared in little magazines, popular sophisticated periodicals such as *Charm*, *Vanity Fair* and the *New Yorker*, or *Theatre Guild Magazine*. A third type can be distinguished as well, a sort deliberately and outrageously employing artifice and mannerism in portraying the *haut monde* of leisure and status as distinct from the mundane world of commonplace effort and pain. The most extreme examples of these sketches are exercises in style.

The personality of the journalist is, of course, least evident in the pieces devoted to daily reportage and in the interviews. When at her most self-effacing, Miss Barnes simply sets a scene and lets the subject speak. Interviewing D.W. Griffith for *McCall's* in 1925, she briefly informs us that she spoke with the film director and proceeds to quote him without intervention. As an aspiring playwright, it was inevitable that Miss Barnes would find the form of the one-act play effective in certain cases. So a meeting with Lou-Tellegen in the *New York Press* becomes "A One-Act Encounter," and an interview with May Vokes is subtitled "Scene From a Play That Took Place in a Dressing Room in the Longacre Theatre." On some occasions, however, the interviewer's own impressions are simply suggested in her accompanying sketch of the subject. Then there are times when there seems to be something in a speaker's personality that is communicative beyond the verbal. In these cases, the eye of the artist takes over. Here is how Miss Barnes sees Jess Willard: "His head, having been overlooked by Sargent, is reproduced in every forest where cutters have been— that gravely solemn thing, the stump of some huge tree staring in blunt Rodinesque mutilation from the ground."[8] Or, in

" 'I'm Plain Mary Jones of U.S.A.' Insists 'Mother' Jones," the reporter's vision penetrates the veneer of plainness:

> And after that she sat down. A little ponderous below the belt, but sitting straightly in a high-backed chair, her hands folded in front of her—gnarled, crooked fingers, bent in a lifelong attempt to straighten things. Shadow beneath her lace, her little chin resting on the beads of her throat. Her black dress leaning about her and the ruffles of her bodice curling and welting over her breast—a small Niagara upon the bosom of a torrent.

The verbal portrait is then rounded off epigrammatically: "Mother's movements proclaim her age—it takes eighty-two years to produce activity of the head with the inactivity of the hips. Upon thinkers, death steals from the feet up; upon laymen, from the head down."[9] Such a literary quality is equally apparent in the various feature articles, particularly in their reliance upon epigram and metaphor. When Miss Barnes states that "Despair betrays itself in epigrams; when one wants to build, one begins to gather. The Bowery boy gathers pictures that express his mind, clippings that express his heart and phrases that express his education," she is laying the foundation of her mature poetic-novelistic method. Here, writing about her visit to an IWW meeting, she approaches the report itself by precise epigrammatic steps:

> There are two classes of people: those who wear caps and badges and those who wear hats and canes.
> There are two kinds of reform: that which is above the collar and that which is below.
> Also there are two types of resignation: that which is gained upon the knees and that which is gained by the fist.

But when the account itself begins, "Coming into this hall, one has no illusions. It is as straightforward as a painted woman,"[10] it is apparent that a private response to the atmosphere is active beyond the reporter's obligation to dispassionate observation.

The most significant of Miss Barnes's newspaper pieces stand as examples of subjective journalism. Besides the elements of literary technique that draw upon visual and poetic terms, certain attitudes and themes that are central in the later works begin to appear. For instance, in "Djuna Barnes Probes the Souls of the Jungle Folk at the Hippodrome Circus," there is the duality of the animal and human, of nature and civilization that is to recur in different contexts: "Animals and children; this is the state of creation, after that it is civilization." Unlike Marianne Moore, however, whose observations of animals were rendered with an almost naturalistic objectivity, Miss Barnes's recurrent fascination invariably tends toward the dark subjective. Although the drawings and poem, "Jungle Jargon," that accompany the account are capricious, as are occasional alliterative touches in description and in the personification of animals, the main note is of awe at the "inquitous past" of the beholder as it is reflected in the beasts. "There are animals which not only possess a presence; they also possess a kingdom," writes Miss Barnes: "Of those are the lions, and, to my mind, as purely tragic is the tiger." But the trained bears, "giggling chorus girls of the jungle," project "banter in the bulk, the jeer from the jungle, the hint of a possible knowledge of those corners of the human mind supposed to be secret." Here is stated what is nearly everywhere implied in subsequent writing: the beast mirroring the dark animal unreason submerged within but out of sight of civilized man. Miss Barnes concludes, "as they came off to descend to the stables below I turned my head away. I'm glad my mother does not know as much about me as those elephants."[11]

This gift for uncommon observation, expressing a need to bring to view the hidden, marginal yet vital aspects of experience is typical of many of these articles. It is the impression of an event rather than the event itself that is predominant. The high point of one backstage visit is when the Picadilly chorus girls, performing in "To-Night's the Night," come off the stage and drop from the stage manner into the human manner, a "passing from sunlight into shadow":

It is all seen through a peculiar gray dusk, thin yet almost impenetrable, yet fraught with a million moving memories, vague yet deeply pregnant with what has been. Almost sombre and still gay, like the laughing face of a widow beneath a veil.

All interiors have this gray dusk. Cathedrals have it, when it becomes profound; stages have it, when it becomes a suppressed giggle.

It is night which has been shattered into laughter; it is also laughter with the restraint of night.[12]

The effect of dusk in an impression which occurs in "Vagaries Malicieux," one of the two essays of 1922 that recount Miss Barnes's meetings with James Joyce. This essay, the bulk of which records in the manner that Hirschman mentioned the author's impressions and sensations upon her arrival in Paris, is particularly notable for its contrasting tones and attitudes which merge in passages descriptive of churches. At one point, Miss Barnes is walking with a companion:

Coming into the lower end of the city, where the shadow of Notre Dame makes all filth and despair holy, we paused. In the darkness of the quai a middle-aged woman worked on a mattress, and nearer at hand, one dishevelled man shaved another, dipping the rusty razor into a shallow bowl of dark water, resting on the steps leading up into the outer world.

These images, sharing the precise quality of those which accompany Madame von Bartmann's passage through Marseilles in the story "Aller et Retour," take on the profundity of the gray dusk of cathedrals. In the shadows in which they are cast, they assume a ritualistic significance and an aspect of timelessness. Earlier in this essay, however, the author writes,

"I put on my cloak and went out to Notre Dame in the sad, falling twilight, and wandered under the trees . . . until, coming upon an old woman selling oranges, I thought how bitter and quick the odor was, and how charmingly unnecessary it was of them to be like that—and on this unnecessity I came into my own."

These contrasting reactions of cathedral profundity and charming unnecessity, then, develop from nearly identical perceptions. Early in the article, Miss Barnes had anticipated going abroad in terms of the familiar opinion, " 'Well, of course, I know that all philosophies contradict themselves in the end, so I have made it a point never to do anything about it, until I visited Paris, then I knew that I just had to express myself.' " That which is expressed follows from a condition of suspension between two opposed philosophies and attitudes, or moods. From the mid point between them, either may be entertained and held viable. The problem is nearly identical to the one that preoccupied F. Scott Fitzgerald in *The Crack-Up*: how to continue to function even while holding opposed ideas in the mind simultaneously.

The next passage further illustrates the author's detachment:

> But Notre Dame somehow leaves you comparatively untouched, you may not remember her for fear of intruding. She is a lonely creature by preference. She is not disturbed by those devotees who fall into two classes; those going toward, and those coming from, faith. She is in the centre condition, where there is no going and no coming. Perhaps this is why, for me, there was something more possible in the church of Saint Germain des Pres, the oldest church in Paris. It is a place for those who have "only a little while to stay"—It too is aloof, but it has the aloofness of a woman loved by one dog and many men. And here one takes one's tears, leaving them unshed, to count the thin candles that rise about the feet of the Virgin like flowers on fire.[13]

From the perspective of a "centre condition" with respect to the contrasts and contradictions in human philosophies and states of being, the author fluctuates between two impulses.

One is to treat experience as a series of what are in essence small epiphanies, as when the squalor surrounding Notre Dame takes on a profound significance in its shadow. The other is to render life in terms of the purely and gratuitously aesthetic.

The pose of the aesthete quickly becomes a familiar one in Miss Barnes's articles. A young girl in her "malicious years" tells Miss Barnes, " 'I hope you will suffer prettily in Paris.' "[14] In "Little Drops of Rain," one of the numerous sketches appearing under the pseudonym "Lydia Steptoe," a nine-teen-year-old girl explains that "suffering is a fine, fine point, and when it's very pointed it purifies."[15] The precocious and high-strung girl in "The Diary of a Dangerous Child," deter-mined to whip her older sister's lover, "stood on the balcony and suffered sideface."[16] A typical figure in Miss Barnes's work, she too is on the verge of early sophistication and poss-essed of an "uncontrollable longing to go to the dogs,"[17] a longing to become a "wanton," a "vixen," a "virago" rather than a wife and mother. She assumes that "One must not look inward too much, while the inside is yet tender. I do not wish to frighten myself until I can stand it."[18]

The attitude is perfectly serious, though it deeply involves the frivolous. It is perfectly summed up in the statement, "After all, life is merely a matter of succumbing becomingly."[19] Suffer-ing becomes tolerable, even purifying, if it is done prettily. "Going down" is bearable if it is within an aesthetic context. The result of such an attempt, not to deny, but to ward off the necessary anguish of mortality is an extraordinary emphasis upon surface and manner, an unnatural stress upon superfi-ciality, upon unnecessity. With the affectation of boredom and world-weariness, the important things of life become elements of facade: the elegant pose, the proper touch of ornamentation in decor or in costume. In "The Woman Who Goes Abroad to Forget," the narrator claims that "a woman never forgets so well as when she is dressed for the part."[20] This is a version of the sensibility of camp, insofar as one kind of camp art has been defined as "decorative art, emphasizing texture, sensuous surface, and style at the expense of content."[21] It is the aesthetic attitude that "sees everything in quotation marks,"[22] that is quick to italicize so as to enhance "the degree of artifice, of stylization."[23] When the "dangerous child" writes, "Ah! What ideas have I not had eating creams slowly, luxuriously,"[24] the experience is one which wears the mask of style, making minor sensation perversely become major. The irrelevant is affirmed to be significant, a stimulus to exquisite fancy, as when Miss Barnes digresses in "Vagaries Malicieux:"

> . . . the bird market filled me with unassuagable emotions. I wanted to have five frail girl friends to send them to. Five little girls who should sit in a row with closed eyes and hands open, to receive five perch-crowding linnets. And failing this I should have liked to send five little pies to five dying queens, each pie the grave of some melancholy swallow, or red-breasted thrush, and to have the death-bed word rise from among the falling of yellow feathers.[25]

Passages of this nature, and there are many, stimulated by initial contact with continental chic and old-world sophistication, echo the art-for-art's-sake detachment of *The Yellow Book*, the mode of the decadents that would render aesthetic all emotions, appearances, and matters of life, including death. Lydia Steptoe in "What Is Good Form in Dying?" suggests that "there is a ritual of good form for death as there is for life!" This parody assumes that there is a "correct manner in which a young lady must die." and that that is determined by a lady's coloring. As she dies by hanging, "A blonde must keep two things in mind—line and color." By contrast,

> For the cold, the cruel, the heavy-lidded vampire of the brunette order, for one who moves slowly, like a wolf-hound, what is alloted to her in the etiquette book of death?
> Poison.[26]

The red-haired woman, however, has alternatives to absolute

death, or to the death by boredom that the really superior person suffers:

> Seclusion, for instance, far, far from the madding crowd; countries one may visit; fourth and fifth dimensions one may overtake. There are . . . all manners of black and white magics, and timeless religions, and faiths that take a red-haired woman out of herself.[27]

Precious though the passage may be, it is impossible to overlook the serious prophetic note that it strikes.

In short, the essential quality of such literary sketches of Djuna Darnes is their dogged unseriousness that rides over the apprehension of human anguish and instability. The play of imagination over the surfaces of things is incessant. The function of this frivolity is not actually to negate seriousness, or to try simply to alleviate it by a dose of wit, but rather to keep it off in some corner in fear of the eventual experience of it. For the red-haired Miss Barnes, journalism seems to have provided a means for getting outside the self, for being of the world and on its surface. The dark subjective, at the same time, could be tentatively investigated through the more personal medium of lyric verse. The anguish of estrangement. of being lost midway between outer and inner being, between the laughter of the virago and the lamentation of the saint, could be explored in fiction and in the theater.

Miss Barnes's withdrawal from the social world and from the popular press which began at the end of the twenties became so total that she is now infrequently remembered as an active, sometimes dazzling, always imposing figure in literary and social circles. On June 5, 1929, Walter Winchell could write in his syndicated column "About New York," "Djuna Barnes, the femme writer, can hit a cuspidor twenty feet away." However, when recently asked about her early years, Miss Barnes summed them up as "'so very, very desperate,'" and explained,

"Years ago I used to see people, I had to, I was a news-

paperwoman, among other things. And I used to be
rather the life of the party. I was rather gay and silly and
bright and all that sort of stuff and wasted a lot of time. I
used to be invited by people who said 'Get Djuna for
dinner, she's amusing.' So I stopped it."[28]

Her impatience with the day-to-day superficiality of her
journalistic work had been indicated in no uncertain terms in
*Ladies Almanack* in the declaration that "Life is represented in
no City by a Journal dedicated to the Undercurrents, or for
that matter to any real Fact whatsoever."[29] Yet Miss Barnes was
not to turn her back upon commercial writing altogether until
after the two years during which she served as a regular
monthly contributor to *Theatre Guild Magazine.*

These articles concerning the on- and offstage worlds of
the theater are indicative of a mature journalistic style, adept
and flexible enough to handle a variety of subjects and assignments while sufficiently individualistic to sustain two regular
monthly columns. In their scope, the pieces fall into the lines of
Miss Barnes's journalism in her broader career. First there are
the articles on emerging or prominent theatrical personalities.
In presenting such figures as Alla Nazimova, the director
Chester Erskin, the young scene designers Jo Mielziner and
Mordecai Gorelik, or the playwright Rachel Crothers, among
many others, the form is that of the biographical interview
which Miss Barnes had continued to develop through occasional articles on various leading figures of the culture of the
twenties in Europe and America. A *New Yorker* "Profile" of Eva
Le Galliene may be taken to illustrate the discipline brought to
bear upon these subsequent theatrical portraits. The author,
while introducing the subject in the context of shifting
theatrical mores, brings her to reflect upon the values implicit
in the changes. A later article on the stage costumer Margaret
Pemberton similarly becomes a little essay on the drama
inherent in fashion and how, in contemporary secular times,
"The Stage Sets the Style."

While certain of Miss Barnes's observations on the
condition of the modern theater will be of particular interest

later when considering her work as a playwright, here it may be observed that a dominant theme emerges in these essays. As Lydia Steptoe tells her butler in "Hamlet's Custard Pie," ". . . Giles, the theatre is on the downward path." But, as Miss Barnes's other writings bear out, the state of drama is only one instance of the decline inherent in civilization's advance. "Giles," Lady Lydia continues, "man was born a fumbler, but he was also born with a brain. Now as we move away from the domain of the mind, that factor which makes of the primitive impluse the civilized action; as we advance on reality without contemplation . . . what do we see?" On the stage a slapstick Hamlet, symptomatic of a condition where "Nobody will inherit today, because we fumble with less, instead of more finesse."[30] In essence, the essays become an effort of restoration, on the one hand to bring back an element of finesse by their style, on the other to revive a diminished sense of contemplation.

A number of the examples are, accordingly, reminiscent. "Portrait of a Crook" assumes that stage crime has come to lose the quality of fancy that actual murder also lacks in modern times (as reflected in the cinema's exploitation of gangland slaughter), and proceeds to sketch out a crime plot with not a few philosophical frills. "The Dear Dead Days" laments how love is portrayed on the contemporary stage; the end effort of Gounod's Marguerite deprived of sentiment, or Wilde's Salomé portrayed without her reverberating evil, is neither a "high" or "low" love, but "the middle class love, which is now a democratic 'grab all.' "[31] And "The Days of Jig Cook" recalls the lost ideals and feeling of communal preciosity that had belonged to the Provincetown Playhouse. In short, the modern theater has suffered a loss of mind, passion, and style, as is revealed by the comparison of the techniques and presuppositions of past and present.

Miss Barnes's illustrated monthly columns "Playgoer's Almanack" and "The Wanton Playgoer" reinforce this theme in their subject matter and in their execution. The drawings are in the manner that had been developed in 1928 in *Ladies Almanack,* a flattened-out style modeled after the vivid and

often playful representations in antique chapbooks and alma-
nacks. The double-page spread of the "Playgoer's Almanack"
offers a decorative proscenium within which, according to an
almanack's diurnal and eternal cyclical character, the author
may introduce bits of legend and past theatrical lore alongside
of timely gossip, observation and reflection, and critical
opinion on the stage and cinema. The mock naiveté of the pictures blends with the verbal wit  that elevates the commentary
above mere offstage chatter. When illustrating, for instance, a
prediction,

> That Dame wit will take some Englishman, in mid-
> career, with the Desire to write Of the American Scene.
> Which play will Be a warre episode, with an all
> Female caste, known as social satire.[32]

a hovering Dame wit embraces the cranium of an Edwardian
gentleman, pen in hand, while a cloud overhead literally farts
in approbation.

Here again the frivolity coexists with an underlying pessimism which surfaces with persisting frequency in the later
articles. When "The Wanton Playgoer" replaces "Playgoer's
Almanack"[33] in April 1931, there appear signs of exhaustion.
The illustrations become fewer, more incidentally and quietly
decorative (but no less delightful), the everyday information
and chatter diminishes, and the anecdotes become more reflective and drawn out, small essays in themselves. The former
world-weariness, initially an affectation, has become a burden;
no longer turned toward parody, it has become charged with a
*plus ça change* awareness that more and more preoccupies the
author. The attitude that "One lives, one wears out, and after a
while one sickens of it all"[34] is sometimes implicit, at others
openly voiced, but present everywhere. The fact of rewriting
certain plays for Negro actors stimulates the protest, "What is
the use of all our days if history is not allowed to stay history?"[35]
Or a production of the opera *The Bartered Bride* reminds Miss
Barnes "of the days when I was young and could still believe
that life was going to turn out like the inside of an easter egg—
those hollow ones with people and lambs in them, roses and

green pastures. For being reminded of the days when we did not know any better, is all that is left to us when we do."[36] And, when relating the tragic death of Poe's mother, she says of the subject "of death and tombs—it has ever been one of my happiest preoccupations . . . ."[37]

These writings also demonstrate that, along with an increasingly bitter struggle under the burden of living there developed an equally forceful reaction against the burden of language, against the sheer weight of words. So Brother Sumac incessantly nags at the tormenting question "Why Actors?" but receives no answer from the wise Doña Barbetta, whose laughter is "massive with long silence."[38] Her words are futile, just as on the modern stage there is not only an unimaginable waste of material and talent, but of words as well. From the past may be recalled a respect for economy of language and the actor's awareness of the value of silence, of the gesture that replaces the word. In the twentieth century, it is in the cinema rather than on the stage that Miss Barnes finds this again. Considering Joseph Rowensky's performance as a mute in a film called *The Girl from the Reeperbahn*, she writes that "So exceedingly painful and poignant he makes silence, that I begin to wonder if we as a race have not made a great mistake in becoming articulate."[39] Predicting in the "Almanack" that dialogue will come to serve merely to accelerate action in films, she states "I like my human experience served up with a little silence and Restraint. Silence makes experience go further and, when it does die, gives it that dignity common to a Thing one has touched but not *ravished*."[40] The reference here is to Joseph von Sternberg's *Morocco*, which Miss Barnes again brings up in relation to a scene in another film,

. . . that scene in *Skippy* where the hero walks home beside his bereaved companion. (The dog catcher has taken the little one's dog and had him shot.) Never have I seen, I think, a better piece of directing, or for that matter acting—than the helpless compassion on the part of the one child as he runs before, then falls behind, then by the side, of the other, who cannot be comforted—though the frantic scene in *Morocco* where Marlene Deitrich is search-

ing the ranks for her lover, now running with, and now
away from the men, is a close second.[41]

The cinema's rediscovery of the silence of experience will
later be seen to be but one aspect of that medium's influence
upon Miss Barnes's work. The years before *Nightwood*, however, involved an effort on her part to experiment with the
expanding and contracting properties of language, an en-
deavor which ran parallel to her alternating impulses to participate in and to withdraw from active experience that determined the dual aspect of her work in whatever genre for years
to follow. For Miss Barnes, the journalistic experience was an
immersion in life and its abundance, and she developed an
active style apt for rendering it. But early in her commercial
career there developed a sense that things were not as they
seemed, that beneath all the talk and activity was an inner
reality that remained to be revealed. One way of getting at it
was to become less the reporter and more the poet-essayist,
trusting to impressions rather than facts, and conveying them
with whatever degree of eloquence the limits of the trade
would bear. Another was to call a hush to all the noise by a
simultaneous involvement with the medium of lyric verse.
Those worldly journalistic writings which become so copious in
verbal extravagance shall be seen therefore to contrast sharply
with Djuna Barnes's restrained, introspective poems, cautious
in their diction and wary of the world.

# 2.

# The Early Poems

Nearly all of the early poems of Djuna Barnes have been forgotten. Her first slim volume of so-called rhythms and drawings, *The Book of Repulsive Women*, originally published in 1915 by Guido Bruno in his series of *Bruno Chap Books*, may be familiar to a few readers as a result of its apparently unauthorized 1948 reprint as an "Outcast Chapbook" by the Alicat Bookshop Press. Her several dozen other poems of the Greenwich Village and expatriate years, however, are lost. Many of the magazines in which they appeared have themselves fallen into oblivion, *All-Story Weekly*, *Munsey's Magazine*, the *Trend*, and *Shadowland* among them. And Miss Barnes is seldom recalled as a contributor to certain others that managed to remain prestigious in American literature, such as Egmont Arens's *Playboy*, *Vanity Fair*, *Smart Set*, and particularly the *Dial* and the *Little Review*. A group of her lyrical poems, along with some of her stories, one-act plays, and line portraits of women, was included in her first collection to follow *The Book of Repulsive Women*, titled simply *A Book* and brought out by Boni and Liveright in 1923. But that volume and *A Night Among the Horses*, its 1929 reprint which included new stories but omitted the drawings, have been out of print since their initial publication. Although William Faulkner quoted lines of Miss Barnes's verse in *Intruder in the Dust* and *The Town*, there is no indication that her early poetry made a lasting impression on anyone else. Faulkner, in fact, when questioned in 1957, remembered Miss Barnes only as a poet belonging to a small expatriate circle in

Paris in the 1920s rather than as the author of *Nightwood*, and he wondered if she was still alive.[1]

It is doubtful that most of the early poems could survive by present standards. Despite some instances of modest achievement, as a group they show the least originality of Miss Barnes's diverse work before *Nightwood*. The earliest efforts were as derivative as the work of most novice poets. Even as maturity of intention and execution increase, the results are so low-keyed and close to traditional that, unlike Miss Barnes's late work, these poems offer nothing to stand up against the best modern writing. The poems in *A Book* seem to be almost incidental parts of an already strangely muted collection and, only a few years later, their presence in *A Night Among the Horses* is further diminished by the addition of three new stories.

The tapering off of Djuna Barnes's productivity as a poet corresponds more or less to the decline in her output of essays and commercial writing. As the twenties advance, fewer and fewer of her poems appear in little magazines, while the sections of verse in *Ryder* and *Ladies Almanack* have little value independent of their contextual function. The poet does not disappear at this point, of course, but moves out beyond the confining mould of lyric verse in order to experiment in fiction with the cadences of prose. When, much later, Miss Barnes returns to poetry, what develops in the intricate lines of *The Antiphon* and the handful of other published poems, has practically nothing in common with her first attempts in the genre. In the late work, the author takes distance upon the emotion that was directly present in the early poems, and through her craft achieves something of permanence rather than transience. In contrast to the early lyrics, new poems like "Quarry" and "Walking-Mort" are oblique and laconic, tightly compressed and resolved units in themselves.

What the early rhythms of *The Book of Repulsive Women*, as well as most of the uncollected lyrics and those in *A Book*, do contain along with the essays are the emerging attitudes and motifs that form the basis of the several major works. Most pervasive is an infatuation with the darker side of experience.

The type of descriptive ornamentation and persiflage characteristic of the personal essays and light sketches is almost
entirely absent from the poetry. Whatever the tonal quality of a
particular poem, whether it intends to render a "Hush Before
Love" or "short sharp modern / Babylonic cries,"[2] it is to some
degree involved with a sense of despair or loss, or a sentiment
which gravitates toward an association of love and death. A
refrain of lost innocence or naturalness recurs, accompanying
the theme of the waning of love or the death of the lover. The
preoccupation is essentially romantic, involved as it is with the
passage of time and its threat to permanence, with an urge to
halt it or to revive past time. The presentation of such sentiments is simple and direct enough in these early poems. There
is at the same time a fascination with dissolution and the
decadent which quite closely corresponds to the lure of the
perverse which the prose reveals at frequent turns but with a
lighter touch. In *The Book of Repulsive Women*, alternating attitudes of fascination toward and repulsion from the spectacle of
human wreckage show up in conspicuous stylistic excesses
which the other poems for the most part, and to their credit,
lack.

It would be impossible to discuss this chapbook without
first taking into account the temperament and tastes of its
publisher. Guido Bruno has been described by Frederick J.
Hoffman as "an extreme case of the Villager wholly committed
to the *fin de siècle*."[3] In fact, to begin to recall the notion of the
Greenwich Village Bohemian in the years approaching the
1920s, one could leaf through the pages of the number of
periodicals and chapbooks that Bruno issued from his garret.
Bruno's prolix reportage, chat, and endless reminiscences, in
combination with his various contributors' poems, stories, and
illustrations, time and again yield up the familiar image of the
artist in poverty, taking a stand against an obtuse, if not hostile,
society while embracing sin and an aesthetic determinedly
above and beyond the claim of economic necessity. As Miss
Barnes herself put it in 1916, "The Bohemian is a man who
knows how to enjoy his poverty."[4] Consistently, Bruno was a
champion of the aestheticism and decadence of the British

1890s and its leading figures—Oscar Wilde, Arthur Symons, Frank Harris, Aubrey Beardsley—and the contents of his several reviews generally reflect his commitment. So when speaking of the "grotesques and arabesques" of the drawings of war subjects by Djuna Barnes that he exhibited in 1915, he was also speaking of a quality of style that he continuously sponsored.

In Bruno's hands it was inevitable that the chapbook would turn out to be an arty and rather garish item. It is as if Miss Barnes had taken a theme of Arthur Symons: "The modern malady of love is nerves."[5] When she declares, "For when a woman lives in awful haste / A woman dies" (*BRW*, 98), Miss Barnes articulates the sense of strain that possesses each member of the whole panorama of "repulsive" women perceived against their urban backdrop, and accordingly grieves upon watching one of them asleep, ". . . that the altars of / Your vice lie deep" (*BRW*, 97). Although the setting is specifically New York City of 1915, the women are as misshapen as the concrete world which they distort by their presence and as likely to appear in sharp profile as to dissolve into shadow. One could just as well be back in "The Harlot's House" of Oscar Wilde where,

> Like strange mechanical grotesques,
> Making fantastic arabesques,
> The shadows raced across the blind.[6]

A degree of the volume's continuity is provided by the titles of three of the eight poems: "From Fifth Avenue Up," "Seen From the 'L,' " and "From Third Avenue On," Guido Bruno's prepublication announcement of the chapbook had described it as "a chant which could be sung by those who are in the daily procession through the streets and highways of our metropolis but which could also be sung by those who are on balconies and house-tops viewing the eternal show of daily life."[7] The poet, however, is determined to disorient the reader's habitual manner of perceiving everyday surroundings. Here the Manhattan locale becomes an expressionistic backdrop for the exposed nerves of those who "live aghast" (*BRW*, 94), much as later in *Nightwood* the concrete Paris of the twenties fades into an interior landscape and becomes part of an anatomy of night. The squalidness of certain details in *The Book of Repulsive Women* is calculated to reflect the decay of the grotesques upon which the poems focus: a "vague molested carpet," a "dusty length of stair" (*BRW*, 95), or a woman walking ". . . on out turned feet / Beside the litter in the street" (*BRW*, 94).

The women of each of these poems have in common their having fallen from a state of innocence into a sort of death in life. Just after the woman of Third Avenue is seen walking in the littered street, an alterate view of her is offered: "Or rolls beneath a dirty sheet / Within the town." Though ambulatory, she is at least spiritually immobilized, as "She does not stir to doff her dress, / She does not kneel low to confess." She is "settled down":

> Ah God! She settles down we say;
> It means her powers slip away
> It means she draws back day by day
>     From good or bad. (*BRW*, p.94)

The first four stanzas build up the sense of withdrawal with such images as the woman in trance, "mouthing meekly in a chair" beside her chinaware, or ginning vacantly into space: "A vacant space is in her face—Where nothing came to take the place / Of high hard cries." Or, on the stairs, her muttered "elements of prayers" break off into swearing while outside, "Somewhere beneath her hurried curse, / A corpse lies bounding in a hearse" (*BRW*, 94). The figure of the corpse, of course, recalls the woman as seen rolling "beneath a dirty sheet" at the beginning, thus anticipating the conclusion:

> Those living dead up in their rooms
> Must note how partial are the tombs,
> That take men back into their wombs
>     While theirs must fast. (*BRW*, p.94)

The woman in "Twilight of the Illicit" similarly has, in living, "all grimaces / Of the dead" (*BRW*, 97). This reiterated motif becomes one element that ties the several women together. A dimly remembered innocence, or awareness of some lost potential, is another; in the same poem there is recollection of "the sweeter gifts you had / And didn't keep" (*BRW*, 97). Varied descriptive patterns which stress corresponding physical traits work to similar effect. The woman "Seen From the 'L' " is combing her hair and,

> Though her lips are vague as fancy
> In her youth—
> They bloom vivid and repulsive
> As the truth. (*BRW*, p. 95)

The Third Avenue woman has "over-curled, hard waving hair" (*BRW*, 94), while the one in "Twilight of the Illicit" has "dying    hair"    and    "Lips,    long    lengthened    by    wise words / Unsaid" (*BRW*, 97). Still elsewhere, the "ruined crimson" of a cabaret dancer's lips "Grew vague and vast" (*BRW*, 99). And so on.

Since the point of view of the narrative "we" in these poems is unvarying, it does not matter whether these women are taken individually or "In General," as this brief poem is titled:

> What altar cloth, what rag of worth
>         Unpriced?
> What turn of card, what trick of game
> Undiced?
> And you we valued still a little
> More than Christ. (*BRW*, p. 93)

The Poem "In Particular" (*BRW*, 96) simply substitues "loincloth" for "altar cloth," and "wrong" for "worth" in the first line; "body" for "card" and "lust" for "game" in the third; and "worshipped" for "valued" in the fifth. The balance is apparent, and the sense of loss equivalent.

The last poem, fittingly entitled "Suicide," concerns two

corpses. Here is "Corpse B" brought into the morgue:

> They gave her hurried shoves this way
> > And that,
> Her body shock-abbreviated
> As a city cat.
> She lay out listlessly like some small mug
> Of beer gone flat. (*BRW*, p. 100)

Jack Hirschman notes that "The word 'abbreviated,' in the context of the poem, serves not only to break up the regularity of rhythmic frame into which the poem is fit; it creates the almost onomatopoetic effect of shuddering or shaking, metaphorically apt for the subject of the poem."[8] Such apt effects, however, do not mark the volume as a whole. The concluding image above is not alone in its triteness. Moreover, the obsessive lurid and grotesque touches lead to excesses in tone and strain in diction: "the over-hearts left oozing / At your feet," or the corresponding configurations in the same poem, "You'd lip the world to madness / On your face," and "Your soft saliva, loosed / With orgy, drip" (*BRW*, 91). Miss Barnes's rather conventional use of metre and rhyme, perhaps intended to provide a neutral ground to counter the strain, only succeeds in magnifying such excess. That a greater control and balance soon emerge in the lyrics only reinforces the impression that in this volume she may have been strongly under the influence of her publisher. Or, like the later Lydia Steptoe, is simply out to shock.

The contrasting attitudes between *The Book of Repulsive Women* and the lyrics in *A Book* that lead to two distinct approaches to verse are paralleled in the sets of drawings which accompany the two volumes. The five drawings of repulsive women draw upon elements characteristic of art nouveau and the neo-rococo patterns typical of the style of 1890's draftsmanship and decor. Guido Bruno frequently calls Miss Barnes "the American Beardsley."[9] As in the drawings of Bruno's other regular illustrators, such as Clara Tice and Coulton Waugh, the elegance of curve and fondness for silhouette that one thinks of as "Beardsleyesque" are reflected, along with sharply contrasting areas of light and dark from which the linear motifs emerge and disappear. This is apparent in three of the drawings which achieve their effect by surrounding distorted human figures coming out of and returning into darkness with oriental elements so as to suggest submergence in vice. In one (*BRW*, 105), the upper body of a young woman curves upward in ecstasy toward a magnetizing Japanese head floating in space. She is posed against a black mass which slopes diagonally like a hill across the upper half of the picture. In the lower half, an Eastern vase in her hand hangs down beside dark strands depending like roots from the dark mass above. The same dark depravity, reflecting the chiché of the mysterious East, is captured in the two other drawings. A demonic, malformed, naked woman with pointed ears and a lewd smile—a vampiric type that Miss Barnes repeatedly sketched[10]—clutches dead flowers (*BRW*,107) in one and in one a woman, nude to the waist and grasping the tail of a serpent, reclines suspended above the activity of figures again suggestive of the evil Orient (*BRW*, 109). This recurrent weirdness is also captured in Bruno's description of an "Ultra Djuna" picture of a Buddha, one which she sold to Frank Harris for twenty-five dollars: "All I had been able to discern . . . was an enormous belly, and claws of gold on ivory white hands, hanging in the black space like the photograph of a successful seance where hands had materialized hanging ghostly in mid-air."[11] It is hardly necessary to add that such work partakes of extreme stylization. Its verbal equivalent might be found in Miss Barnes's answer to the question, "What Does 291 Mean?"

Blinking on your part, oh, holy Asiatic pottery, with square fists and untutored toes. And now, a sense of an ineffable thumb reaching stealthily like a gigantic misshaped shadow with four clenched fingers as a background, a thumb that turns down—a preoccupied yet profound dismissal of a blinking set of preoccupied porcelains, almost any abysmal foreboding.

A hand that still holds the odor of a moment's pulsing
of some dethroned heart.
Also a space.[12]

The six later drawings in *A Book*, however, are marked by a
complete reversal of technique. Like the understated poems in
their company, they eschew showy effects of any sort. All are
portraits, titled simply "Portrait," "Study," etc., and all employ
subtly modulated lines instead of heavily blocked masses of
light and dark. The means are so minimal that it appears that
the artist has taken all steps to conceal her attitude toward the
subjects. Deprived in reproduction of the delicate pastel coloring that some of these portraits originally possessed, the
unidentified women seem stark, dehumanized. One critic
wondered "why was it illustrated by those strange, unearthly
pictures of drawn, haggard, Ibsenish persons, all of whom look
weary of life, deeply embittered and starved?"[13] The ambiguity
is further increased by a hint of undetermined sexuality in
most of the subjects, enhancing the sinister aspects they already
have. As there are no backgrounds to the sketches, the figures
seem stripped of identity and of time and place.[14] Thus they
seem to universalize the polar types, rustic and aristocratic, that
populate the stories, poems, and plays. In their elusiveness,
they finally convey much the same impression as the subject of
the verse portrait "Antique" in *A Book*:

A lady in a cowl of lawn
With straight bound tabs and muted eyes,
And lips fair thin and deftly drawn
    And oddly wise.

A cameo, a ruff of lace,
A neck cut square with corners laid;
A thin Green nose and near the face
    A polished braid.

Low, sideways looped, of amber stain

The pale ears caught within its snare.
A profile like a dagger lain
      Between the hair.[15]

Here a chaste approach to rhyme and metre perfectly corresponds to the chaste management of line in the portraits. The
suggestiveness of "oddly wise" is extended in two directions: by
the precision of description which invests the subject with a
quality of perfect measure or composure, and by the ominous
implications of "snare" and "dagger."

The quiet effect of "Antique," like the other poems in *A
Book*, is much more typical of Miss Barnes's early work than the
garish, expressionistic style of her first volume. Most of the
lyrics, however, do draw upon elements present in the 1890s in
a fashion that connects with Wylie Sypher's description of the
"arabesque and neo-rococo" quality of much of minor late-
Victorian and Edwardian poetry: "a verse on the verge of
becoming functional, purifying its language and treating the
poem as a series of stanzas carefully worked up into a decorative field." Wylie Sypher also observes that "the motif in such
poetry is carefully chosen and freed from the encumbrances of
Tennyson's elegance—the impression is enough."[16]

The eleven poems gathered in 1923 in *A Book* could be
categorized as 'a poetry of impressions, verging on the
functional but comprised of the hints or "fragments of sensations" of which Natalie Clifford Barney spoke. The most
uncomplicated of these and other poems of this period are
concerned with the poet's relationship to her natural environment.

In such earlier uncollected poems as "The Dreamer" and
"Call of the Night" of 1911, the response to nature had been
simplistic enough, and the mode of expression of a sort that
would have been available to any youth versed in lyric poetry of
the past century:

Mist, the dust of flowers.
    Leagues, heavy with promise of snow.

And a beckoning road 'twixt vale and hill:
With the lure that all must know.[17]

It is not impossible that Miss Barnes was under the influence of
the poetry of her paternal grandmother Zadel (Barnes)
Budington Gustafson, author of a collection called *Meg: A
Pastoral* consisting of competent though conventional,
protracted and often saccharine lyrics, the kind suitable for
family reading. Whatever the case, here the poet is a romantic,
a dreamer, "madly drunk on shadow wine," taking "for my
love, the meadow at my side."[18] A few years later, however, the
poet has awakened and is at some greater remove from the
landscape surrounding her. "Pastoral" (*AB*, 74–75), first published in the *Dial* in 1920, depicts the breaking of dawn upon
the rural scene:

A frog leaps out across the lawn,
And crouches there—all heavy and
                    alone
And like a blossom, pale and over-blown,
Once more the moon turns dim against the dawn.

The faintly oriental descriptive motif in this first of nine stanzas is carried through by such touches as "The mushrooms
flare, and pass like painted fans," and the imagery alternates
between the seen and the unseen. While,

Here in the dawn, with mournful doomed eyes
A cow uprises, moving out to bear
A soft-lipped calf with swarty birth-swirled
                    hair
And wide wet mouth, and droll uncertainties.

simultaneously, "Thin, dusty rats slink down within the grain,"
and "The wheat grows querulous with unseen cats." The total
impression is of motion in stillness ("The stillness moves, and
seems to grow immense."), framed by a more abstract concern

with the eternal in the temporal: "All the world is patient in its plans— / The seasons move forever, one on one." The paradox of simultaneous progression and recession in recorded time is a concept to be greatly refined later. Here,

> And so it is, and will be year on year,
> Time in and out of date, and still on time
> A billion grapes plunge bleeding into wine
> And bursting, fall like music on the ear.
>
> The snail that marks the girth of night with slime,
> The lonely adder hissing in the fern,
> The lizard with its ochre eyes aburn—
> Each is before, and each behind its time.

Some attempt to come to terms with the fact of temporality is involved in nearly all of Miss Barnes's early poems. On occasion, as in "Lullaby" (*AB*, 179), the theme is presented in a way that strikes the predominant note of *Nightwood* and certain of the stories:

> When I was a young child I slept
>                 with a dog,
> I lived without trouble and I
>                 thought no harm;
> I ran with the boys and I played leap-frog;
> Now it is a girl's head that lies on my arm.

The following two stanzas sustain the discrepancy between past and present: "Then I grew a little, picked plantain in the yard;/ Now I dwell in Greenwich, and the people do not call. . . ." "Then" was a time of simplicity, of union with nature and response to life. "Now" is a state of death in life not unlike the Third Avenue woman's. The last lines render explicit the dilemma of enduring time's duration. There is an echo of lost innocence in the shock of rhyming "thistle" with "pistol":

> Then I pricked my finger on a thorn, or a thistle,

Put the finger in my mouth, and ran to my
                mother
Now I lie here, with my eyes on a pistol.
There will be a morrow, and another, and
                another.

Love does not in every case imply degradation, as it does here
in "Lullaby," but it is invariably treated as fugitive. The brief
"Hush Before Love" (*AB*, 116) is able to render an impression
of the fullness and purity of a moment:

A voice rose in the darkness saying
            "Love,"
And in the stall the scattered mice grew
           still,
While yet the white ox slept, and on the sill
The crowing cock paused, and the grey house
           dove
Turned twice about upon the ledge above.

But, almost as if in aftermath, the lover in the poem "Paradise"
hears "the echo of the Kiss that Slew" (*AB*, 131). The pastoral
setting for many of these lyrics of the early twenties—"Song in
Autumn," "I'd Have You Think of Me," and others—is far
from the defunct urban background of *The Book of Repulsive
Women*. Here the atmosphere is filled with the subtle transfor-
mations in nature that are instantaneous and fugitive but yet
belong to an eternal cycle. Love, by contrast, is subject to the
erosion of time. A sonnet of 1923 about the estrangement of
lovers, "To One Feeling Differently," begins, "To-night I
cannot know you and I weep . . . ," and concludes, ". . . on
high lamenting wings / Cold time screams past us, shedding
sparks of pain— / Of which you are the core and the refrain."[19]
The mute sorrow of the beloved is compared to the dress of
one in mourning, again reinforcing the inevitability of death in
love.
    This central theme, the constant awareness that "The
mortal fruit upon the bough / Hangs above the nuptial bed"

(*AB*, 219), often takes on a particularly morbid complexion. When the figure of the dead lover is central, as is often the case, the descriptive field is apt to become a Gothic tapestry. In "The Flowering Corpse," one of the more lugubrious poems in *A Book*, a "closed place apart" is the setting for a "ghostly tryst," where " . . . beneath her armpits bloom / The drowsy passion flowers of the dead" (*AB*,209). As in an uncollected poem of 1918, "The Lament of Women: Ah My God!" ("Ah my God, what is it that we love! / This flesh laid on us like a wrinkled glove?"),[20] a stanza from the later "Six Songs of Khalidine" (*AB*, 145–46) evokes Donne in its reminder of mortality:

> It is not gentleness but mad despair
> That sets us kissing mouths, O Khalidine,
> Your mouth and mine, and one sweet mouth
>                    unseen
> We call our soul. Yet think within our hair
> The dusty ashes that our days prepare.

These six stanzas to a dead lover primarily employ a sort of Gothic imagery to fill out a sense of "the dark funereal:" "And here the black bat cowers / Against your clock that never strikes the hours." The whole is a poem of sick, haunted passion, in resistance to which the poet is able to offer a single moment of purer passion in recollection: "And now I say, has not the mountain's base / Here trembled long ago unto the cry/ 'I love you, ah, I love you.' "

At times, touches of chinoiserie may enter as decorative flourishes if not as the basic descriptive motif. "To the Dead Favourite of Liu Ch'e," which appeared in the *Dial* in 1920, is a delicate lament which achieves its fragility by developing in small touches a sense of hush and halt:

> The sound of rustling silk is stilled,
> With solemn dust the court is filled,
> No footfalls echo on the floor;
> A thousand leaves stop up her door,
> Her little golden drink is spilled.[21]

And in an earlier poem, "The Yellow Jar," white butterflies creep about the china tomb of "blossoms past," which, by a death bed, recalls "That other bowl of dust. . . ."[22]

All in all, the early poems of Djuna Barnes are, without exception, minor works both in terms of their restricted emotional range and the conventional prosody they employ. This is not to say, however, that they aspire to be more than they in fact are. As they develop over nearly two decades, the poet's intention clearly becomes to render, with increasing fragility of impression, not an event or state of mind, but the nuances thereof, as in the typical "Vaudeville" of 1923:

> Her little feet half sought the dizzy ground
> And half they rose like sun motes spent in
> > space;
> A whirling rhythm in a shower of lace,
> Between the music's silence and its sound.[23]

In suspension between silence and sound, between ground and space, the most fugitive impressions are caught out of the flux of experience: "More delicate than leaf-light on a lake / The dimples that made shadows in her chin." It is as if the most delicate and transparent of screens were illuminated to reveal patterns and traces lost to customary vision. Taking alone these personal, muted lamentations, still essentially ornamental, that Djuna Barnes continued to publish through the twenties, one might have assumed that she was unaware of the distinctive new poetics evolving from *imagisme* through Eliot's *The Waste Land* and Pound's experiments with transliteration and juxtaposition. But it would soon be apparent in two unusual novels that a modern voice was developing, along the lines of Joyce's, in the rhythms of a prose expanded, not according to the dictates of a current aesthetic rationale, but by a new application of abandoned traditions.

# 3.

## *Ryder* and *Ladies Almanack*

The work discussed so far reveals an author still in search of her proper voice. Djuna Barnes's development during the course of the twenties appears to be in two directions that are so sharply divergent as to be nearly directly opposed. Dual attitudes toward style and experience are at work, whether the attempt is in the genre of verse, literary sketch or essay, illustration, or, as subsequent chapters will indicate, the short story and one-act play. In the broadest view, the divergence is between the author's going into and withdrawing from life. The latter tendency had operated behind nature poems of a personal quality on a reduced lyrical scale, the quiet, static line portraits, and reflective anecdotal articles on theatre, all of which mainly held to traditional principles in their composition. Alternately, however, the poet became brazen, stridently chanting the decadence of city women, illustrating their depravity in bold, Beardsleyesque touches, and, as Lydia Steptoe, going to hell in the most decorous way, totally serious about being unserious. The restrictive melancholy of the poems seemed in mood a world apart from these prolix and witty sketches. Stylistic excess was the issue of all this, the cultivation of preciousness and ornamentation for their own sake. This was the iconoclastic side of the author, subversive of meaning and traditional literary decorum to the point of affirming only the pointless and perverse. *Ryder* and *Ladies Almanack*, two illustrated novels of 1928, were the logical results of this iconoclasm.

The shift to a broader genre may have been prompted in part simply by a feeling of having reached an impasse. By the mid-twenties, Miss Barnes's writing began to seem repetitious at times, to fall into a monotony of tone, theme, and situation. Her commercial writing and plays became increasingly slick and mechanical, while her poems depended more and more upon affectation, whether Gothic or *chinoise*. Perhaps because of the necessary brevity of the forms in which she had been working, her growth as an artist seemed temporarily blocked, with reiteration a momentary resort. But a deeper reason for taking on the novel may have been that Miss Barnes needed to try for the first time to achieve a synthesis of experience and ideas, a coordinated vision developed out of what had existed before in literary bits and pieces. In the same way that she went from the line portrait sketches to finished oil portraits, with her novels she moved upon a larger generic scale offering richer possibilities and risks to the restless imagination.

In manner of publication, the one novel could be said to be public, the other private. In the autumn of 1928, Brentano's New York bookstore listed *Ryder* as among its six best-selling novels. *Ladies Almanack*, however, was privately and pseudonymously published in an edition limited to five hundred fifty copies without the least expectation of its ever becoming available for a trade edition—which it eventually did in America in Harper and Row's 1972 facsimile. Both works appeared as a sudden new departure on the part of their author, at least insofar as style is concerned. Miss Barnes's most successful short stories of the twenties, with which the next chapter will be concerned, were characterized by a carefully limited scope and an economical quasi-naturalistic manner in the telling. They bore a similar air of restraint to the poems interspersed among them in *A Book*. But in these novels, all is expansive and abundantly artificial. *Ryder*, in the course of its fifty chapters, attempts to bring into play nearly every literary mode or tradition since the holy scriptures. *Ladies Almanack*, a cameo alongside *Ryder*, is a virtually plotless exercise in technique, adapting a form of Elizabethan prose and scrupulously sustaining it throughout. Both books, for reasons that will soon appear, put the term *novel* to a test. In spite of this, however, they do demonstrate that, upon a deeper level than the author's apparent split between introverted and extroverted states of mind, she had been working toward a new thematic consistency, managing to make elements that had developed out of the earlier efforts begin to cohere. Along with the short stories, the two novels importantly prepare the way and clear the air for *Nightwood*. Although they seem to retreat to the past for inspiration, shunning the demands for naturalness or commonness of diction which were a central part of the expatriate literary enterprise of the decade, paradoxically they begin to indicate their author as a modern.

In an attempt to single out the particularly "modern" elements in *The Antiphon* in 1958, Howard Nemerov brought out three points that now appear to apply to *Ryder* and *Ladies Almanack* with equal import. For Nemerov, the verse play involves "An art of serious parody," or perhaps travesty, serious in that the parody has a desperate quality which shatters the old idea of the well-made work of art and causes style to mock at itself in the mirror. The second element he outlined as "A breaking-up surfaces; a destruction of the conventional sequences and coherencies of 'plot'. . . . " In addition, as a result of the author's "Treatment of language as an independent value,"[1] the poetic dimension rather than the dramatic is involved. There is no question, of course, that in *The Antiphon* these factors exist in closer fusion than in the early works. The diffusion of the effects they result in accounts in part for the failure of *Ryder* and for the limitations of *Ladies Almanack*. But to look at *Ryder* to begin with is to observe an author beginning to find a voice and sense of direction after some apprentice years of minor, occasionally derivative, creation.

*Ryder* is ostensibly a family chronicle[2] which has as a central figure Wendell Ryder. Its odd thread of progression, however, follows his mother, Sophia Grieve Ryder, from her prime to her deathbed. The narrative begins sometime in the first half of the nineteenth century and in its course, works into the early years of the twentieth. As background, it is established that Sophia is of New England Puritan descent, of "great and humorous stock,"[3] and one of many offspring of Jonathan Buxton Ryder and his bride Cynthia, glimpsed briefly upon their wedding night and, once again abruptly, upon the mother's death at the birth of her fourteenth child. Of Sophia's first husband John Peel, little is told; of the union, the only issue of note is Wendell, born in 1865 (the youngest child had died in infancy, and of another, Gaybert, a surgeon, there is little more than mention). Wendell recalls that Sophia was a fond and doting wife to a second husband, a Swede named Alex Alexon, but this marriage had been overshadowed by the splendor of Sophia's marvellous travels, her social eclat, and her role as mistress of a wandering salon attended by, among numerous others, Oscar Wilde, where she had "moved among the Pre-Raphaelites as accustomed as a glint of steel" (*R*, 43).

The bulk of the novel follows the embarkation of Sophia, Wendell, and his wife Amelia for America, where they come to settle in a small log cabin at "Storm-King-on-Hudson." Amelia de Grier, formerly of the British country seat of Tittencote, had come to London in 1886 for the first time, enrolled as a student of violin and singing at the Conservatory of Music, and found herself adopted by Sophia with her embracing invitation, " 'Call me mother' " (*R*, 42), and married to Wendell. Ten years elapse in America before the coming of Kate-Careless in 1897. The probably illegitimate daughter of a buxom street contralto from Cork and a Pre-Raphaelite painter of seascapes, in her wanderings she had come finally to Storm-King-on-Hudson where she too had called Sophia "Mother." With wife and mistress, five legitimate and three illegitimate offspring, Wendell goes along living a life of polygamy, idleness, and free-thinking, against the social repercussions of which he must repeatedly put up verbal frontage. All the while, it is Sophia who must maintain the stability of the family and, through elaborate clandestine begging, work industriously against the dwindling family fortune. At her death, Wendell is left to an unpromising future, to his inevitable fall without the support of women. "Whom should he disappoint now?" is the novel's final question.

The above may seem straightforward enough in the

sketching, yet becomes anything but so in the telling. In the
first place, chronological dissociation is a first guiding principle
of narrative here. Very few specific dates are given at apparently random moments, but these are so engulfed in the narrative that the reader must withdraw from its flow in order to link
them. The principle of consecutive arrangements of events
that dominated the type of fiction that this parodies, at least on
the level of plot construction, is submerged—allowed to surface only enough to arouse the reader's distrust. The transition
from Cynthia Ryder's nuptial bed to death-childbirth bed, for
example, takes place in a single sentence. Early in the novel,
Sophia's entire career is so sharply telescoped as to emphasize
its unreality. By contrast, the events in America, occupying
nearly two-thirds of the book's 323 pages, seem almost entirely
without calendar sequence, creating an impression of timelessness within which the book's interrupted narrative can
proceed.

The forward movement of the novel is blocked at nearly
every turn of event by passages or entire chapters which relate
only tangentially to plot, or, as the plot works out, to the static
situation. This permits Miss Barnes to carry out her intentions
as parodist in divergent directions. On one level she is suggesting the death of the social or domestic novel of generations that
had dominated the nineteenth century. Beyond the narrative
disjunction, it will appear that Miss Barnes replaces historical
perspective with mythic perspective, incorporating a view of
the life span that reaches back beyond the solid faith in continuity and progress implicit in that type of novel to the terror
that went out with the eighteenth century. There is a finality in
the fact that Sophia holds a copy of *Adam Bede* on her deathbed.

In other places, Miss Barnes reaches back to incorporate
narrative patterns of the eighteenth century. In the chapters
that consist of letters to Amelia from her sister in England,
mostly filled with domestic travail and exclamations over the
supposed horrors of the primitive New World, there is a
tongue-in-cheek acknowledgement of the epistolary mode.
Chapters or passages in which Wendell is treated in a mock
heroic fashion seem to satirize loosely the picaresque tradition

of Smollet or Fielding, with the frequency of disgressive chapters again recalling the latter. All in all, however, the novel's planned chaos and stress on folly recall the Sterne of *Tristram Shandy*.

Beyond this point, the adventure in style becomes even wider ranging. Poems of diverse types may serve as brief chapters punctuating the narrative flow. Echoes of even earlier styles now and then are heard. "The Occupations of Wendell," a long chapter on Wendell's lustiness and his closeness to nature and animals, is cast in a pastiche of Chaucerian verse:

> Eft Wendell pondered, and he say him "Sooth!
> What is this swims like dregs within the truth
> That animal and man be set apart?
> I hear not muchë difference in the heart
> That beatës soft and constant under hide,
> And this same hammer ticking in my side!" (*R*, p. 77)

Certain chapters recall Renaissance styles of narrative, such as "Rape and Repining," a lament for a girl's loss of virginity in Tittencote, a bit of facetiae that is sufficiently independent of the main narrative to have appeared in *transition* in advance of the novel. Or the monologues of Doctor Matthew O'Connor, who makes his first appearance in *Ryder* as the family physician and whose speech, as later in *Nightwood*, is filled with Elizabethan conceits and timbres, echoes now of Lyly, now of Burton's *Anatomy of Melancholy*. A biblical style is employed initially in "Jesus Mundane," an altogether earthy gospel that stands as an introductory chapter, and, like the other stylistic threads introduced, brought into play later in various contexts. Finally, there are variations on myths throughout, alternate myths of creation and cosmogonies, occasionally with an Eastern touch, and moral fables that wind into non sequiturs, all willfully distorting the reader's inherited orientation toward mythology and legend. In short, Miss Barnes has broken up surfaces and conventional sequences to create a final impression of a novel hidden in a massive stylistic display case.

Language, then, has independent value, is the means by

which the novelist, as she had before as journalist, elaborates the irrelevant. *Ryder* is filled with lengthy passages devoted to catalogues of objects, descriptions of clothing, enumeration of nicknames and catchwords, all of which work against the reader's immediate involvement in the human situation. There are frequent leaps without transition from plain narrative and common speech to eccentrically punctuated, syntactically convoluted streams of prose compounded of archaisms, puns, double entendres, and so on. Just as the novel's events are edited in a cinematic fashion and thus freed from spatial-temporal fetters, language is treated as a montage. So the doctor may speak in his best passages in the language of the present and of the past simultaneously. The virtuosity is irritating, antiempathic. It arouses the conviction that the author, while trying to master and assimilate the bypassed elements of her literary tradition, is mocking that tradition in the process. The illustrations bear this out. One reviewer appropriately described them as "decided of line, neatly blocked and frequently minute," and further asserted that "they hint queerly, now at William Blake, now at Rowlandson or the Dutch or Picasso. The women seem Augustan, but the whole tone is decidedly American primitive, and one gets in looking hard at them as one senses likewise in the overtones of the prose, a degree of Puritan gentility at odds with itself."[4] Wildly unrealistic in conception, they yet suggest an earthy "primitive" quality that makes them seem both in and out of time.

Finally, with respect to style, *Ryder* represents an approach to genre that is characteristic of all of Miss Barnes's work to come. It aims to open up what had been a redundantly rulebound form, to expand its limits and awaken a new sense of possibility. By inserting poems, illustrations, and even at one point dialogue in the form of a one-act play, Miss Barnes is attempting to give the novel a new breadth of scope while bringing her diverse skills into focus. In later work the transgeneric elements become forced into a tighter coherence, but here they either stand side by side on display or are made to intrude conspicuously into the middle of things. For this novel is designed to befuddle its audience and reorient it. On a basic level it aims ostentatiously to shock and bewilder. One even wonders at times if it is not also a part of the author's program to bore the reader.

In response, the public had a best-seller, a development not so surprising in view of the book's concentrated bawdiness. Having been subjected to censorship, as Miss Barnes explains in a brief foreword, at her insistence the points of excision were boldly marked by asterisks so that the havoc would be evident. In a novel that had interruption as its keynote, the result hardly mattered, and what remained was, though predominantly indirect or masked by innuendo or double entendre, pungent enough for the decade. As for critical opinion outside of Boston, reviews in the popular press were mixed, running the gamut from a Newark, New Jersey, reviewer's conclusion that the novel can be read in any random direction and "she never writes well,"[5] to the opinion of the *Saturday Review*, "the most amazing book ever written by a woman."[6] Reviewers were quick to conjecture about the novel's possible sources and debts, citing Chaucer, Sterne, the King James Version, Rabelais, Fielding, Cabell, and Joyce and the group around him most frequently, but also detecting traces here and there of Jane Austen and Mary Lamb, the Martin Marprelate Tracts, Lyly, Gertrude Stein, and Sherwood Anderson. But relatively few critics recognized the novel's true parodic intent. A writer like Eugene Jolas, of course, could write in *transition*, "Instead of choosing the dessicated language matter of her contemporaries, Miss Barnes gives us what at first sight seems an archaic style, but which is merely the resuscitation of a highly charged word mechanism that succeeds in electrifying us."[7] Ironically, however, a number of reviewers insisted upon reading *Ryder* in the very terms against which its thrust was directed, resulting in interpretations such as the following from the *Nation*: " . . . it fails of the true picaresque quality in that the scenes and characters and dialogue are not tied down to one definite homely locality, as in 'Don Quixote.' They are abstracted so that in the end the impression given is of an allegory, which is in a sense the very antithesis of the picaresque novel."[8] Likewise, the opinion often recurs that, as the story rushes off in constant streams of technical display, Miss Barnes "mistakes the technical article of apparel for the true tissue of creation."[9] Here it must be admitted that there is a degree of justice in the judgement. The preciousness of the diarist of dangerous children is still present, though *Ryder* is a more purposive and intricate exercise in style and manner, with Miss Barnes's poetic infatuation with language evident everywhere. As few of *Ryder's* critics, however, acknowledge the thematic substance that its style is in the service of, the majority are in the odd position of being altogether more preoccupied with style than the author they are treating.

The reviewer for the *New Republic*, who finds the novel bloated and the characters thinly pressed "between the listed contents of their clothes-presses, their mantelshelves, and their outhouses,"[10] does at the same time indicate the novel to be a tragedy of women. Indeed *Ryder*, like *Ladies Almanack*, is matriarchally oriented, but unlike the latter it is so in contradiction to its appearance. The presentation of the fecund Wendell as hero and adventurer, as active master of himself and his domain, is one of several deceptions that are practiced in the book. " 'It takes a strong woman to die before she has been a fool' " (*R*, 40), Amelia is told by her mother, and it is Sophia who is no fool. Contrary to the way the narrative makes things seem, it is women upon whom the tragic burden of mortality rests and who must cope as they can.

If, as one review pointed up, the novel is "the very backlash of all Puritanism,"[11] it is primarily evident in the act of reversal of the doctrine of original sin. Molly Dance, one among many incidental characters, relates to Wendell how a midwife learned in a vision that the orignal sin was not woman's: " 'It was an apple, surely, but man it was who snapped it up, scattering the seeds, and these he uses to this day to get his sons by' " (*R*, 259). In an early chapter, two "Sisters Louise" discuss Wendell and how " 'He paints a rosy picture . . . of polygamy for—she stressed, 'the *man*—' " (*R*, 49). In her fantasy, one sister imagines several girls engaged in erotic play in a field that is " 'a perfect prostrate tapestry of fecundity' " (*R*, 50). Suddenly in the mind of each arises the figure of a winged

Wendell ascending into the clouds, with " 'thundering male parts hung like a terrible anvil, whereon one beats out the resurrection and the death' " (*R*, 51). With this breach in nature the girls turn upon each other in bloody combat. Thereafter, Wendell moves through the novel as a kind of rampant Adam, the spreading of his seed his guiding principle. It would be a mistake, however, to claim without qualification as does Eugene Jolas that "Ryder will go down in American literature as the archtype of the imaginative, swashbuckling super-male."[12] For in the end, Wendell turns out to be " 'bloody mortal' " (*R*, 321), to have gone about through fear of extinction, as Doctor O'Connor says, in and out of wedlock " 'multiplying his own nothing' " (*R*, 308).

When appearances are gradually stripped away, Wendell appears as an example, not of the super-male he has conceived himself to be, but of androgynous man. The doctor's insight follows from his being Wendell's counterpart. Although the homosexual doctor is cerebral and resolutely celibate in type, while Ryder is instinctual and compulsively polygamous, both are " 'much mixed . . . of woman and man' " (*R*, 310) as partly appears in the spontaneous compassion they share toward children and animals, or anything in nature that is vulnerable—in short, a maternal tenderness. Wendell himself, whose body even in the cradle was like a girl's, admits that he is " 'all things to all men, and all women's woman' " (*R*, 214). Proclaiming himself the diverse soul, he goes along frequently ringing changes on the theme of the number of men in himself. As Wendell is so broadly made out to be the compound creature, the aspects of his duality ultimately become undifferentiated. There is strength in his weakness and vulnerability in his strength. He is both creative, a writer and composer of operas (Sophía relates to him a dream of hers in which he was conceived by the mirage of Beethoven), and idle, preferring to indulge in his capacity for fancy while leaving the practical needs of his family to the women. He is capable of exercising the most advanced free thought, but is also susceptible to the mindless identification with nature that makes him at one with the animals. Yet in his fear of mortality he has lost what they possess, what men in innocence had once long ago possessed, the "holy look," with eyes on either side that " 'are apart and contrive not together' " (*R*, 245). Though his children inherit his traits—Julie, who is " 'simple and great' " with her " 'wide-set uncalculating eyes' " (*R*, 165), Timothy with his lust to whore, Elisha with his infatuation with the maiden and his drive to recreate the music of the romantics—Wendell, in wanting to be God and the father, has by his promiscuity in the end "unfathered" himself. And the dying Sophia tells him that he must fall because there is no resistance for his kind of strength: " ' . . . you lust openly and sweetly like . . . the beast of the field, because you are nature, all of you, all of you, and nature is terrible when law hunts it down' " (*R*, 317). Wendell's multitudinous nature is finally his flaw and, much as O'Connor later in *Nightwood*, he must at last acknowledge his mortality.

Wendell, equated in his role of fecundator with all of nature, stands as the agent of woman's suffering. At the beginning, the bed upon which Sophia is born is called "a terrible suffering centre without extremities" (*R*, 8), the first of many references to childbearing in terms of pain. As Amelia later insists, it is no pleasure to scream oneself into motherhood. While Wendell is a sensitive man, " 'racked with women, and with beasts' " (*R*, 292), wisdom belongs to women, racked with the anguish of childbirth and ever aware of the pangs of mortality. Incidental images of dolls point this up all the more sharply, the doll being symbol now of sinlessness or virginity, now of playful maternity. In reality, the mother is cursed with intimate knowledge. As Amelia's sister writes, "This, now I do think on it, is the matter with the world, that a man's greatness do come right out bang upon us, a woman's is in her flesh and hidden" (*R*, 198). The sexual difference is borne out in a corresponding spiritual distinction. Wendell comes to realize that there are no good women for they see too much from the beginning: " 'They look into their hearts . . . and in their hearts is the whole drama of man' " (*R*, 300).

Only Sophia in the novel fully incorporates the insight that is the hidden greatness of women. In her the hardiness and humor of her Puritan forebears continues. Miss Barnes speaks

of humor in this connection as "ability to round out the inevitable ever-recurring meanness of life, to push the ridiculous
into the very arms of the sublime" (*R*, 10), the gift that Amelia
and Kate-Careless cannot grasp in their self-limiting roles.
Kate is Mistress, and her lust turns against itself as she becomes
wholly addicted to the habit of childbearing. Amelia is Wife,
the passive victim of Wendell's illusions. The two together
become almost coarse representatives of the sadomasochistic
element in Puritan domesticity. Sophia, however, is Mother,
the cohesive force in the story and, by extension, the universe.
When she signs her begging letters "Mother," she is asserting a
claim against which there can be no refusal. She is the novel's
vessel of compassion, and it is for love of family that she begs
and lies to hold together the splintering generations of Ryders.
For her, the lie is more enduring than the truth. As she tells
Wendell when his own lying has put him at odds with the law,
his mistake has been to lie beautifully. " 'The people will accept
anything but beauty,' " she says. " 'You must lie near the heart,
and the heart of man is an insulting shape' " (*R*, 317). It is this
dark perception of Sophia's that lies beneath the view of history and the condition of man in advanced Western civilization
that *Ryder* advances.

The walls themselves of Sophia's salon tell the story.
Originally they had been covered by innumerable crayons and
prints of both the sublime and abhorrent in history. There
were pictures of those she admired, George Eliot, Beatrice
Cenci, Ouida, Dante, Pepys, Wilde, Browning, and Proudy the
railroad magnate, to name but a few in the inventory. There
were also prints of "the rack, the filling of the belly, known as
the Extreme Agony, the electric chair" (*R*, 15). In time, these
came to be covered over so that they finally stood two inches
from the wall, giving way at last to clippings from newspapers
in a "conglomerate juxtaposition" resembling the content of
the novel itself. As in Sophia, and "like the telltale rings of the
oak," there was "nothing erased but much submerged" (*R*, 15).
History, it is suggested, is lost to man, leaving him forlorn in a
diminished, cheapened present. Late in the novel, Timothy
comes to realize that once there were great fables, when " 'the

gods and their customs were beneath and above, but the times have come down,' " and in the day at hand, " 'We are unlearned of our greatness and lost of our destiny and foredone of our inheritance' " (*R*, 244). The fate of Sophia's chamber pots is significant here. Originally she had possessed five splendid vessels, upon four of which were inscribed one of the following lines:

"Needs there are many,
Comforts are few,
Do what you will
'Tis no more than I do." (*R*, 11)

The fifth, whose belly bore the single word *Amen*, became the only survivor of the destruction of the years. It is the age, Miss Barnes seems to be saying, of the lost axiom and the forsaken ratification.

The illustration that serves as frontispiece suggests a picture of things as they once could have been imagined. Atop a tree, an angel holds a scroll which reads "The Tree of Ryder," and several generations of Ryders sit upon its limbs. On the ground linger several of the novel's secondary characters surrounded by birds, sheep, and horses. Off to the side is a gravestone bearing the legend, "Like any ewe." The impression is of pastoral serenity in an orderly universe with everything in its place, quite like the lost-childhood, Easter-egg vision of the world with its people, lambs, and pastures that Miss Barnes recalled in one of her theater pieces. But this is another of the author's deceptions, and all order and stability vanish in the New World. Inevitably, it is the male Wendell, who by his polygamy turns backward the "Just Proportion of Generations," wrecking the continuity that woman must fight to preserve:

Who sets the Child backward upon the Beast of Time? Who makes of his Son no Kin but the Tomb, no Generation but the Dead, nay, bequeaths him no Dead and no Living, no Future and no Past? He must move foreward seeking, and backward lamenting. He is whirled about in an Uncertainty . . . . (*R*, p.35)

But in Miss Barnes's broader conception, the human heart is an insulting shape and a cauldron of evil. Given its terrible nature, the progress of civilization becomes a grotesque illusion, and one might best look back to the submerged myths and religions that once were created out of and for the sake of a sense of order. In *Ryder*, though, the parodic treatment of fable and scripture only points up to the absurdity of civilized man's attempt to resuscitate them.

Without a sense of history or a cohesive world view, the human life span appears as a coming " 'out of the eternal whim of time' " and going " 'into the eternal maw of its caprice' " (*R*, 303). Along the way all is tentative, and Miss Barnes repeatedly brings into play terministic patterns that recall this to the reader. Moving forward and backward, going and coming, coming and going: intermediate motion that falls within the broader limits of birth and death. In a chapter titled "Going To and Coming From," Wendell confounds the local authorities who are incensed by his ways by telling an apocryphal story about Moll and Eva which revolves around the rhetorical question of which of the two was holier, the one who was always seen going to or the one seen coming from church. In the end, beneath a picture of the bleeding heart, the answer is given: Moll dies and goes to the Lord, Eva gives birth and thus comes from the Lord. A similar effect comes from the repeated contextual variation of the term "go down," a phrase that is carried with resonance into *Nightwood*. Here, as later, to go down ultimately refers to the act of being born or to going to the grave, with intermediate associations in varying directions: to the sexual act, to debasement or humiliation, devaluation, or sometimes humility, as in going down upon one's knees in prayer. This "Vocabulary of Movement" (*R*, 32), this leitmotif evolving out of the novel's central themes, strives for a certain unity beneath the often bewildering variety that is everywhere.

It objectifies the uncertainty of passage from the mystery of birth to that of death in a novel that counsels by way of introduction, "Thou knowest not."

Is nature, then, the only balm for the tortured heart in a civilization that is disinherited of its ideals and beliefs? If so, it is a consolation that is as tentative as all of human experience. As the animals surround Ryder in the last scene, we are aware simultaneously of his closeness to and distance from them. Like Robin in *Nightwood*, he is composite of animal and human, and from this comes his beauty along with his terror. Sophia knows that "'a woman can be civilized beyond civilization and she can be beast beyond beast'" (*R*, 317). At the same time, the opaque eye of the beast marks a line that cannot be crossed. So when Suzanne C. Ferguson writes that "the apparent longing for the freedom and peace of the beasts is nowhere more in evidence than in . . . *Ryder*, and Miss Barnes's inability to come to terms with its difficulites is one of the main causes of the novel's failure,"[13] she fails to consider how ambiguity is thematically pivotal in all facets of the book. Miss Ferguson does recognize that in the case of the short stories it is misleading to speak lightly, as critics have, of her sympathy and identification with the simple animal, but *Ryder*, does in fact demonstrate a more complex attitude toward nature and the beast than had emerged out of the earlier pastoral poems. In those, nature's cyclical rhythms afforded some solace for the pain of fugitive love. And the "Rape and Repining" chapter does, after the breach in time and nature, close on this healing note: "It is Spring again . . . the Waters melt, and the Earth divides, and the leaves put forth, and the Heart sings dilly, dilly, dilly!" (*R*, 36). Yet nature is Wendell himself, involving all of life in risk, but in the end becoming fearfully inscrutable, a final enigma.

Mystery, in essence, is the subject of *Ryder*, the ambiguity of suspension between nature and humanity, life and death, man and woman. The novel conceives of being as dichotomous, wherein there is no state that does not partake of its opposite. In its attempted scope, it represents a major advance for the journalist-poet who had begun with an attraction to sharply polarized points of view and sentiments. Here is an effort to operate *at once* on high and low levels, to convey simultaneously vivid concrete experience and abstract uncertainly. The constant shifts in style and tone occur in response to the vast complex of human points of view and feelings that are crammed into the novel. What is finally missing is the balance that some of the stories and all of the late work attain. The changes are often so rapid that the effects seem isolated or showy, as indeed they are sometimes meant to be. The author fully succeeds only in the long rhetorical monologues of the doctor, but they too seem divorced from context and merely inserted on a whim, part of the novel's unnecessity. One eventually suspects that, although Miss Barnes wants to reformulate narrative design by means of "conglomerate justaposition," at the same time she wants an effect of simultaneity that she attains only in places, and with difficulty. What is discordant and disjointed in *Ryder*, however, coalesces afterwards, and *Ladies Almanack* seems to be a move to gain the equilibrium lacking here.

On a much reduced scale, *Ladies Almanack* involves the same experiment with style and language that *Ryder* initiated. Although many of Miss Barnes's articles had been characterized by a detached infatuation with language, with the poetic potential of words aside from content, none of the poems or early stories anticipated this new fascination with archaic patterns of prose composition and terminology. One decisive factor in the shift, it is clear, was the influence of James Joyce.

Djuna Barnes had met Joyce in Paris early in the 1920s, and had the occasion to write of him in 1922 in "Vagaries Malicieux" and in an article in *Vanity Fair*. Primarily concerned with rendering her impressions of Joyce the man, she has little to say in them concerning the work itself. Miss Barnes does make it known, however, that her impression of Joyce as singer had been confirmed finally by *Ulysses* as it had appeared in the *Little Review*, by its passages that arranged "in the necessary silence, the abundant inadequacies of life, as a laying out of jewels—jewels with a will to decay."[14] Late in 1941, Miss Barnes recalled that when *Ulysses* appeared in February 1922, "Expatriate pens stood still," that the novel "had, overnight, changed the perspective of all who embraced the hope of a literary career."[15] Indeed, at that time Miss Barnes is supposed to have said, " ' I shall never write another line . . . Who has the nerve to after that?' "[16] But only a few years later, *Ryder* and *Ladies Almanack* came as evidence that Miss Barnes had adapted certain techniques of Joyce's for purposes of her own. While one can only conjecture that her poems had been influenced by "the thin sweet lyricism of *Chamber Music*," or her stories by "the casual inevitability of *Dubliners*," it does seem clear that the novels of 1928 grow out of the example of "that great Rabelaisian flower *Ulysses* . . . , with impartial addenda for foliage."[17] Joyce's observation that " 'All great talkers . . . have spoken in the language of Sterne, Swift or the Restoration,' "[18] could be taken as the inspiration for *Ryder*.

Miss Barnes's mention in 1922 that Joyce was never without his book of saints is suggestive when the question arises of the form chosen for *Ladies Almanack*, for its thin narrative line concerns the sainthood of its lesbian heroine Evangeline Musset, with full attention to saints' days in managerial gloss. That the book's style itself is a degree derived from Joyce has been closely considered by Jack Hirschman.

Hirschman views Djuna Barnes's attraction to Joyce as that of one poet to another, a poet who, moreover, had been developing in a variety of genres. Consequently, "in Miss Barnes's raciest and most abandoned passages, the verbal intricacies, the rhythmical varieties, and even the imagery itself are directly influenced by Joyce's *Work in Progress*," as it had appeared in *transition*, a review to which Miss Barnes herself was contributing at the time. In *Ladies Almanack*, throughout which a fairly uniform Elizabethan style prevails (in contrast to *Ryder*'s stylistic medley), Hirschman singles out three characteristic passages. One is a description which employs a catalogue method comparable to the opening description of Shem as it appeared in *transition* in 1927. The second Hirschman calls "a philosophy," a highly "involuted rhetorical statement, complete with parentheticals," A third type is a verbal tapestry echoing certain passages of word play in *Work in Progress*, but lacking Joyce's "neologistic innovation" and the "polysemantic evocative quality"[19] of his language. At this point before *Nightwood*, Hirschman is saying, Miss Barnes still lacks Joyce's skill in orchestrating the novel.

The three verbal strains that Hirschman cites were, of course, present in *Ryder* but in a scattered and generally unassimilated fashion. Falling far short of Joyce in erudition, according to one reviewer, the novel nonetheless held its ground by virtue of Miss Barnes's more unified and "virile" personality.[20] In the last analysis, what is missing from both *Ryder* and *Ladies Almanack* is a single grand coordinating principle like Joyce's intention to record simultaneous levels of human consciousness in their interaction with the subconscious. In *Ladies Almanack*, style discovers its own values and, as in *Ryder*, gradually turns upon itself in parody.

The parodic framework of *Ryder* was virtualy limitless, leaving ample room to emulate as well as satirize any and all aspects of human development with its religions and systems of knowledge, with their modes of expression through the course of history. Its pretense, in short, was to be both encyclopedic and lexical. A corresponding duality of intent lies behind *Ladies Almanack*, which in its narrowed scope seems an afterthought to the longer novel. It is content to evolve one style, develop one thematic-philosophic line, and as its point of departure to satirize one particular social group.

In *Ladies Almanack*, Miss Barnes is again concerned with the nature of women, but the sexes are even more sharply polarized. The universe of *Ryder* was one in which the matriarchal impluse toward unity and order was ceaselessly contending with the patriarchal drive toward disorder and division. The duality was incorporated in Wendell, who appeared as Adam both before and after Eden. With his vestigial feminine psychic component which manifested itself in maternal warmth and empathy with nature, Wendell embodied an androgynous Adam not unlike the Adamic figure in hermetic philosophies, but his historical role in the novel became that of Adam the progenitor. Implicitly linked to the notion of post-Edenic man was that of the decline of civilization. Adam's sons and the world they created were both subject to an almost deterministic inevitability, the dominant male principle wearing away the old order through successive generations by imposing its systems of free thought (later allied with commerce in *The Antiphon*) and practice of polygamy. By default, the man of *virtu* in *Ryder* became the homosexual O'Connor. And in *Ladies Almanack*, *virtu* becomes a Sapphic trait, the property of women alone.

Among the diverse literary and artistic cliques of Paris in the 1920's was a noteworthy circle of intellectual lesbians, with its crusaders and aesthetes alike. Representative among them were such individuals as Radcliffe Hall, author of *The Well of Loneliness*, the painter Romaine Brooks, and especially Natalie Clifford Barney, the famous "Amazone" whose influence on Miss Barnes's work would be evident later. Well known for her salon of long standing and great repute in the rue Jacob, frequented over several decades by the artistically and socially prominent, Remy de Gourmont principal among them, the totally expatriated American "N. C. B." was recalled by Miss Barnes years later as follows:

> Miss Barney entertained French statesmen, aging philosophers, poets, and haggard ladies of the faubourg St. Germain and the Proust tradition. Here titles and courtesans swayed among the callas, balancing sea urchins or sherbets, as the case might be, as fair blond ladies in flowering robes plucked at harps.[21]

Miss Barnes had had the opportunity to attend and observe these select and esoteric gatherings and ironically, not long before Miss Barney wrote admiringly of the work of Djuna Barnes in *Aventures de l'esprit*, Miss Barnes chose to write *Ladies Almanack*. It has been alleged that Miss Barney appears in this "slight satiric wigging" as its pivotal figure, Dame Musset.

The dust-jacket notes of the recent American edition make it clear that Miss Barnes considers the book as a piece of fun apart from her serious work. Created for the amusement of a limited coterie, the original edition had been published for Miss Barnes by Robert McAlmon under the imprint of

Darantière at Dijon, passed about in page proof in Parisian cafés, and sometimes brightly hand colored by its anonymous author, "A Lady of Fashion." The element of *blague* immediately comes across in the cover illustration, depicting ranks of lesbians charging on horseback across the clouds, holding aloft a banner bearing the book's title. The title page itself reads,

## LADIES ALMANACK

showing their Signs and their tides;
their Moons and their Changes;
the Seasons as it is with them;
their Eclipses and Equinoxes; as
well as a full Record of diurnal
    and Nocturnal Distempers (*LA*, p. 1)

Then begins the story of Evangeline Musset, couched within the twelve calendar months of the almanack. We are told of her birth, when she came forth missing an inch, and learn of the steps by which she became sainted. The bulk of the book's eighty-five pages presents glimpses of her and the members of her entourage, reports their discussions and disquisitions, and surrounds them with a thick verbal decor. In the final month, her death and burial befitting a saint are recorded. All of this is presented facetiously. Dame Musset is, of course, a mock saint.

Part 2 of *Aventures de l'esprit* is entitled "Une Académie de Femmes." and *Ladies Almanack* is a satire on the notion of a cultural aristocracy of women with its rituals and credos, its chic and its intrigues, its esoteric predispositions. In her new foreword to the Harper and Row edition, Miss Barnes cryptically presents her chronicle to the public:

Neap-tide to the Proustian chronicle, gleanings from the shores of Mytilene, glimpses of its novitiates, its rising "saints" and "priestesses," and thereon to such aptitude and insouciance that they took to gaming and to swapping that "other" of the mystery, the anomaly that calls the hidden name. That, affronted, eats its shadow. (*LA*, 3)

The work that follows is enveloped in obscurity, filled with superstitions, half-truths and credible falsehoods. As in *Ryder*, the bare narrative is overwhelmed, buried here in the novel's "fearfully punctuated" (*LA*, 3) rhetoric, distracted now and again by poems, illustrations, and even at one point a "Lullaby for a Lady's Lady" complete with its music. The setting is Paris in the twenties, where characters talk of wandering on the Champs Elysées or toward the church of Saint-Germain-des-Pres, but time is once again out of hand.

One 1972 reviewer compares the ornate style of Miss Barnes with John Barth's in *The Sot-Weed Factor*, finding that Barth's artificiality was handled brilliantly but "Miss Barnes, with no believable or interesting characters to help her out, does it poorly." It is hardly a novel, Larry McMurtry, himself a narrative-bound novelist, concludes, but "merely a piece of fluff."[22] Why, then, use the term *novel* for what is essentially a work of style, a protracted literary sketch? The justification is in the book's Elizabethan texture itself, for it recalls the antecedents of the novel proper in the fiction of the Renaissance, the period when narrative was enmeshed in a rhetorical web, when the tale told was frequently drawn thin in the elaboration of its telling. The June section, a poem of "Portents, Signs and Omens" refers to "the Bird of Memory lost,/Late roosting on the Hollow tree of Time,/Which only backward can the Scaler climb" (*LA*, 40), and Miss Barnes appears to be reaching backward to the sources of a form that, along with all else, had acquired "a stink of Advancement" (*LA*, 69). Just as *Ryder* was an effort to revitalize the novel by calling a halt to its development along traditional lines and going back to past forms, *Ladies Almanack* returns to a point where style still had the grip on narrative and stories were marvelous, ornate, and possessed of wonderment. The illustrations, done "with apologies to ancient chapbooks, broadsheets, and *Images Populaires*" (*LA* 3), likewise reach back with deliberate flattened perspective and naiveté of draftsmanship to a time prior to the mandates of realism.

The themes along with the style of *Ladies Almanack*, almost in continuation of *Ryder*, develop from an awareness that "In the Salt Earth lie Parcels of lost Perfection . . ." (*LA*, 15). In consequence, it too belies its appearance. Beneath its surface levity it is a pain-racked comedy, aware of a lost Eden and a confused present. Before "the Earth sucked down her Generations" (*LA*, 62),

> There was a time when still rhymed to the wild Rib that had made her, Woman was atune to every Adder, every Lion, every Tiger, every Wood thing, every Water-wight, every Sky-wanderer; every Apple was to her a whole Superstition, and to quiet and to tame that Bone, she whispered "Lord! Lord!" (*LA*, p. 61)

Miss Barnes seems to presume an hermaphroditic Adam, from which would follow what one Low-Heel recalls to her companion High-Head from her reading, that woman must originally " 'have had a testes of sorts, however wried and awander; that indeed she was called forth a Man, and when answering, by some Mischance, or monstrous Fury of Fate, stumbled over a Womb, and was damned then and forever to drag it about, like a prisoner his ball and Chain, whether she would or no' " (*LA*, 53).

Since the sunderance of Eve, the pain in the world is rooted in sexual difference, the fact of woman that "near to a Man or far from a Man, she will not be of him!" (*LA*, 53). Whereas *Ryder* treated the tension of this separation in domestic terms, here Miss Barnes focuses upon the condition of women who turn to women, and in doing so becomes once again deeply involved in anomaly.

In a rather salacious opening chapter, Dame Musset, who had been intended in the womb to be a boy, tells her father when her inclination finally becomes revealed that she should be commended all the more for managing to eventuate according to his wishes without the "Tools for the Trade." The chapter becomes a panegyric extolling her Sapphic virtues, her ability to administer " . . . the Consolation every Woman has at her Finger Tips, or at the very Hang of her Tongue" (*LA*, 6). Then the January section brings in by contrast Patience

Scalpel, who cannot understand the ways of her sisters. " 'Do they not have Organs as exactly alike as two Peas, or twin Griefs . . . ?' " (LA, 11) she asks. ' "Where, and in what dark chamber was the Tree so cut of Life, that the Branch turned to the Branch, and made of the Cuttings a Garden of Ecstasy?' " (LA, 12). This is the end of generation to her eyes, a blind alley, and certainly not for her daughters.

Here and there Patience Scalpel is brought in again as a foil, all the more to point up the point of view of sexual dichotomy that is the lesbian's. At moments, the narrative takes on the tone of a Sapphic manifesto, arguing the prerogatives of Sisters in the social patriarchal world from which they are outcast. Most of the time, however, the book is a lamentation amid much laughter. Man's role in the universe is seldom considered, and when it is, it is either in concrete terms of physical difference or in abstractions. To Lady Bulk-and-Balk, for example, brutal men have only death between them while women share " 'Pity only, and a resuscitating Need!' " (LA, 20). Or, as Maisie Tuck-and-Frill has it, "Love in Man is Fear of Fear. Love in Woman is Hope without Hope' " (LA, 23). Evangeline Musset is her own revenge against men. In general, men are despised and, in the inversion upon which the book's philosophy partly depends, women become the standard.

Yet "'Love of Woman for Woman should increase Terror'" (LA, 20), according to Dame Musset. It is women's unity in similarity that is at the same time her superiority and her curse. The horror is in the experience of coming back upon oneself: " 'A Man's love is built to fit Nature. Woman's is a Kiss in the Mirror,' " as Maisie Tuck-and-Frill goes on speaking in " '. . . that Voice which has been accorded ever to those who go neither Hither or Thither; The Voice of the Prophet' " (LA, 23). The lesbian weeps " 'for Loneliness estranged—the unthinking returning of themselves to themselves' " (LA, 58), the finding at the end of nature and generation the image of the double.

Furthermore, when "Planets, Stars and Zones/Run girlish to their Marrow-bones" (LA, 60), there is the additional horror of being neither here nor there, neither this nor that, but a compound creature mirroring itself. Like the lesbians in the

distempers of August, "they swing between two Conditions like
a Bell's Clapper, that can never be said to be anywhere, neither
in the Centre, nor to the Side, for that which is always moving,
is in no settled State long enough to be either damned or transfigured" (*LA*, 48). Not wholly woman but mixed of man, at the
same time "God-Haunted and Demon-Seeking" (*LA*, 66), they
go neither hither nor thither and few can speak with the
tongue of the prophet. Their cult is a cult of mystery. She who
"thaws nothing but Facts" has no place in the circle.

Ladies Almanack, finally, revolves in enigma. Our only
proof of God, Miss Barnes says, is what we know not of Him. It
is in this paradoxical vein that the book attemps to render
"unfathomed Mystery" as more tangible than concrete fact. As
the "Jesus Mundane" chapter in *Ryder* has stated, "For some is
the image, and for some the Thing, and for others the Thing
that even the Thing knows naught of; and for one only the
meaning of That beyond That" (*R*, 2). The elaborate obscurity
is justified first by the object of the book's satire, and secondly
by the author's conviction that there are few philosophers, that
the grand systems of thought in the past have become muzzy or
distorted. In its play on the almanack tradition, it reaches back
to the medieval mode of creating systems out of cosmic uncertainly, all the while aware of the repository of wit that the
almanack later became. In its treatment of the anguish of
unknowing with harsh humor, *Ladies Almanack* stands beside
*Ryder* as a step toward merging the frivolous and the serious,
the attitudes that had appeared irreconcilable in the earlier
articles and poems. Perhaps due to its more limited scope,
*Ladies Almanack* achieves a greater unity of effect so that the
recurrent echo of the lamentation is laughter.

Along with this resolution, the novels of 1928 mark an
important point in Miss Barnes's development in other
primary respects. They both begin to shape an attitude toward
recorded history, discovering that time revolves back upon
itself and that progress is an illusion. They also develop a conception of human relationships as haunted by "Loneliness
estranged," and proceed to reveal this primarily through the
condition of women. While working out these themes which

become central in *Nightwood*, Miss Barnes, largely through Joyce's example, was also becoming aware of the liberating properties of language and the possibilities of style that had predated the past century and its inflexible forms. *Ryder* and *Ladies Almanack*, however, find Miss Barnes still in an experimental phase, only beginning to struggle out of the binding limits of the novelistic genre. They amount essentially to a reaction against traditional form, only half of the process of reconstruction preceding *Nightwood*. It was elsewhere, in the form of the short story, that Miss Barnes was taking another perspective on her craft that would equally determine the course of her later work.

# 4.

# The Short Stories

After the discursiveness of *Ryder*, the stories of Djuna Barnes appear as extraordinarily tight constructions. Those carefully revised and sharpened ones that form the later *Spillway* hold together almost as chapters of a planned whole. In view of its resemblance to a story sequence in which each distinct part, through interrelated or recurring symbols and literary techniques, contributes to a central purpose or vision, a further similarity to James Joyce may be noted. Both *Spillway* and *Dubliners* convey a whole rather than a fragmented impression. Both deal with the suppressed life of a particular culture and the moments in which it spills over into daily experience. In *Dubliners*, Joyce is specifically concerned with Ireland's frozen political, social, and historical position and the consequent repression of spirit. Miss Barnes's locale shifts and is less specific, but it no less concretely incorporates the dead forms that remain in a twentieth-century wasteland after the severance of all historical and spiritual connections, leaving a terrible restlessness underneath. Similiar polar types appear in the books of each writer: in Djuna Barnes's case, peasants and continental aristocrats, in Joyce's the common men and the elite of Dublin. And of course each is the sole short story collection in the two authors' bodies of work.

Before *Ryder* and *Ladies Almanack* appeared, Djuna Barnes's reputation as a developing artist centered upon her achievement with the short story. By any standards, the articles, drawings, and poems that Miss Barnes was publishing in the

1910s and later were secondary creations. And just as she was becoming recognized as a playwright, sometime in the early twenties she evidently found herself blocked in trying to round off two three-act plays to her satisfaction. In the meantime, a career that had begun in the pages of the *Morning Telegraph* was continuing steadily, as Miss Barnes's stories appeared in *All-Story Weekly*, the *Little Review*, the *Dial*, *Smart Set*, *Vanity Fair*, Ford Madox Ford's *Transatlantic Review*, and other little magazines and anthologies of the twenties. In 1923, *A Book* brought together twelve of these, and three more were added to the reissue, *A Night Among the Horses*, in 1929. Then, having become deeply involved in the early thirties in the long composition of *Nightwood*, Miss Barnes stopped publishing new stories almost completely.

None of the short stories of Djuna Barnes, however, is presently available in its original form. A number were never collected or anthologized. With one exception, the ten which appear in the 1962 Faber and Faber edition of *Spillway* are carefully revised versions of stories from the 1923 and 1929 editions, leaving six of those still out of print. From this it may be assumed that it is Miss Barnes's choice, as a writer of short fiction, to be represented by *Spillway* alone. Accordingly, this chapter will take *Spillway* as its primary subject but also, in the absence of any significant critical attention to Miss Barnes's fiction before *Nightwood*, try to convey a sense of what comparable qualities the early stories had.

An examination of the stories allows a reader to discover nearly all of the techniques, ideas, and motifs that are basic in Miss Barnes's work. The early examples quite closely parallel her work in other genres, while the late *Spillway* stands as a volume with a high degree of unity, built almost as if intentionally as a story sequence which would suffer from the removal or displacement of any of its members. Placed at the beginning of *The Selected Works*, also of 1962, and preceding *Nightwood* in the volume, it serves as an ideal means of approaching that novel. Neville Braybrooke writes that many of the stories in *Spillway* act as bridges between *Nightwood* and *The Antiphon* because "they are part of the same imaginative landscape, relayed at the same order of intensity."[1] They are also a strong link between the early work and the mature work, bridging the gap between *Ryder* (and *Ladies Almanack*) and *Nightwood*. By the very fact of their revision, they are at once the creations of the developing and the mature artist.

Defining the particular quality of these stories would require relating them to Miss Barnes's work in other genres. In the first place, they have none of the rhetorical excess of either the novels of 1928 or the earlier *Book of Repulsive Women* and the Lydia Steptoe vein of literary sketch, although from the last follow the stories that are narrated by a precocious and perverse "little girl." The affinity of the majority is rather to some of the more stylistically restrained articles and essays and, in certain cases, to the lyrical-bucolic poems. Like those, the stories demonstrate the author's ability to observe and render the natural world, the world outside, with a certain degree of objectivity. In their mode of narration, excepting only the two stories in *Spillway* told in the first person by the girl, they hold to an omniscient third-person voice that has no patience with verbal decoration or gratuitous fancy. Pointedly economical, concise both in exposition and metaphor, the narrative voice delivers a terse, often epigrammatic, often either elliptical or involuted, version of common speech. The verbal condensation results in something both elusive and concrete, as will readily appear in quoted passages.

As might be expected, the stories are not confined to any conventional approach to plot. Much different in manner from *Ryder* and *Ladies Almanack*, they are no less of a departure from the great storytelling tradition. In fact, Miss Barnes's least successful stories are those few that do depend upon the elaboration of a plot. For instance, in *Vanity Fair* at the end of the twenties, she attempted a few light ironic tales of European aristocracy somewhat in the manner of de Maupassant or Schnitzler. The results, however, lacked their primary interest in character, and the irony remained merely on the surface, plot-bound. In one of these, "The First of April," two longtime lovers are pesuaded by their respective spouses to terminate the affair on the grounds that they have become visibly old and ridiculous. The parting messages that Baron Otto Lowenhaven and Contessa Mafalda Beonetti wire each other are indeed received, but, irresistibly reunited in Rome, the lovers thank each other for not wiring, feigning unbroken trust. In "The Letter That Was Never Mailed," the Baron Anzengruber and the Vicomte Virevaude, friends since childhood, share a "wild, lyric, rococo"[2] infatuation with Vava Hajos, a Viennese dancer, and their rivalry reaches a comparable ironic dénouement. Rather more successful is "A Duel Without Seconds," which has to do with repeated thefts at society affairs given over the years by the Baron and Baroness Otterly-Hansclever. Its measure of success, however, comes from the fact that it creates a precise sense of faded, impoverished nobility that remains after the mechanics of its anecdotal plot are forgotten.

Although this milieu is present in parts of *Spillway*, the *Vanity Fair* stories relate more closely to Miss Barnes's formulaic one-act drawing room dramas of the twenties than to the majority of her stories. Equally atypical is a much later story, "The Perfect Murder." Written in 1942 and published in the *Harvard Advocate*, it concerns a Professor Anatol Profax, whose field is dialectology and whose special interest is in the effect of environment on speech ("The inarticulate had proved particularly satisfactory; they were rather more racial then individual."). Love to him is love of sound, and ridiculously he conceives himself a man of violent passions: "Certainly at some time in his life he must have curbed an emotion, crushed a desire, trampled a weakness." In any case, in his tabulations he has yet to find someone who defies classification.

One day on the streets of New York, he observes a circus poster depicting "the one True and Only Elephant Woman." Shortly he stumbles into a woman who claims that she had just died from a fall from a trapeze and come back: "'I'm devoted to coming back, it's so agonizing.'" She announces herself as a *Trauma*, saying that she is sometimes the elephant girl, some-times the trapeze artist, sometimes a milliner, and sometimes hungry. Her speech is a string of nonsense statements, epigrams, and non sequiturs. She calls herself " 'as aboveboard as the Devil,' " and " 'the purest abomination imaginable.' "

Perverse and irrational, she walks the streets with the train of her velvet dress dragging cigarette butts and theater ticket stubs in the dust. They proceed to his rooms and agree to marry, but later. When the elephant girl stumbles amid sheet music and caramels, the professor, abruptly feeling something entirely new, happy yet "cold, dedicated, and gentle," slits her throat with a penknife. After putting her in a trunk piece by piece, "He did not know what to do; he had destroyed definition; by his own act he had ruined a great secret; he'd never be able to place her." Immediately finding that she has vanished from the trunk, he rushes out and climbs into a hansom cab, only to discover that she is at his side in the neighboring one. A traffic light presently separates them.

Those who would argue the influence of surrealism upon Miss Barnes could find no better support than this story, with its juxtaposition of incongruous elements and its management of dream as reality. "The Perfect Murder," different though its style may be, relates to the earlier stories directly through its theme of the subjugation of logic by the great force of the irrational, of the suppressed life of the imagination. True knowledge, Miss Barnes repeatedly implies, is intuitive and cuts through rational philosophies. Human language, especially ordinary discourse, is powerless to express it. If language is to achieve a higher synthesis of experience, it must be restored to its living sense through the image. In effect, Miss Barnes is after the same thing as Professor Profax, who hopes to recapture "that great band of sound that had escaped the human throat for over two thousand years":

No theories for or against; no words of praise or of blame, only a vast, terrible lamentation which would echo like the "Baum!" of the Malabar Caves. For after all what does man say when it comes right down to it? "I love, I fear, I hunger, I die." Like the cycles of Purgatory and Damnation.[3]

The satiric approach of "The Perfect Murder" is unique in Miss Barnes's short stories. Its schematic method mocks itself, the end result of a reaction against the sort of mechanical plot-ting attempted in the *Vanity Fair* tales. While the *Spillway* stories and their early versions react against the conventional plot, however, most of them do have affinities to certain types of narrative fiction or drama. One story involving the tortured relations between a lady and her ostler shows the conscious influence of Strindberg.[4] More often, Miss Barnes's way of fleshing out small situations in her mordant, spare prose recalls some of the Russian short stories of the late nineteenth and early twentieth centuries. The naturalism of Chekhov in partic-ular comes to mind. But there also appears a quality that is more difficult to define. Natalie Clifford Barney may have come the nearest to capturing it when she commented, in con-nection with passages of Miss Barnes's prose that she was intro-ducing in translation, "Ses pensées ne vont jamais jusqu'à la pensée. Ce sont des bribes de sensations, miriors brisées à la joie de vivre ou l'on se coupe."[5] It is in this sense that the stories may be called experimental. They amount to an attempt to get in touch with "the Undercurrents," ignored in journalistic writ-ing, by capturing "fragments of sensations," the very elements that the literary naturalists might have suppressed in expec-tation of conclusive action, the effective climax of character development in time. They suggest the way which the silent moving picture found to pick and isolate significant details from the stream of sequential action and, by the technique of montage, transcend the frequently mundane requirements of story and dramatic structure. By ordering such fragments, not to reinforce some abstract idea or promote some sequence of events, but to render in a concise image or turn of speech the tentativeness of being, they cohere rather independently of the reader's preconceptions. One can begin to get a sense of how Miss Barnes manages the refractive elements of experience from a look at two of the stories in *A Book* that were excluded from *Spillway*.

In "The Nigger," a Southern gentleman who has lived well and scornfully, who "hated negroes with that hate a master calls love,"[6] is dying in the presence of Rabb, the nigger. She had served John Hardaway's mother also at her deathbed, and had tried to do something for her. "But the thing she was trying to touch lay in some hidden corner of Mrs. Hardaway, as a cat hides away under a bed, and Rabb had done nothing after all" (*NAH*, p. 174). The son wishes to tell Rabb something, but only whispers, " 'Keep your place' " (*NAH*, p. 177). When he is near the point of death, Rabb assists him by placing her mouth to his and breathing one powerful and deadly breath into him. Like the stories in *Spillway*, this tale builds upon the indirect, stressing the unsaid and the implied. Between Hardaway and Rabb there has been no communication, yet a feeling of quite frightening intimacy is conveyed. The final result is ambiguity, for their relationship cannot be defined in familiar terms.

Equally elusive and marked by fragments of sensations is "Mother," which returns to Miss Barnes's familiar drab, somewhat seedy urban milieu which is in keeping with the physical descriptions of the characters. Lydia Passova, the pawn shop mistress, is "excessively tall," and "her eyes were small, and not well focused. The left was slightly distended from the long use of a magnifying glass" (*NAH*, p. 164). As for her lover, he is "a little nervous fellow . . . a roundfaced youth with a deep soft cleft in his chin, on which grew two separate tufts of yellow hair. His eyes were wide and pale, and his eye-teeth prominent" (*NAH*, p. 165). Less garish than the women in *The Book of Repulsive Women*, these characters—and there are many of them in Miss Barnes's stories—have a powerful aura of waste about them, a sense of having been bypassed by life and condemned to a semi-isolated existence of unfulfilled or inarticulate love. So, although her lover astonishes himself by thinking Lydia Passova a great woman,

> He never knew where she had come from, what her life had been if she had or had not been married, if she had or had not known lovers; all that she would say was, "Well, you are with me, does that tell you nothing?" and he had to answer, "No, it tells me nothing." (*NAH*, p. 168)

Their relationship even seems to rest directly upon its obscurity as the basis of its endurance. Eventually she dies, and he beholds that she is an old woman: "He felt as one feels who has become conscious of passion for the first time, in the presence of a relative" (*NAH*, p. 171). That night he weeps in bed with knees drawn up.

A sense of elusiveness is gained here by moving around the outer edges of a human relationship. Most of the stories in *A Book* and its reprint, *A Night Among the Horses*, deal obliquely with experience. They make the reader a furtive observer of something that he cannot logically understand, that he finds himself in the middle of and yet not of. Insinuative rather than explicative, Miss Barnes's method is perhaps most effective in "Aller et Retour," the story that opens *Spillway*.

Perhaps the best known of all her stories, "Aller et Retour" was remembered by Graham Greene as it had first appeared in *Transatlantic Review* as "an impressive story with a cruel, visual wit and dialogue curiously precise and suggestive, like the imagery of a Jacobean dramatist."[7] The opening one-sentence paragraph, as if in rebuttal of Gertrude Stein's pronouncement, "A Sentence is not emotional a paragraph is,"[8] forecasts the directness and precision that are to follow: "The train travelling from Marseilles to Nice had on board a woman of great strength."[9] Her journey itself, following the death of her estranged husband, is from Paris to Nice, back to a daughter she has not seen for seven years. The opening description places an unusual emphasis upon her dress, her jewels, which hint of her self-contained demeanor. She surveys the passing countryside through a lorgnette, having tried with difficulty to read a few sentences of *Madame Bovary*. "A middle-aged and rather absurd Madame Bovary,"[10] Graham Greene calls Madame Erling von Bartmann herself.

There is a two and a half day pause in Marseille. Madame von Bartmann walks the dirty streets holding up her skirt in a way that is described as at once careful and absent. As foul odors reach her, "she looked neither pleased nor displeased" (*S*, p. 10). From her aloofness, what she observes seems both charged with significance and oddly disconnected:

A gross woman, with wide set legs, sprawled in the doorway to a single room, gorged with a high-posted rust-

ing iron bed. The woman was holding a robin loosely in
one huge plucking hand. The air was full of floating
feathers, falling and rising about girls with bare
shoulders, blinking under coarse dark bangs . . . .

At a ship-chandler's she stopped, smelling the tang of
tarred rope. She took down several coloured postcards
showing women in the act of bathing; of happy mariners
leaning above full-busted sirens with sly cogged
eyes . . . . A window, fly-specked dusty and cracked,
displayed, terrace upon terrace, white and magenta
funeral wreaths, wired in beads, flanked by images of the
Bleeding Heart, embossed in tin, with edgings of beaten
flame, the whole beached on a surf of metal lace. (S, p. 10)

The next morning she enters a church alone. Kneeling,

She turned the stones of her rings out and put her hands
together, the light shining between the little fingers;
raising them she prayed, with all her vigorous understanding, to God, for a common redemption.

She got up, peering about her, angry that there were
no candles burning to the *Magnifique*—feeling the stuff of
the altar-cloth. (S, p. 11)

Upon arrival in Nice, Madame von Bartmann announces to
Richter, her daughter, that she plans to stay for quite a while.
Between the two, all is hesitation. The girl is reticent, embar-
rassingly immature, and the mother's resentment clearly
stands between them. "'A queer, mad fellow'" (S, p. 14), she
says of Herr von Bartmann.

That evening, however, Madame von Bartmann attempts
to speak to her daughter. Her words pour out in a barely interrupted monologue. Life, she begins, is filthy and frightful.
"'There is everything in it: murder, pain, beauty, disease—
death'" (S, p. 16). She tells her daughter she knows nothing,
and continues:

"You must know *everything*, and *then* begin. You must have
a great understanding, or accomplish a fall. Horses hurry

you away from danger; trains bring you back. Paintings give the heart a mortal pang—they hung over a man you loved and perhaps murdered in his bed. Flowers hearse up the heart because a child was buried in them. Music incites to the terror of repetition. The cross-roads are where lovers vow, and taverns are for thieves. Contemplation leads to prejudice; and beds are fields where babies fight a losing battle." (*S*, pp. 16–17)

Man, she then says into Richter's silence, is rotten with virtue and with vice alike.

"He is strangled by the two and made nothing; and God is the light the mortal instinct kindled, to turn to, and to die by . . . . I do not want you to turn your nose up at any whore in any street; pray and wallow and cease, but without prejudice . . . . Do not be vain about your indifference, should you be possessed of indifference; and don't . . . misconceive the value of your passions; it is only seasoning to the whole horror."

" '*Think*,' " Madame von Bartmann at this point concludes:

"Think everything, good, bad, indifferent; everything, and *do* everything; *everything*! Try to know what you are before you die. And . . . come back to me a good woman." (*S*, p. 17)

This remarkable passage, marking the peak of intensity in the story, is described by Jack Hirschman as a "rhythmical and rhetorical elaboration"[11] evoking a poetic response, and then just avoiding the poetically pretentious by virtue of the universal statements framing it. Likewise, the dissociated images that accumulate in montage in the Marseilles passage might have appeared merely esoteric without the verbal extension they are given here. When Richer asks her mother if there had been anything nice in Marseilles, Madame von Bartmann smiles and replies, " 'The Bleeding Heart—sailors—' " (*S*, p. 13), recalling instantaneously the whole poetic tableau of pain and eroticism that she had beheld earlier.

What follows is abrupt. A few days later Richter shyly reveals her engagement to a government clerk that had been prearranged by the father. When he comes to dinner, Gerald Teal speaks as follows:

> "I shall do my best to make your daughter happy. I am a man of staid habits, no longer too young . . . . We hope to have children—Richter will be occupied. As she is delicate we shall travel, to Vichy, once a year. I have two very fine horses and a carriage with sound springs. She will drive in the afternoons, when she is indisposed—though I hope she will find her greatest happiness at home." (*S*, p. 19)

Two months later, the wedding having taken place, Madame von Bartmann boards the train back to Paris. " 'Ah, how unnecessary' " (*S*, p. 19) is all she says to herself in conclusion.

Once again it is apparent that Miss Barnes is working in style and theme alike with the dualities that continue to preoccupy her. Here there is an interplay between two orders of experience which relates to a comment of Miss Barnes in her theatre article, "The Dear Dead Days":

> I had written that there are only two kinds of loneliness: love and imagination. I said that only two classes knew love, the high and the low; the high because of their fancy, and the low because of their need. The middle classes dabbled in that simple intrigue which takes itself out in what I called the "home condition"; they never suffer the agony, or discover the ecstasy of the "emotional return." By this was meant that no associations displace their caution; they could, in other words, scarcely be betrayed because their little sardine of love has been decorously sandwitched (sic) between forethought and afterthought.[12]

Hence the inability of Madame von Bartmann to touch her daughter. Richter is vacant, while her mother is overflowing. The two stand parallel to Miss Barnes's aforementioned contrast between Gounod's Marguerite, a total blank or "matter without structure" ("There was no ego, therefore one could come upon her so easily."), [13] and Oscar Wilde's Salomé, in whom one feels the reverberation of past events. Here it would seem in order to question Suzanne Ferguson's claim that for all her knowledge, "Mme. von Bartmann is not a person, either."[14] The strength with which Miss Barnes initially endows her heroine is not in doubt, but there is a gap here between particular orders of being, on a level beyond the individual characters. Like Sophia in *Ryder*, Madame von Bartmann is one of Miss Barnes's women who have come to some terms with the mortal agony. The end note of unnecessity, in her terms of coping, has to be not flippant, but profound. The title itself, recalling the repeated "going to and coming from" pattern in *Ryder*, is a forecast of the irony of her experience.

Two languages play in counterpoint throughout. One is the language of plain narrative, though extremely concise and highly charged, which is capable of lending credibility to the social comedy in the situation. The other is a compact metaphorical poetic construction, a series of striking images reflecting the terror of the impossibility of being with an impact comparable to the final exclamation of horror in Conrad's *Heart of Darkness*. In their particular ways, each of Miss Barnes's stories is involved with what happens when what is dark and suppressed spills out into the deceptive world of daily events and rational motives.

"Cassation," the next story in *Spillway*, contains a significant extension of this theme. Originally titled "A Little Girl Tells a Story to a Lady," it is the monologue of a young girl in a café, addressed to a silent lady who is again the presumed interlocutor in "The Grande Malade," formerly called "The Little Girl Continues" when it appeared in *This Quarter* in 1925, its only publication prior to *Spillway*. A third of these stories, "Dusie," appeared in *Americana Esoterica*, an anthology of 1927, but was never reprinted.[15] The narrator is again one of Miss

Barnes's young girls on the verge of womanhood, part innocent yet insouciantly and intuitively involved in adult perversity and sophistication. In this case the models for Katya and her sister Moydia (in "The Grande Malade") were actual figures in the Parisian café scene of the twenties, and Miss Barnes had already drawn attention to them in an article for *Charm*:

> From Holland come the tiny sisters Bronja and Tylia, eighteen and twenty. They speak four languages, they have sat to Marie Laurencin, Princess Lucien Murat, Boussingault. . . . They are part of the movement *Cigale*, the "*Boeuf sur le toit*." They all call Cocteau "Jean"; they talked with Radiguet as he dropped and replaced his monocle in those days before his death. They danced to the rhythm of the jungle beaten out by a "dusky" on the drum; they sat in their capes at the bar drinking *Yvette* and *Menthe* for its color.[16]

Like their fictional counterparts, they are intoxicated with their preciosity.

The story that Katya tells a lady is a bizarre one indeed, and it is easy to see why certain critics incline to characterize Miss Barnes's stories as "gothic and melodramatic."[17] In a Berlin café, Katya observes a magnificent woman, " '. . . savage with jewels, and something purposeful and dramatic came in with her, as if she were the centre of a whirlpool, and her clothes a temporary debris' " (*S*, p.21). With her is a small, oddly fragile man, her broken husband who remains in the background throughout, but whose presence, once established, hangs in the atmosphere like a ghost. Eventually the woman, Gaya, takes the girl to her home, where, in an expensive but disorderly and melancholy bedroom, a child of about three lies in the center of a tall, massive bed making a thin buzzing noise like a fly. The bed is disheveled and "devastated," and over it hangs a great painting of foreign battle, in which warriors on horseback seem to be charging the battlefield of the bed. The reader is directly thrust into the same landscape that Madame von Bartmann had created through her distilled experience. The woman tells Katya that she will stay here, forgetting her ambitions for the theater, her passion for the dance, everything.

During the course of a year, the girl becomes a *"religieuse"* of a sort, embracing, as she says, " 'a religion, Madame, that was empty of need, therefore it was not holy perhaps, and not as it should have been in its manner' " (*S*, p.25). As for Gaya's religion, it involves the philosophy that " 'one should be like all people *and* oneself, then . . . one was both ruined and powerful' " (*S*, p.26).

One night, in the presence of the buzzing child, Gaya tells the girl that she must stay forever and forget everything. Reversing Madame von Bartmann's advice to think everything, she begins a terrifying monologue devoted to the theme of nothingness: " 'The whole world is nothing but a noise, as hot as the inside of a tiger's mouth. They call it civilization—that is a lie' " (*S*, p.28). Becoming wilder, she says that Katya must learn that there is nothing but herself and that then she will manage. At last totally and schizophrenically dissociated from herself, she cries " ' . . . she has no claws to hang by; she has no hunting foot; she has no mouth for the meat—*vacancy!*' " (*S*, p. 20). In the end, she is helpless to conceive of living out the beast within her, having failed of life on any other plane.

Katya departs. The fancy takes her to visit Paris, but before leaving she returns to the strange house once more. On the bed, the woman and child are both making the same dehumanized buzzing cry. Gaya says, " 'Forgive me—I trusted you—I was mistaken. I did not know that I could do it myself, but you see, I can do it myself' " (*S*, p. 30). In other words, she has accomplished her cassation. " 'Things are like that, when one travels, *nicht wahr*, Madame?' " (*S*, p. 30), Katya concludes.

The weird, seemingly catatonic child is a perfect symbol for Gaya's alienation from herself and from life. As Katya says, " 'It was beautiful in the corrupt way of idiot children; a sacred beast without a taker, tainted with innocence and waste time; honey-haired and failing, like those dwarf angels on holy prints and valentines' " (*S*, p. 26). Indeed, the child's name is Valentine, a touch which is in part Miss Barnes's way of heaping on the decadence again, but which also recalls in oblique fashion the image of the Bleeding Heart. Along with the helpless husband Ludwig, the three, in a configuration anticipating the Volkbeins in *Nightwood*, embody the historical cassation that Miss Barnes had dealt with in *Ryder*. Even Katya too is corrupt with "innocence and waste time." In the course of her narrative, she repeatedly disgresses into the charm of the seasons in Germany, a leitmotif[18] acting in witty counterpoint to the theme of seasonless horror in nothingness, and pointing up her rootlessness, her distance from life, in a word, her estrangement.

In the only scholarly article on the stories of Djuna Barnes, Suzanne C. Ferguson accurately observes that their world is one of displaced persons who "have abandoned national, racial, and ethical traditions; their human contacts are laceration,"[19] and they are finally even estranged against themselves. Madame von Bartmann is prepared for this estrangement, carries it like a shield, while Gaya allows the same perception of life to drive her into a void. Whatever their destiny (and Gaya denies that man has a destiny), the characters are all radically dislocated. Correspondingly, their stories, in Miss Ferguson's terms, "have their being outside society and historical milieu, and indeed the vacuum that surrounds them is responsible for not a little of their impact."[20]

As "the little girl continues" in "The Grande Malade," a story said to be based on the death of Radiguet, [21] she tells Madame, " 'We are where we are. We are Polish when we are in Poland, and when in Holland we are Dutch, and now in France we are French, and one day we will go to America and be American' " (S, p. 32). At fifteen Moydia wishes to become " ' *"tragique"* and *"triste"* and "tremendous" all at once' " (S, p. 31), to become effectively consumed in her youth. So as a lover she takes a Monsieur X, " 'beastly with *finis*' " and a " 'product of Malaise' " (S, p.36), yet the " *'belle-d'un-jour'* " of that season in his role as the protegé of a certain Baron. While Moydia is in Germany visiting her father, Monsieur X becomes ill and, after drinking all night in the company of the Baron, dies. " 'The

Baron wanted it that way: "For that," he said, "he might die as he was born, without knowing" ' " (S, p.39).

When Moydia learns of this, she herself drinks all night and before sleeping says, " 'Now I have a great life!' " Wearing X's cape, she goes about " 'gay, spoiled, *tragique*. She sugars her tea from far too great a height' " (S, p.40). As Katya says of her, " 'She had a *great memory in the present*, and it all turns about a cape, therefore now she wears a cape, until something yet more austere drives the cape away' " (S, p. 33).

In "The Grande Malade," Miss Barnes slips into parody, a parody which is double-edged. First the story satirizes the café view of life with its italics and its inclusion of everything in quotation marks, which is also meant to involve immediately the tone of certain writings of Raymond Radiguet and Jean Cocteau with which it was infected in the epoch. Secondly, Lydia Steptoe is seeing herself clearly, perhaps for the first time, in a mirror. In context, however, the story can be taken (and is taken on the first reading) as perfectly serious. Moydia is estranged from life and from her own emotions. Her malady is obviously chronic. Her early sophistication is its symptom, and as it is obviously incurable, all she can do is move on. In her internationalism, she is everywhere and nowhere, perpetually going to and coming from, her own "aller et retour" deprived of necessity.

The next story, "A Night Among the Horses," was anticipated thematically by "Renunciation," published in 1918 in *Smart Set* but uncollected. In "Renunciation," a man tires of his rootlessness and returns to New York twenty-five years after running away from his wife and home. Feeling strange that he, a Pole, should be there, Skirl Pavet stops in a church to pray. He ends, however, by acknowledging the sweetness and power of sin. Hating the sordidness of the city and the commonness of the restaurant that his wife operates, he had fled to the country and open fields, to love in far-off places. In the story's present time, he renounces his freedom for the sake of what is familiar and unvarying and his. In the end, having hoped to return to his inner self, he is dimly aware that he belongs nowhere. Like Pavet, the groom in "A Night Among the

Horses" is caught between alternate possibilities and states of being, but in a situation much more complex.

While a story like "Aller et Retour" depended for its impact upon reaching a level of verbal intensity, "A Night Among the Horses" succeeds through the purposefulness and compactness of its more traditional narrative form. Opening with the spectacle of a man in full evening dress creeping through the underbrush at the edge of a pasture as the sound of horses' hooves approaches, the story proceeds to work up to this moment in flashback. The relationship between John, the ostler, and Freda Buckler, the mistress of the house, is pure torment. In "a game without any pleasure" (S, p.45), she lashes at him with objects of culture, with the very promise of stepping him up " 'from being a "thing" ' (S, p. 44) But he vigorously insists that he likes being common, and lashes out at her with his whip. His violence pleases her in turn, and her cruelty consists of debasing him further by the very prospect of making him a gentleman. Freda Buckler is described as a "small fiery woman, with a battery for a heart and the body of a toy, who ran everything, who purred, saturated with impudence, with a mechanical buzz that ticked away her humanity" (S, p.44). With this trait, which links her grotesquely to the child in "Cassation," she is less a human being than a force of mindless intensity against which the comparatively simple groom is powerless. He is intelligent enough, however, to perceive that with Freda, "he'd be neither what he was nor what he had been; he'd be a *thing*, half standing, half crouching, like those figures under the roofs of historic buildings, the halt position of the damned" (S, p.46).

Finally she tells him to come to her common-dress masked ball in his customary clothes, to serve as "whipper-in." Perversely, he appears in evening dress, with top hat and cane. As his mistress dances with him, he sees her as a praying mantis. At that point he steps back, with a primitive gesture draws a circle around her in the rosin, and flees. Back running among his horses, where he feels he belongs again, he attempts to mount one of them, fails, and is trampled to death.

The drawing of the circle recalls another passage in a

theater piece by Miss Barnes where, speaking of the Provincetown Playhouse, she mentions effects which created atmos-
sphere "as a chalk line on the floor of a magician's home makes
terror and expectation—atmosphere and a dead line over
which the public could not go."[22] In this story, magic seems to
be the last hope, the last possible resort against a consuming
inhuman force. The irony, of course, is that the ostler is marking himself out of a life circle, for he cannot go back to nature
either. Descriptive touches at the beginning had pointed up the
actual indifference of nature to the man: "A frog puffed forth
its croaking immemoried cry; the man struggled for breath,
the air was heavy and hot; he was nested in astonishment" (*S*,
p.42). At the end, the horses do not know him. After they
trample him, "Presently the horses drew apart, nibbling and
swishing their tails, avoiding a patch of tall grass" (*S*, p.49). No
longer close to nature, unable to participate in a civilization
that produces monsters like his mistress, he ends up nowhere
in his damnation. And nature proves to be as blind a force as
the oblivious mechanical drive of his mistress.

The tension between forces of nature and civilization is
brought up again and handled with a degree of similarity in
"The Rabbit," but something rather different occurs in
between in "The Valet." Djuna Barnes's poems had shown a
fascination with civilized decadence on the one hand, with
nature on the other, and *Spillway* again moves between these
poles with particular interest in those moments when the two
tragically conflict, as they do in "A Night Among the Horses."
"The Valet," however, seems almost an interlude in the collection. It has to do with the gradual dying of Louis-Georges, a
proud and self-assured farmer described as "a man who all but
had a 'hand in being' " (*S*, p.51). His intimacy with Vera Sovna
causes many to speculate as to its real nature, much as the
townspeople in *Ryder* wondered about the ladies going to and
coming from church. Completing what turns out to have been
a triangle is Vanka the Russian valet, totally devoted to his master and to the service and order their relationship required.
When Louis-Georges dies, Vera Sovna pleads with Vanka to
tell her what his master had been like. " 'He let you touch him,

close, close, near the skin, near the heart' " (*S*, p.59), she cries, revealing the intensity of her suppressed passion.

Little happens in "The Valet." It seems overpopulated with incidental characters, and so little is said of Vera Sovna that one can hardly be moved by the end of the story. "The Passion," which closes *Spillway*, corresponds to "The Valet" in its central purpose. However digressive and drawn out "The Valet" seems, it is typical of Djuna Barnes's way of working that Natalie Barney indicated. It does convey to a degree the subtle quality of a long unspoken relationship by touches that indirectly reveal the hesitation of character. It might have gained if "The Nigger" or possibly "Mother" from *A Book* had been included in the sequence of *Spillway*.

In the following story, "The Rabbit," Miss Barnes shifts to a contrasting squalid milieu. It is made clear at the beginning, however, that her character Amietiev was once a gentle, simple man like Louis-Georges in "The Valet," whose farming existence had been a steady reassuring one. But, left a tailor shop in lower Manhattan by a dead uncle, his people convince him that he must leave Armenia and become a "man of the world," a "boss," come up in the world like John, the ostler, was commanded to do. Having "let Armenia slip through his fingers" (*S*, p.60), he becomes ailing and sallow in the foul air of his New York shop, fly-specked and facing a butcher shop whose colors are "a very harvest of death" (*S*, p.62). In an affair that recalls the one between the groom and Freda Buckler, he falls in love with a "small, ill, slender" Italian girl: "The sharp avaricious cruelty of her face pleased him; he confused the quick darting head with brightness" (*S*, p.63). She taunts him viciously, saying, " 'You'll never *be* anything,' " and " 'You are hardly a *hero!* ' " (*S*, p.65). In his stupidity—he is consistently portrayed as a man of little wit—he arrives at the conclusion that a hero is one who kills or is killed. In short, he steals a rabbit from the neighboring butcher and, in terror, strangles it. The girl Addie laughs at him but is suddenly afraid of the way his mouth swings "slightly sidewise" and of his walk, "loud and flat." At this point the story ends, as she pushes him toward the door: "He did not seem to know where he was, he had forgotten her. He was shaking, his head straight up, his heart wringing wet."[23]

This is *one* ending of the story, that is, and it stands as such in the American edition of *Selected Works of Djuna Barnes*. It implies that the tailor is estranged from himself by his absurd deed, as far outside of his own former world as of the girl's. The early version of the story, however, ends with Amietiev looking into the air, smiling as he sniffs it. Addie says to him, " 'Come . . . we are going to have your boots shined' " (*NAH*, p.208), and Suzanne Ferguson is probably correct in assuming that for the first time he has entered her world and is at home in it.[24] The British edition of *Spillway* on the other hand has this one sentence as a final touch: "She said tartly, 'At least shine your boots!' " (*S*, p.71). So it is clear that Addie is unaffected, and the tailor therefore appears all the more grotesque. In any case, both later endings make it apparent that he has become a part of the deathscape about him, one more figure in Miss Barnes's gallery of the living dead.

With the seventh story, "The Doctors," Miss Barnes sustains this theme and once again reaches the level of her best stories, "Aller et Retour" and "A Night Among the Horses." The trouble with "The Rabbit" is that its tension mounts in a conventional way, with an end result that is so close to melodrama that it is out of key in *Spillway*. But in "The Doctors," the tension is implicit from the opening sentence and is deeply involved in a developing sense of a terror of the heart beyond all rational comprehension. The doctors of the title, Otto and Katrina Silverstaff (the original title was simply "Katrina Silverstaff"), have lived for ten years on Second Avenue in Manhattan with their two children, and are well liked and trusted by the people. Formerly they had been doctoral students in gynecology at Freiburg-im-Breisgau, "but Katrina lost her way somewhere in vivisection, behaving as though she were aware of an impudence" (*S*, p.72): "She never recovered her gaiety. She married Otto but did not seem to know when; she knew why—she loved him—but he evaded her, by being in the stream of time; by being absolutely *daily*" (*S*, p.73). In his dailiness, and from his liberal point of view, Dr. Otto sees nothing out of order in his wife's severe detachment. In his terms, "she was 'sea water' and 'impersonal fortitude' " as well as "compact of dedicated merit, engaged in a mapped territory of abstraction, an excellently arranged encounter with estrangement" (*S*, p.72). She frequently remarks to herself, however, without apparent relevance to anything, " 'We have fashioned ourselves against the Day of Judgement' " (*S*, p.72).

One day a book salesman comes to the door. He is selling the Bible, having missed that part of the city the year before with Carlyle's *French Revolution*, and appears "a slight pale man with an uncurling flaxen beard, more like the beard of an animal than of a man" (*S*, p.75). Katrina takes him to the waiting room, and begins to speak of religion. Religion, she says, is " 'claimed by too many.' " " 'I must have religion become out of reach of the *few*; I mean out of reach *for* a few; something impossible again; to find again' " (*S*, p.75). She then proceeds to announce her purpose, saying that she needs his hindrance rather than help in it, that he is merely a means: " 'You can do nothing, not as a person' " (*S*, p.76). In short, he will become her lover, and he experiences a foreign sense of fear.

For several days his calls are rebuffed. When Katrina finally admits him, she begins undressing while speaking to him in a precise, unemotional, in fact cold manner: " 'There is something in me that is mournful because it is being.' " And again, " 'It is the will . . . that must attain complete estrangement' " (*S*, p.77). Her procedure is quiet and gentle, yet icy and calculated. She will not let him suffer while she is in the room, she announces. " 'You see,' she continued, 'some people drink poison, some take the knife, others drown. I take you' " (*S*, p.78). Oddly, it is the voice of Lydia Steptoe still speaking of good form in dying, but now from a point of spiritual alienation on the far side of decadence.

At dawn, Rodkin feels a new ease and admits, " 'Last night I almost became somebody' " (*S*, p.78). He quotes from his Bible, " 'Shall the beasts of the field, the birds of the air forsake thee?' " Finally it dawns on him that she is altogether unaware of his presence. A man "so colorless as to seem ghostly" (*S*, p.75), he hardly exists for her, had perhaps at no point been more to her than a ghost. " 'I'm nothing, nobody,' " he realizes: " 'I can't feel—I don't suffer, nothing you know—I can't—' " (*S*, p.79). In a typical ending that Suzanne Ferguson accurately calls a "flattened out coda,"[25] Rodkin returns a few days later, "his heart the heart of a dog," only to find a length of crepe hung on the door. Thereafter he becomes a drunken nuisance around the quarter, and seeing Doctor Otto once with his children, bursts into laughter and tears.

As Miss Ferguson observes, "The fantastic spiritual vivisection that Katrina performs upon herself and her action is among other things a complete reversal, an overturning, of Christ's symbolic action in his passion and sacrifice; it is willful, desperate denial of all that is human."[26] It is a mad decision to hasten the Day of Judgement, with sex as the instrument of destruction, by the utter negation of the religion that exists for the many. In the early version of the story, the phrase that Katrina mutters out of context is " 'We have eaten a great deal, my friend, against the day of God' " (*NAH*, p.104), and when she says, instead of speaking of a will to estrangement, " 'It takes more than will to attain to madness' " (*NAH*, p. 111), it begins to appear that she, like Robin in *Nightwood*, is seeking her apotheosis in the very reverse terms of apotheosis, that she is out to attain a state of spiritual exaltation in her own madness and through the degradation of another. She has " 'deliberately removed remorse from the forbidden' " (*S*, p. 77), and more. It is not difficult to understand her choice of Rodkin for her purpose. He is nowhere and nobody to begin with (the early version presents him as conceivably "of any nationality in the world" and of such "fluid temperament" that "little was fixed or firm in him, a necessary quality in a salesman" (*NAH*, p. 109), but perhaps more importantly, he is less than realized as a person. Before revision, the animal in him was even more prominent. As he begins to realize Katrina's complete withdrawal into herself, he wants to kiss her feet but flees with "a soft, swift running gait" (*NAH*, p. 114), and as in the later version, reappears with the heart of a dog. In a reversal similar to when Madame von Bartmann's insistence upon thinking everything is twisted into Gaya's reversion to nothing, John in "A Night Among the Horses" is taken out of his natural element while Rodkin is returned to nature at the basest level. In both cases, (and in "The Rabbit" as well), the men are victims of the women, who are in some degree conceived as predators. It is as if in these stories, Miss Barnes were taking a revenge upon the Ryders of the human race.

In "Spillway," the title story of the collection, Julie Anspacher is the agent of her husband's destruction also, but here alienation or noncomprehension replaces aggression in the situation. At the beginning of the story, Julie is returning to her husband's country estate, having survived five years beyond a fatal diagnosis in a sanitarium for the tubercular. With her is an excited but bewildered daughter whose father had died of the same disease in the sanitarium, and of whom Paytor is unaware. Talking to the coachman, she betrays her distraction. " 'Corruption!' " she interrupts, and then, " 'I was saying nothing. I said, all is lost from the beginning, if we only knew it—always' " (S, p. 88).

The central part of the story is constructed almost as a one-act play, consisting in the confrontation between husband and wife and building more upon dialogue than any of Miss Barnes's other stories—except, perhaps, "Aller et Retour," of which the center is actually a monologue. The tension develops out of Julie's wild hope beyond her actual knowledge, that Paytor, a rational man, would be able to divide her against herself, " 'Personally I don't feel divided; I seem to be a sane and balanced whole, but hopelessly estranged' " (S, p. 95), she tells him in foregone hope that he can see " 'where the design divides and departs.' " Her life is at deadlock; only the prospect of death, nothing else, lies ahead, and division would be merciful as it would return her to tangible conflict. Her estrangement is further expressed through water imagery. She says that she is alien to life, " 'lost in still water' " (S, p. 94), and thinks:

"Water in the hand has no voice, but it really roars coming

over the falls. It sings over small stones in brooks, but it
only tastes of water when it's caught, struggling and
running away in the hands." (S, p. 96)

What she needs is some release, as Miss Ferguson indicates, the
spillway of the title. [27] But she knows that Payton lacks the
"grace" she would invest him with in her despair, that his heart
is empty of " 'perception, that strange other "something," that
must be at the centre of everything (or there wouldn't be such a
passionate desire for it), that something secret that is so near
that it is all but obscene' " (S, p. 94). She goes on to Paytor in
one of those monologues that is itself a spillway:

"I've been on my knees, I've beaten my head against the
ground, I've abased myself, but . . . it's not low enough,
the ground is not low enough; to bend down is not
enough, to beg forgiveness is not enough; to receive?—it
would not be enough. There just isn't the right kind of
misery in the world for me to suffer, nor the right kind of
pity for you to feel; there isn't a word in the world to heal
me; penance cannot undo me—it is a thing beyond the
end of everything—it's suffering without a consum-
mation, it's like insufficient sleep; it's like anything that is
without proportion." (S, p. 92)

"Beyond the End" was the first title of "Spillway," and Julie
cannot keep hold of a religion or faith that could carry her
beyond. She seeks " 'something more fitting than release' " (S,
94), and her search is futile.

Paytor cannot reach her any more than Otto Silverstaff
could reach his wife. His life had been all proportion, as sym-
bolized by the concentric circles of the targets he shoots at.
Julie's return turns all upside down for him and at first he tells
her that he can do nothing at all for her. Later, having insisted
that one must not arrive too hastily at a conclusion, he admits
that his torment is in his coming to conclusions instantly and
having to fight to destroy them. At the end of their confrontation, Paytor goes up to his shooting loft, saying " 'I'm human,

but frugal. Perhaps I'll be able to tell you something later—give you a beginning at least. Later' " (S, p. 96).

Alone downstairs, Julie realizes that her capacity to feel what she should feel has been destroyed by " 'the interminable discipline of learning to stand everything' " (S, p. 98). Becoming dizzy, she murmers, " 'It's because I must get on my knees, But it isn't low enough . . . but if I put my head down, way down— down, down, down, down . . .' " (S, p. 98). At this moment, hearing a shot from above, she thinks, " 'He has quick warm blood—' " (S, p. 99).

Existence, then, appears in Miss Barnes's terms as an incessant struggle, not to understand, but to "stand everything" beyond the end of rational comprehension or under-standing. Only Madame von Bartmann in the stories discussed to this point is a woman of great strength, although there is a reverse sort of integrity in Katrina Silverstaff's managing of her own fate, however grim and final that may be. Julie Anspacher, Gaya, the ostler, Amietiev: all are truly caught in the "halt position of the damned," and the stories gain their compressed power in dramatizing the restlessness of their con-dition. Katya's reference to her sister's restlessness, comparing it to " 'a story that has no beginning and no end, only a passion like flash lightning' " (S, 34), sums up the quality of intensity that the best of the stories possess. They take characters out of the ordinary routines of their lives and focus upon highly charged situations in which their suppressed dread and passions can no longer remain unbidden and so pour out into the spillways of their lives. Then all is risk and chaos, against which reason is no effective agent.

The venting of repressed emotion calls for a dramatic shift in tone and style. The world these characters inhabit may be rendered in plain language, but the inner life expresses itself with an anguished eloquence. Usually the common language Miss Barnes employs, with its sharp terms of tangible perception, makes her passages of numinous, poetic prose stand out all the more prominently. In "Aller et Retour," for example, Madame von Bartmann's journey remains in the foreground; the emotional drama is treated almost as a secondary factor, much as in the early lyrics the lover's anguish is almost incidental upon the pastoral surface. The effect is not unlike W. H. Auden's use, in "Musée des Beaux Arts," of Breughel's *Icarus* to suggest something of the human position of suffering. At the story's core, however, is a distilled vision of suffering that takes on heightened significance as a result of the mundanity surrounding it. A metaphorical poetic precision then plays against a concrete precision which is applied to the prosaic, and the reader is suspended between dualities along with the characters before him.

"The Passion" is the final story in *Spillway*, serving in its brevity as a fitting coda to the volume as a whole. It too is a little work of precision, developing with the same "measured excellence" with which Princess Frederica Rholinghausen's carriage moves through the *Bois*. It is mentioned that on Thursdays in her absence it is driven at a "smart rocking pace," a touch which marks her distance from the world outside, from ongoing life. Most of the story is descriptive of her and the environment surrounding her, its immaculate visualization bringing to mind Miss Barnes's skill as a draftsman and portraitist. Take, for instance, the princess in her carriage, "erect, in the dead centre of a medallioned cushion":

> The tall figure, with its shoulders like delicate flying buttresses, was encased in grey moiré, the knees dropping the stiff excess in two sharp points, like the corners of a candy box. No pearl in the dogcollar shook between the dipping blue of the veins, nor did the radiance on the finger-nails shift by any personal movement; the whole glitter of the jewelled bones and the piercing eye, turned with the turning of the coach . . . .(S, p. 100)

What is conveyed here is shortly made perfectly explicit: "At times . . . she had surprisingly, the air of a *galant*, a *bon-vivant*—but there was a wash of blue in her flesh that spoke of the acceptance of morality." "She was in the hand of a high decay: she was *sèche*, but living on the last suppuration of her will" (S, p. 103). Her aura of regularized decay is borne out in various ways: by the periodic and perfunctory visits of palsied aunts and a dandyish nephew, by the unvarying visits of Kurt Anders, a widower and Polish officer, one Thursday each month for thirty years, by the habitual movements of servants, and now and again by the state of the furniture:

> The spinet in the corner, covered with a yellow satin throw, embroidered by her own hand, was crumbling along the bevel of the lid, signifying silence of half a century. The scores, lying one above the other were for soprano. One was open at *Liebeslied*. (*S*, p. 102)

And so on. The atmosphere built up here, and the characters as well, bring to mind some of the tales of Isak Dinesen, but it is a texture of greater density that Miss Barnes is creating.

Attention shifts to Kurt Anders and his visits midway through the narrative. "Imposing, high stomached, spatted, gloved . . . " (*S*, p. 105), Anders is a man with a history both "*éblouissant* and dark" (*S*, p. 104), surrounded by the sort of scandal that is common to the "*demi-monde*." In his past is a relationship with a tinge of rumored homosexuality, comparable to the liaison between Monsieur X and his Baron. All in all, "He had the bearing of one who had abetted licence, he looked as though he had eaten everything: but though elegant in his person, there was something about him not far from the stool" (*S*, p. 104). His calls upon the princess have a distinct formality. They discuss dogs, races, the autumn (the majority of Miss Barnes's stories are autumnal in setting, often in tone), cathedrals, etchings, drama ("Then Anders would plunge into the uses of the fool in Shakespeare . . . , weighing a point the princess had made, regarding the impracticability of maintaining tradition, now that every man was his own fool" [*S*, p. 106]) or literature in general. No matter how gossips construe their relationship, everyone assumes that the princess is his life's one passion, a notion that Miss Barnes dismisses with a lovely touch:

**All of this was nonsense.**

They were pages in an old volume, brought together by the closing of the book. (*S*, p. 106)

The manner of this story is the precise opposite of that of the *Vanity Fair* stories of aristocracy mentioned earlier. Here the only thing that can be said to happen occurs in the last four brief paragraphs. One day Anders speaks of Gesualdo and the sorrows of the assassin, and then of "the passion of Monteverdi 'at the tomb of the beloved' " (*S*, p. 106).[28] When he says to her, " 'The "walking straight up to dreadfulness" . . . that is love' "[29] she replies,

> . . . "The last attendant on an old woman is always an 'incurable.' " She set her teacup down with a slight trembling of the hand, then drawing her eyeglasses up, she added with mordant acerbity, "But—if a little light man with a beard had said 'I love you,' I should have believed in God." (*S*, p. 107)

A typically terse conclusion follows, stating that "He called only once after that, and only once was the princess seen riding in the *Bois*, a mist behind a tight-drawn veil. Shortly after, she did not live" (*S*, p. 107). Thus from accumulated impressions finally emerges an oblique but comprehensive view of the ambiguity of unacknowledged passion, a theme that had been introduced in "Aller et Retour," sustained in "The Valet," and held as the end note of the volume. "The Passion" presents "only the simple story, told by everything" (*S*, p. 85).

The last phrase quoted occurs in "A Boy Asks a Question," a story that exists in uneasy relation to *Spillway*. Included in the Faber and Faber edition, it was omitted from *The Selected Works*, evidently by an editorial decision with which Miss Barnes readily complied. There is no doubt that it is a slight piece, and its placement between "The Doctors" and "Spillway" tends to diminish the impact of the latter. It is thematically relevant, however, and one moment in it serves to prepare for the somewhat ambiguous last line spoken by the princess. The boy in the story, like everyone else, is fascinated by Carmen la Tosca, a worldly actress possessed in high degree of the by now familiar chic. Relating to her how one of his brothers had cried when his girl died, feeling that he could have stopped her, the boy says, " 'I would have said "I love you." Is that a power?' " The lady replies, " 'Yes, it is innocence. We are all waiting for someone who will learn our innocence—all over again' " (S, p. 84). But the broader question, never fully articulated, involves the knowledge of all of life to come. The lady's summation is, in effect, a condensation of Madame von Bartmann's monologue into three simple words: " 'Dignity—and despair—and innocence' " (S, p. 86).

It is again the vision of a lost Eden, of innocence and unity out of time, that lies behind each of Djuna Barnes's short stories. The gap, the vacancy that Gaya suffers in extremity is experienced by all the characters wherever they may be. For Miss Barnes's twentieth-century wasteland is a purgatory where all suffer the middle condition, being at home neither here nor there, being neither one thing nor the other, all fashioned against the Day of Judgement. The groom, the tailor, the doctor, the aristocrat: theirs is a collective damnation, which is a radical physical and spiritual dislocation. Being is a terrible state of tentativeness or suspension, never resolved but certainly terminating in death, ending in the mystery that initiated it. The remarkable thing about the stories is the immediacy and concentration that they gain by abandoning all frills and moving directly in style and content toward a central vision. In *Spillway*, the milieu and the subject of *Nightwood* are finally created. However, *Nightwood* is the world of *Spillway* as if seen in a mirror.

# 5.

## *Nightwood*

*Nightwood*, appearing in 1936, suddenly towers over all of Djuna Barnes's previous work, excelling it in organizational perfection, intensity of conception, and power of phrasing—the same broad qualities that would later distinguish *The Antiphon* and, less imposingly, *Spillway*. But it should not be assumed that it is discontinuous from the earlier work, a result of a sort of literary immaculate conception. It is in fact the convergence and refinement of Miss Barnes's hitherto somewhat contrasting styles and scattered themes. *Nightwood* is a distinct advance in treatment of narrative and character, achieving a new unity and reaching a plateau upon which Miss Barnes has since insisted upon remaining. It goes beyond the early versions of the short stories in its extreme concentration and richness of ambiguity, and it is also much more successful in transcending literary period and fictional genre than was *Ryder*.

The greater unity of *Nightwood*, to give but one preliminary example, is apparent in Miss Barnes's management of parody and the new prominence given to Matthew O'Connor. *Ryder* meant to disrupt and parody its own narrative by insertion of dialogue in play form, poems, and illustrations. It aimed for scattered effects rather than one dominant effect. *Nightwood*, however, manages to achieve an intense single-mindedness comparable to that of the *Spillway* stories in their final version, and the urge to parody is strictly contained in the doctor's inexhaustible flights of rhetoric. This is not to say that, with the doctor offstage, Miss Barnes is incapable of regarding Felix Volkbein's passion for nobility and the Catholic church, or Jenny Petherbridge's "squatter" tactics, without irony. The fact is that these attitudes culminate in O'Connor's own vision, and the parodic tone belongs to his choral monologues. So if, say, Burton's *Anatomy of Melancholy* is echoed somewhere in the novel, it is in the doctor's own words that it, along with the spirit it represents, is parodied. It is this associative resonance that *Ryder* and *Ladies Almanack* never fully achieved.

But this is only one element that contributes to the greater cohesiveness of *Nightwood*. A particular new factor in Miss Barnes's work that appears here is a preoccupation with the nocturnal, with sleep and dreaming, which, insofar as the characters in the novel become immersed in it, provides a new perspective upon the familiar themes of the earlier work: the nature of time and history, the condition of women and particularly women in love, the Bleeding Heart as a religious and secular symbol for universal suffering, and the "middle condition" as the measure of being. It is possibly the last of these that furnishes the broadest understanding of the novel's exceedingly close and complex texture.

In *Spillway*, the state of being at halt, neither here nor there, is one of intolerable anguish. Yet for Madame von Bartmann, it is the source of illumination, of the tragic vision of life. In the intermediate position, dualities are abolished. The distinctions that the rational intelligence habitually makes, as it analyzes and categorizes experience, become erased. The characters in *Nightwood* hover between night and day, dream and reality. It is a middle region that they inhabit, and implicit in their situation are the novel's intertwined themes. This condition also determines the form of the novel, giving rise to its unique structure, imagery, and language. As the need to be in the middle of experience equally affects *Nightwood*'s relationship to the novelistic genre, it should first be understood how style is made to serve as the foundation for character and theme. One passing statement in the novel points to a primary aspect of Miss Barnes's method.

In the book's sixth part—it would almost be a misnomer to

call the eight sections "chapters"—Felix Volkbein, the sham Baron, says to O'Connor, " 'An image is a stop the mind makes between uncertainties' " (*N*, p.111). He is making a distinction between idea and image with reference to Robin Vote long after she has left him and their son, explaining how an image of her had taken the place of a clear idea of her from the beginning. His statement is a suggestive one when considering the novel as a whole, as it is in considerable part the imagery that continues to puzzle readers. T. S. Eliot notes parenthetically in his introduction to *Nightwood* that the reader finds Robin quite real without, however, completely understanding how Miss Barnes has made her so.[1] Felix's experience and the reader's are alike: it is only through the images and sensations aroused by Robin in others that she paradoxically becomes the central presence.

One passage from the scene in which Felix and the doctor first encounter Robin should give a preliminary idea of how this happens. Describing the emotions that come over Felix as Robin is revived from her faint, Miss Barnes writes,

> Sometimes one meets a woman who is beast turning human. Such a person's every movement will reduce to an image of a forgotten experience; a mirage of an eternal wedding cast on the racial memory; as insupportable a joy as would be the vision of an eland coming down an aisle of trees, chapleted with orange blossoms and bridal veil, a hoof raised in the economy of fear, stepping in the trepidation of flesh that will become myth. (*N*, p. 37)

It is not difficult to see how the passage works contextually. The image of the eland is dreamlike, almost surrealistic, and the references to "an image of a forgotten experience," "racial memory," and "myth" that enclose it form part of a movement that will culminate in Nora Flood's nocturnal obsession and Doctor O'Connor's fantastic disquisitions on night, sleep, and dreams. Robin, moreover, is explicitly termed beast turning human. This perception is then obliquely reinforced by the image of the eland in its trepidation, thus beginning a circle that the end of the novel will complete. But the image is such that these recognitions are not exhaustive in themselves. An ineffable quality remains that analysis not only cannot diminish, but cannot even touch.

In *Creative Intuition in Art and Poetry*, Jacques Maritain quotes a passage from the section "Watchman, What of the Night?" in order to exemplify

> . . . the *immediately illuminating image*, without the intermediary of any concept—illuminating because it is illuminated both by the Illuminating Intellect and by poetic intuition or spark of intuition. Everything, here, comes about in the depths of the preconceptual life of the intellect and the imagination. Two things are not compared, but rather one thing is made known through the image of another. One thing already known is not brought near to another thing already known. One thing which was unknown—only contained in the obscurity of emotive intuition—is discovered, and expressed, by means of another already known, and by the same stroke their similarity is discovered . . . .[2]

The point is that poetic intuition draws upon both preconscious life and the intellect, and that this takes place instantaneously by overleaping intermediary concepts. In Djuna Barnes's case the poetic cast of the imagery would seem to derive less from any particular philosophy of aesthetics that treats art in terms of intuition than from Ezra Pound's *imagiste* definition of an image as "that which presents an intellectual and emotional complex in an instant of time."[3] It is this approach to imagery that should be kept in mind when considering the observation that Eliot brought to bear upon his assertion that the novel would "appeal primarily to readers of poetry."[4] In saying that it is "so good a novel that only sensibilities trained on poetry can wholly appreciate it," but that "Miss Barnes's prose has the prose rhythm that is prose style, and the musical pattern which is not that of verse," he is correcting the impression that he might have implied that it is written in "poetic prose." Although Eliot speaks of how Miss Barnes frequently brings her characters to life in a sudden phrase, he never explicitly acknowledges the book's most essential poetic quality, its devotion to the image that is the product of intuitive illumination. It goes without saying that the more literal the reader's approach to *Nightwood*, the less accessible are its means of revelation.

Felix's comment on the nature of images calls attention to another factor contributing to their obscurity, or inaccessibility. It has already been noted that even the earliest work of Djuna Barnes contained a view of experience as indeterminate, of life as a movement from initial uncertainty on to a terminal mystery. In this flux there is nothing absolute or final, but rather a continual participation in duality of being. To call a stop between uncertainties is to perceive man in "the halt position of the damned," to halt the flow of experience in order to observe what is lost in custom or in the multiplicity of things. It is an act of poetic detachment that illuminates the "middle condition" (*N*, p. 118)—the term is the doctor's—where one is in constant suspension between the dualities of existence on the " 'grim path of "We know not" to "We can't guess why" ' " (*N*, p. 101). It is essentially a verbal equivalent of the photographic image in its way of abstracting from ongoing activity and juxtaposing dissimilar elements, the known with the unknown. As the images intertwine in a complex pattern to render a higher reality, the daily world and its consequential developments begin to dissolve to a great extent. The effect is suggestive of a waking dream.

Added to the imagistic nature of the novel is the fact that *Nightwood* continues to bear out the tendency that Natalie Clifford Barney had found operative in the stories and poems of *A Book* and *A Night Among the Horses*: "Ses pensées ne vont jamais jusqu'à la pensée." When Nora surprises the doctor in the disarray of his "appallingly degraded" room, in bed with wig, facial make-up, and woman's nightgown, it flashes into her head, " 'God, children know something they can't tell; they like Red Riding Hood and the wolf in bed!' " Miss Barnes immediately adds, "But this thought, which was only the sensation of a thought, was of but a second's duration as she opened the door . . ." (*N*, p. 79). By snatching the *sensation* of a thought out of the conscious thought process that would ordinarily erase it,

Miss Barnes is again attempting to transcend the prosaic, to attain a level of reality above the commonplace temporal, an "eternal momentary" (*N*, p. 127), to borrow a phrase that O'Connor uses to characterize Robin. So, again, Robin is seldom directly available to the reader, but is nearly always presented in terms of the sensations she arouses in those with whom she becomes involved. The seeming illogic of the doctor's harangues and monologues becomes another consequence of the procedure. As he himself says, " 'I have a narrative, but you will be put to it to find it' " (*N*, p. 97).

It would be well to pause here to consider the content and shape of *Nightwood*'s main narrative and just where it stands in relation to Miss Barnes's earlier experiments with plot and structure. The novel is divided into eight titled parts, and Joseph Frank has observed that "the eight chapters of *Nightwood* are like searchlights, probing the darkness each from a different direction yet ultimately illuminating the same entanglement of the human spirit."[6] The term *chapter*, however, may be misleading if one assumes its customary reference to marked phases of sequential development in time. The eight sections of *Nightwood* at first seem curiously disassociated, removed from each other in time and place. Each seems to initiate a new movement, not unlike a story in a sequence, and the relation of each event to what has preceded is initially obscure. Nonetheless, the central situation of the novel is built up in chronological time. "Bow Down," which opens the book, begins with the birth of Felix Volkbein in precisely 1880 and proceeds to sketch as background the historical elements that have formed him as the Wandering Jew in the assumed guise of a baron who is obsessed with rendering perpetual homage to nobility or whatever titular authority. Exact chronology ends, however, as early as the ninth page, after Felix is established in Paris in 1920 amidst the "splendid and reeking falsification" of a group of circus people. At an affair given by a Count Onatorio Altamonte in Berlin which he attends with a trapeze artist, Frau Mann, three of the characters in the novel's quadrangle—Doctor Matthew O'Connor, Nora Flood, and Felix—first come together.

In "La Somnambule," the second section, Felix and the doctor are in Paris again, and are summoned to the Hotel Récamier in order to revive a young girl, who closely resembles a boy, from a faint. It is Robin Vote who is the "somnambule," and Felix falls in love with her with the involuntary force which is his destiny. "When he asked her to marry him it was with such an unplanned eagerness that he was taken aback to find himself accepted, as if Robin's life held no volition for refusal" (N, pp. 42–43). After the birth of their sad, weak child, an event which Robin had approached with "a stubborn cataleptic calm" (N, p. 45), her wanderings from café to church (she had abruptly turned Catholic) become more frequent. Robin finally disappears for months, eventually to reappear with Nora. Then in "Night Watch" we learn that Robin has been in America with Nora, having first been drawn to her at a circus in New York in 1923. This third section summarizes the deterioration of their relationship over several years, with Nora's anguish and helplessness mounting in proportion to Robin's estrangement, as manifested by her strayings and by her constant promiscuity. All of this reaches a climax in " 'The Squatter,' " when Jenny Petherbridge, the lesbian of the section's title who has "a continual rapacity for other people's facts" (N, p. 67) and more, finally appropriates Robin. The section closes with a scene (the time is now 1927) in which Jenny, in the presence of the doctor, an unnamed English girl, and a little girl named Sylvia who is in love with Robin, viciously attacks Robin in a carriage. The strange event assures Nora and Robin's final separation, with the subsequent departure of Jenny and Robin for America.

As Sharon Spencer notes, "At this point the book's 'time' begins to slow down and to stand still."[7] What had been presented dramatically so far had been done so out of a need generated not by plot demands but by the emotional necessities of a mounting subjectivity and indirection of approach to indivdual characters and their complex involvements with each other. A sense of chronological time had been gradually receding and the fifth section of Nightwood, "Watchman, What of the Night?," is out of time altogether. Here Nora, rigid and

distraught, comes in the night to the doctor's fantastic lodgings
to seek consolation. Whereupon " 'Dr. Matthew-Mighty-grain-
of-salt-Dante-O'Connor' " launches into a lengthy, overwhelm-
ing discourse on night, sleep, and " 'the peculiar polarity of
times and times' " (*N*, p. 80). His words immediately go beyond
Nora, who is numb with her obsession, and eventually come
around to his recollection of the night of the altercation
between Jenny and Robin in the carriage. His reversion to the
scene is a reminder of the point where waking time had finally
ceased, while a resumption of chronological time is forecast by
his concluding prophecy, " ' "Nora will leave that girl some
day; but though those two are buried at opposite ends of the
earth, one dog will find them both' " (*N* p. 106).

In the following part, "Where the Tree Falls," Felix reappears with his mentally deficient and estranged son Guido, now
age ten. The boy's spiritual condition is largely the subject of a
dialogue between Felix and O'Connor. At one moment, Felix
recalls a bitter incident in which Jenny had approached him.
The section concludes in a Viennese café with a glimpse of the
"odd trio" of Frau Mann, Guido, and a drunken Felix, still
seeking nobility to render homage to.

"Go Down, Matthew" complements "Watchman, What of
the Night?" Nora's new understanding of her love for Robin
has brought her no consolation or release, and the doctor talks
on helplessly of night and the human condition from his own
parallel anguish. " 'I talk too much because I have been made
so miserable by what you are keeping hushed' " (*N*,
pp. 162–63), he exclaims as much to himself as to a defrocked
priest he encounters in his habitual Cafe de la Mairie du VI$^e$,
having turned away from Nora in his confusion. Drunk and
spiritually infected, he finally cannot rise: " 'Now . . . the
end—mark my words—now *nothing, but wrath and weeping!* ' "
(*N*, p. 166)

"The Possessed" closes the novel in four brief pages. After
Robin abandons Jenny in America, she wanders into the
countryside, circling closer and closer like an animal to Nora's
estate. Finally, at the summons of her dog, Nora surprises
Robin in a chapel on her grounds. Robin goes down before

Nora's dog and, emulating the dog herself, ends by carrying out a bizarre ritualistic ceremony with the beast which brings her down to its level.

So much for the events themselves of *Nightwood*. Narrative movement here is essentially a new application of what had been operative in *Ryder*. It, too, began with a sequence of discontinuous vignettes in a context of historical time prior to the birth of the principal characters. Although anecdotes, extraneous forays, and summaries of events began to break down a sense of predictable development in time, at least some attention was given to the passage of years, dates of determining events, etc. But once established at Storm-King-on Hudson, the narrative became in effect timeless and the present became a receptacle for the historical past. In *Nightwood*, time is marked with diminishing regularity up to the point of the separation of Robin and Nora, after which there is a descent into night and the unconscious, and ultimately the preconscious and ahistorical.

Although the doctor claims to have a narrative, Joseph Frank insists that his is a static situation, one which is explored from different angles by eight sections that are "knit together not by the progress of any action—either narrative action or, as in a stream-of-consciousness novel, the flow of experience—but by the continual reference and cross reference of images and symbols that must be referred to each other spatially throughout the time-act of reading."[8] The structural principle is spatial form, the "unit of meaning" in the novel being seldom more than a phrase or several phrases in a sequence, "independently of any time-sequence of narrative action."[9] To the frame of cross-reference described by Frank must be added a series of repeated or varied terms which recur in different contexts. Shifting forms of the phrase "to go down," for example, form a pattern as they appear throughout the novel, and in such terms the main themes cohere. Because this technique is so closely allied to character and theme, however, a fuller consideration of its use will follow later.

Walter Sutton takes exception to Frank's argument with respect to two points. In the first place, he points to the specific determining factor of the spatial and temporal location of the story. Secondly, there is movement in the novel which, as should be apparent from the preceding summary of chapter content, is a "relatively simple narrative sequence of events which are related in time and causally . . .,"[10] a sequence which in addition metaphorically parallels the movement of the novel's theme. Nonetheless, as Sharon Spencer observes at the point when Felix's son reappears, "Time has not seemed important to the circular movement of this tale of perpetual loss."[11] It may be concluded that *Nightwood*'s narrative circularity involves its beginning in, departure from, and conclusive return to chronological time. Both motion and stasis exist within this framework.

What actually happens to the narrative as a whole follows from the function of thought sensations and images throughout, from the gradual breakdown of rational and sequential perception. Just as an image emerges from a stop between uncertainties, a dark but universal insight comes out of the static and timeless situation that Nora and the doctor are eventually trapped in. The Dante in O'Connor is a chronicler of purgatory. *Nightwood* is a study of mixed being, of the estrangement that is the state of being neither one thing nor the other. The novel's time sense is determined by this state of suspension. Joseph Frank states that the reduced unit of meaning brings the novel's spatial form to the point where it nearly belongs to modern poetry. It also contributes to the reader's impression of time in the process. As his perception of the novel's progress is retarded by the weight or concentration of a phrase or paragraph, there exists a complementary subordination of action to sensation and reflection in the book. As in Eliot's "Love Song of J. Alfred Prufrock," the daylight narrative is effectively submerged and an interior reality rises to the surface of the work.

The reader's disorientation, as Frank's remark suggests, extends to the matter of genre as well. After "Bow Down," or perhaps even after that opening part of it which is devoted to Felix's ancestry, the forms of fiction begin to dissolve and the sensations commonly aroused by a poem, or a painting, or a drama, or a musical composition come into play. One begins to realize that the narrative is gradually "going down" or under, and that the pleasures experienced are no longer simply the familiar ones of the novelistic genre. The poetic nature of the imagery is evident from the first page, but it is only gradually that the associational principles of modern poetry appear to be operative, as is strikingly the case in the monologues of O'Connor in which images and epigrams seem to pour chaotically forth but are actually linked by a sense of intuitive order. Thus Kimon Friar and Malcolm Brinnin saw fit to include a lengthy excerpt from "Watchman, What of the Night?" in an anthology of modern poetry,[12] and critics are time and again, despite Eliot's corrective note, inclined to treat this book, not only in poetic terms, but in those of other genres as well.

For *Nightwood* is more purely trans-generic than any other work of Djuna Barnes, combining as it does the distinctive aspects of former efforts with a greater unity than *Ryder* or *Ladies Almanack*. The diverse generic properties become contributing factors to a powerful overall impression. In the first place, *Nightwood* is theatrical as a whole, not in flashes. Graham Greene finds it to be as akin as "Aller et Retour" to the Jacobean dramatists in its language and dramatic substance; its ending he finds "as horrible as anything conceived by Webster or Tourneur."[13] T.S. Eliot suggests that "the final chapter is essential, both dramatically and musically."[14] Prompted by this observation, Jack Hirschman attempts to describe the novel's dramatic properties in terms of the structure of a five-act play. His analysis, however, is so literal that it ignores *Nightwood's* fluidity and this distorts its meticulous eight-part structure.[15] But the true dramatic aspect of the work is suggested by A. Desmond Hawkins in a review for the *New English Weekly*. After the concrete narrative of the opening loses momentum, he says,

> Whatever action there is occurs as something now being relived in dialogue. The book is a work of sibylline sensibility, a relentless confession counterpointed with oracular pronouncement. Once the stage is set we do not know

what has happened until the characters involved begin their post-mortem.[16]

This post-mortem effect is the same dramatic principle that is operative later in *The Antiphon*. It is characteristic, not of the contemporary stage deplored by Lady Lydia Steptoe in "Hamlet's Custard Pie," but of a stage enlivened by rhetoric and reflection such as that of the Elizabethan period where *Ladies Almanack* and now *Nightwood* seem to have their source. It follows that the doctor, in his much commented on Tiresias-like choral role, becomes most prominent as time and action slow down. It is through Felix, however, that the reader is first prepared for what is to follow dramatically. Once he is in Paris, writes Jack Hirschman, "history (time) comes to a dead stop and the reader discerns that the description of his life in 'real' time was a pretext for getting him onstage, for the drama of his part in the night to unfold.[17] With his pretense to noble lineage, he naturally gravitates toward the sham world of the circus and theater, the milieu within which he first encounters O'Connor, whose stage role is not solely declamatory but is also manifested in his various impostures, in his role as a " 'dumb-founder' " (*N*, p.35). The impression of life as theater once established, the work proceeds to take on what Wallace Fowlie calls "the pure depiction of tragedy": "Without the theatric floodlight [in which a tragic character invariably exists alone], *Nightwood* succeeds in presenting characters of deep solitude illuminated by the very darkness of their world," and it takes on "the excessive luminosity of a circus"[18]—which, as a debased form of theatre, fits perfectly within the novel's scheme of paradox and inversion of values.

Fowlie also suggests that at the end of the novel action and setting are so perfectly fused that "as in some classical fugue, the elements answer one another in even, controlled tones."[19] Hirschman's analysis, more credible in musical than in dramatic terms, also chooses to focus upon the fugue, composed of three main segments, of Exposition, Episodes, and Coda. Demonstrating how the novel's structure approximates this form, he further notes that the "spatialized" imagery implies a counterpoint of various motifs, and that a central theme is presented by counterpoint of characters, with the factor of overlapping temporality in the structure further illustrating the musical figure.[20] He concludes:

> As the fugue form is involved with intricate over-lapping, so . . . the character introductions and entangle-ments centering around the major theme involve a similar overlapping. As the fugue form, by means of counter-point, allows for the existence of two or more elements simultaneously in time, so *Nightwood* possesses such simultaneity.[21]

It should be indicated, however, that *Nightwood*'s structure is far from rigidly bound to the form of the fugue, and that the effect of simultaneity is just as strongly served by nonmusical elements, such as visual design and other techniques, syntactical and conceptual, which accomplish poetic resonance. Also, the novel is musical in a much broader sense. Clifton Fadiman pointed this out in his comparison of it with *Ulysses*, *The Waste Land*, and certain poems of Hart Crane. These several works, he wrote, "approach the non-representative condition of pure music, in that they defy description in other terms. Everything that they are is immovably contained in and identical with the original phrasing of the author."[22]

But *Nightwood* does to an extent specifically imply the tex-ture and the inevitability of movement of a fugue, and its musical nature is enhanced by numerous references to music in the text. Many of these are incidental, as when they sustain the doctor's *blague*, or seem to serve no other purpose than that of simply extending the musical frame of reference. In certain cases, as earlier in "Aller et Retour," they may strike accord with thematic points bearing upon character.

At one point in *Nightwood*, for example, the theme of the decay of nobility is enhanced by musical references. In his last appearance in the novel, the drunken but correct Felix calls from his café table for "military music, for *Wacht am Rhein*, for *Morgenrot*, for Wagner" (*N*, p.122): He keeps time to the music by drumming his thumb and little finger on the table, the low and high notes of the imagined octave corresponding to the low and high range of the music he has demanded. The span between military music and Wagner reflects the tonal polarity that the novel sustains from its opening. But it also recalls the strains of militarism and royalty in Felix's remote past. These had been introduced in the beginning among the many details portraying Felix as the end of aristocracy, and then ironically sustained in the figure of Frau Mann. A blind eye, we were told parenthetically, had kept Felix from the army and his residual and unconscious emulation of the warrior accompanied his absurd obsession with nobility. So finally, as he listens to military music, he sits "erect, his neck holding his head at attention" (*N*, p.122). This last touch is typical of many that contribute to the effect throughout. Much earlier, the statement, "On the tenth day, therefore, Felix turned about and re-entered Paris" (*N*, p.44), struck a similar note of ludicrousness in the manner of its phrasing, as if to imply the decisiveness of the military hero when actually Felix was wandering in a limbo with Robin at that point. Such effects, again, sustain an opening theme with a regularity that evokes musical composition.

*Nightwood*'s visual dimension is no less striking than its dramatic, poetic, and musical ones and no less essential to the feeling of the whole work. Take, for instance, this opening description of Hedvig Volkbein's house, the "fantastic museum" of the encounter of Hedvig and Guido:

> The long rococo halls, giddy with plush and whorled designs in gold, were peopled with Roman fragments, white and disassociated; a runner's leg, the chilly half-turned head of a matron stricken at the bosom, the blind bold sockets of the eyes given a pupil by every shifting shadow so that what they looked upon was an act of the sun.[23] (*N*, p. 5)

Once again the creative touch is primarily a visual one. The scene itself, a tableau of disassociation, most immediately resembles the irrational or incongruous compositions of certain surrealist painters such as Max Ernst, René Magritte, or Giorgio de Chirico,[24] or the prose images of Lautréamont in *Les Chants du Maldoror*. Such scenes are frequent in the novel and are inseparable from its basic orientation toward the dream experience.

At other times, certain effects recall the *fin de siècle* decadence of *The Book of Repulsive Women*. Particularly representative is the scene at the end of "Night Watch" where Nora perceives the embrace of Robin with one of the nameless women of her nights as a double shadow falling from a garden statue, whereupon she experiences an intense sense of evil followed by an "awful" happiness. The theme of decadence is of course everywhere in the novel, Robin being another in the long line of vampiric women in Miss Barnes's work, but is more fully realized here conceptually and visually than in prior work. A more subtle and oblique treatment replaces what had earlier been strident, ostentatious, or coy. The paradox of transcendence through decadence represents a conceptual refinement in Miss Barnes's work at this point, and *Nightwood*'s stylistic refinements follow in its course.

The term *rococo* in the passage quoted above is crucial in describing the book's manner. In the first place, the whorled pattern, common to rococo design, relates to the circularity of the novel, its plot and central themes. It applies to Robin and her relationship to the other characters who are "whorled" about her in the novel's design. The also frequently employed arabesque pattern with its intricate interlace is simultaneously operative, a figure for the novel's interlaced and recurring images, terms, and symbols. Robin's centrality is enhanced by the floral, plant, and sometimes animal motifs of rococo arabesque, the very ones that operate metaphorically upon Robin throughout.

More broadly speaking, *Nightwood* resembles rococo art as an art of ornamentation, where a sense of pattern is uppermost. But decoration here is involved with "occult balance rather than with mathematical symmetry. Among the reasons for the vitality of rococo ornamentation is the fact that one side of a panel never exactly repeats the design of the opposite side; there is equivalence, not mere restatement."[25] Confusion is avoided only by virtue of a substructural symmetry. Similarly, *Nightwood* possesses a surface mutability, with its recurrent visual and verbal components marked by approximation or equivalence, as in the images of statues with the play of shadows upon them, rather than repetition. It achieves a fictional quality of space, reminiscent of the effect attained by use of multiple mirrors in rococo architecture, that of a "constantly changing infinity"[26] ordered by the balanced central structural elements of the space. Just as the fugal orchestration of theme keeps several elements in simultaneous interplay in *Nightwood*, the novel's central vision allows for the coordination of numerous mutually reflecting details.

The distinctiveness of *Nightwood* in contrast with Djuna Barnes's earlier work is its striking correspondence to the last phrase of rococo in particular, the *genre pittoresque*, the beginning of "a new subjective art that tries to suggest, not to state."[27] Wylie Sypher indicates that this brief movement appeared in France around 1730 in the work of Nicholas Pineau, only to end about twenty years later.Its new fantasticality, represented by the work of such artists as Boucher and François de Cuvilliés, and soon approximated in verse by William Collins, stressed distortion and an "exaggerated asymmetry" in design to a point where "the occult balance of rococo art is changed into the freakish contours of a dream."[28]

The development of Miss Barnes's art is a parallel to this shift. She had begun in *The Book of Repulsive Women* to develop a chic, an art of decoration for its own sake with stress upon grotesque and arabesque figuration. Her drawing, not without its verbal parallel, began to display a greater subjectivity and purposiveness of effect in *A Book*, and by the time of *Ryder* had crystalized in a new sort of amalgamation of disparate elements, deliberately fantastic but capturing the uncluttered space and simplicity of effect of the work of the period it derived from. *Nightwood* is a turn toward a more suggestive and complex design in which the recognizable world is distorted in appearance by a grotesque dreamlike perspective which brings its clarity of outline into and out of focus, with its profuse decor endlessly mirrored within its fictional spatial frame.

The novel's fantasticality persistently yields an impression of beauty in barbarity or degradation. The note is struck in O'Connor's description of the black Nikka of the Cirque de Paris, "tattoed from head to heel with all the *ameublement* of depravity":

> "Well then, over his belly was an angel from Chartres; on each buttock, half public, half private, a quotation from the book of magic, a confirmation of the Jansenist theory . . . On each bosom an arrow-speared heart, each with different initials but with equal drops of blood . . . Over his *dos*, believe it or not, and I shouldn't a terse account in early monkish script—called by some people indecent, by others Gothic—of the really deplorable condition of Paris before hygiene was introduced, and nature had its way up to the knees. . . I asked him why all this barbarity; he answered he loved beauty and would have it about him." (*N*, pp. 16–17)

The effect is approximated by later descriptions of two rooms, Robin's hotel room and the doctor's squalid lodgings. Robin as first encountered is surrounded by palms, potted plants, flowers, with the sound of unseen birds coming from somewhere:

> Like a painting by the douanier Rousseau, she seemed to lie in a jungle trapped in a drawing room (in the apprehension of which the walls have made their escape), thrown in among the carniverous flowers as their ration; the set, the property of an unseen *dompteur*, half lord, half promoter, over which one expects to hear the strains of an orchestra of woodwinds render a serenade which will popularize the wilderness. (*N*, p. 35)

The doctor's miniscule room, as Nora perceives it, is no less fantastic:

> On a maple dresser, certainly not of European make, lay a rusty pair of forceps, a broken scalpel, half a dozen odd

instruments that she could not place, a catheter, some
twenty perfume bottles, almost empty, pomades, creams,
rouges, powder boxes and puffs.

. . . A swill-pail stood at the head of the bed, brimming
with abominations. There was something appallingly
degraded about the room, like the rooms in brothels,
which give even the most innocent a sensation of having
been accomplice; yet this room was also muscular, a cross
between a *chambre à coucher* and a boxer's training camp.
(*N*, pp. 78–79)

Even the derogatory connotation of the term *rococo* as pretentious or overdecorous, as applied to Renaissance or baroque art
in its decline, suits this novel of disciplined and necessary
excesses. And from rococo and its *genre pittoresque* phrase in
particular, it would be possible to trace the influence upon
Djuna Barnes of late nineteenth-century symbolist and *fin-de-
siècle* styles, insofar as these revive certain characteristics of late
rococo art. For our purposes, it can be generally concluded, as
one reviewer put it, that "Miss Barnes has substituted pattern
and texture for the structure one most often expects as the
main convention of a novel."[29]

*Nightwood*'s unity results in great measure from the intricate interlacing of visual, musical, theatrical and poetic motifs.
Ulrich Weisstein's description of the novel as "transition incar-
nate" may be taken to include its trans-generic design: "Everything in *Nightwood* would seem to participate in several actions
at one and the same time."[30] Indeed, part of the sensation of
simultaneity comes from the closeness of interweaving of
effects throughout. Once led into what is properly a novel by
rather traditional narrative steps, the reader's experience
gradually becomes at once novelistic, poetic, musical, visual,
and dramatic. But *Nightwood*'s mutable character does not only
come from its manner of incorporating several artistic genres.
The work seems to relate to and derive inspiration from
diverse literary types and periods as well.

That *Nightwood* possesses contemporaneity is beyond question. It holds up as a rendering of continental bohemia of the

twenties, a distillation of the despair and estrangement of expatriation, its verisimilitude undoubtedly boosted by the fact that there was an actual model for the doctor, known to most frequenters of Parisian literary and artistic circles of the period. As will soon be apparent, the work relates directly to specific trends of literary experimentation of the decade. But at present, it may be fitting to shift away from the image of its author as an avant-garde figure in order to consider her as a writer belonging to a classic tradition. *Nightwood* is steeped in the literary-historical past as thoroughly as it is grounded in its concrete present. Through sleep and dream, it moves back to get in touch with pre-Christian attitudes, with the primitive, blood-rooted rituals and cycles that predate civilization. Its grasp on literary history begins in its taking two section titles out of the Old Testament, and it goes on to draw as freely, though less obtrusively, from the antique as did *Ryder*.

The frequency with which critics associate the novel with the Elizabethan and Jacobean periods is a sufficient signal of its overriding tone. Graham Greene, it was mentioned, found *Nightwood* to possess the same Jacobean tones as the stories, while Eliot concluded his introduction by speaking of the novel's "quality of horror and doom very nearly related to that of Elizbethan tragedy,"[31] and both are members of a larger group of critics holding similar views. The frame of reference, however, becomes expanded when, for instance, one begins to hear echoes of the metaphysical poets. When the doctor says, " ' . . . we all carry about with us the house of death, the skeleton, but unlike the turtle our safety is inside, our danger out' " (*N*, p.130), the impression that he sounds like Donne here is soon confirmed by his direct quotation from Donne. In addition, the element of compassion in O'Connor's faith is not unlike that expressed by George Herbert. But more frequently his bombast is punctuated by concise epigrams yielding striking conceits, juxtaposing dissimilar elements which create a black humorous effect.

To continue, Janet Flanner assumed that Djuna Barnes's source in *Nightwood*, as in *Ryder* earlier, was eighteenth-century fiction: "Certainly only she would have so thoroughly and deliberately steeped herself in the eighteenth century in order to have conveniently in hand its richer vocabulary, and to grasp . . . those early novel-patterns in which the amitive, ribald, and melancholy states of man's mind were plot enough and to spare."[32] And it may have been a converse perception that prompted another critic later to speak peremptorily of *Nightwood's* "congested neo-Georgian prose."[33]

The novel's critics also refer frequently to the nineteenth century. Bringing things back around to where Miss Barnes began with *The Book of Repulsive Women,* a critic for the *Saturday Review* asserted that, while the early chapters of *Nightwood* recalled Wilde and Pater, "the atmosphere of decay in *Nightwood* stems from the *fin-de-siècle* Frenchmen rather than from the Elizabethans."[34] Hilton Kramer provides a more extensive argument that the novel's affinity is with the symbolist tradition. He quotes Jacques Rivière's remark that a symbolist writer, rather than telling the story that he probably begins by imagining, " 'vibrates ahead of time as he comes in contact with the work that he has not yet written,' " and, after absorbing the materials and emotion that the story might have produced, then begins to write. " 'In other words . . . more than half takes place only in the mind of the author.' "[35] By its narrative indirection that prohibits the reader from judging or observing for himself, *Nightwood* becomes a "series of memorable symbolist vignettes,"[36] the term *vignettes* seeming quite appropriate for expressing the discontinuity of its composition.

With *Nightwood* in mind as an important twentieth-century work, Melvin Friedman nonetheless recognizes its debt to symbolism in its "devotion to the word." In his analysis, both the tradition of Mallarmé and Joyce, and that of stream-of-consciousness prose have influenced *Nightwood,* and each movement has evolved directly from French Symbolist poetry.[37] Not that *Nightwood* is a stream-of-consciousness work; as Friedman points out, its construction is based upon a pattern of cross-reference of image and symbol rather than upon the "index of thought." However, like *Ulysses,* it does depend upon borrowings from poetry and is constructed upon a spatial rather than temporal conception.[38] And Kramer goes on in his article to indicate a similar link with symbolism in reference to the poetic work of T.S. Eliot, who set a precedent for Djuna Barnes in his stylistic conjunction of Elizabethan imagery and rhetoric with the aims of French symbolism. "Her book is thus," writes Kramer, "among other things, a gloss on the literary taste that Eliot's poetry and criticsm found for an entire generation."[39] That Eliot was Miss Barnes's editor at Faber and Faber during the composition of *Nightwood* and *The Antiphon* is a fact that cannot be overlooked.

With its affinities to the modern work of Joyce and Eliot, *Nightwood* has moved through centuries of literature up into its present time, transcending style and period as it had artistic genre. The novel is a kind of echo chamber, wherein faint and distant echoes of literary voices merge simultaneously and reverberate continuously. It would thus seem to be an error to attempt to link it too closely to a single tradition. *Nightwood* is a protean example of the novelistic genre. It is protean too in its characters and themes, insofar as its dominant ones involve the "middle condition" as perceived as a halt between uncertainties. Before a consideration of *Nightwood*'s central themes and characters, however, it must be shown how the novel relates immediately to its time, how, beyond the influence of Joyce and Eliot, the work is rooted in the thirties.

It has been noted in passing that there are some resemblances to surrealist art and its imagery in Djuna Barnes's work. Although the notion of Miss Barnes partaking of automatic writing or the politics of the movement is ridiculous, it is as an art of dissociation and incongruity that the comparison suggests itself. In such art, ordinary relations cease to exist and the subconscious becomes the region of wonder and insight where the objects and events of every day become transformed. *Nightwood*'s imagery often recalls the art of surrealist collage, of Miro or André Breton, for example, which combines elements out of an instinct for inner truth rather than coherent order of concept or surface. In this novel one recalls, among other images, those of the eland, of the fantastic rooms encountered, and of the boyish Robin surrounded with her dolls and toys, or sitting in bed eating eggs and crying " 'Angel, angel!' " Such images are all rendered with a visual accuracy which, like that of the paintings of Magritte, works toward the sharpening rather than softening of details, toward exactitude rather than fuzziness. But Miss Barnes's relation to the surrealists could never have been more than tangential, and, by the late 1920s, interest in the unconscious and its application to aesthetic principles was by no means exclusively the surrealistic. *Nightwood* evokes even more directly the involvement with dreaming and the poetics of the night mind in the pages of *transiton*.

Miss Barnes herself was a contributor, though not a frequent one, to *transition*, having chosen it for her "Rape and Repining" and for a presentation of posthumous "Selections from the Letters of Elsa Baroness von Freytag-Loringhoven" with a brief tribute. As a contributor she was one of many in the company of Joyce, as his "Work in Progress" continued in its pages. As in the case of *Ulysses*, its influence upon her may have been significant. *transition*'s involvement with dreams and the racial unconscious extended far beyond Joyce's work, however, and by the 1930s it had become, under Eugene Jolas, a symposium for investigation of the subject and the poet's relation to it. Typical were large sections of the magazine under headings such as that of November 1929, "The Synthetist Universe: Dreams and the Chthonian Mind," "Dream and Mythos" in 1930, or, continuing as late as 1938, "Night, Myth, Language" with a subsection, "Inquiry Into the Spirit and Language of Night." Jolas's study of dream and night language had evolved out of familiarity with the German romantics[40] such as Novalis and Tieck as well as the poetics of Mallarmé,[41] and had found in psychoanalysis a new perception of unconscious phenomena that the poet could not afford to ignore. As Jolas wrote in "The Language of Night" in 1932:

> Modern psychology . . . has discovered that the subconscious is the basin into which flow all the inhibited components of our being. According to Freud, they are mostly sexual in character. Dr. Jung . . . found, however, that into the subconscious flow not only the unfulfilled ele-

ments of our personal lives, but that it contains also the continuation of a collective mythos. He finds in it a connection with the social organism and even with cosmic, mythological forces. We stand in contact with the entire evolution of mankind, with all the demonish and benevolent powers, and from this inner world emerge both the religious and the bestial phenomena of life.[42]

This inquiry was largely Jungian in inspiration, and valued those states of mind where, however briefly, the "wisdom of the ages" revealed itself—hypnosis, dreams, and half-sleep—and where the rigid dualisms of logic dissolved.[43] The movement of "vertigralism" saw language and syntax as the means of pursuit of the world soul; it stressed verbal innovation rather than automatic writing. While Djuna Barnes never appeared as a participant in the movement as such,[44] its spirit and substance are pervasive in *Nightwood*.

Finally, *Nightwood* takes a prominent place in the "subjective-feminine"[45] tradition in modern fiction. As a work in the broad tradition of the novel of sensibility, it is able to stand on its own while also forming a kind of bridge between the stream-of-consciousness novels of Virginia Woolf and the "interior" novels of Anaïs Nin. As a work of the nineteen thirties, it seems to share Natalie Clifford Barney's faith in "The inspired intelligence, the feminine intelligence of the poet, the intelligence of intuition, of receptivity . . . . " It is likely that Djuna Barnes was familiar with Miss Barney's own subjective novel of 1930, *The One Who Is Legion or A.D.'s After-Life*, the wholly amorphous "plot" of which is capable of summation only in the author's condensed "argument":

A.D., a being having committed suicide, is replaced by a sponsor, who carries on the broken life, with all the human feelings assumed with the flesh, until, having endured to the end in A.D.'s stead, the composite or legion is disbanded by the One, who remains supreme.

In the reading, the book is esoteric enough to justify its subsequent neglect. But certain resemblances to the later *Nightwood* are suggestive. First there is a correspondence of intent. In Miss Barney's statement, "For years I have been haunted by the idea that I should orchestrate those inner voices which sometimes speak to us in unison, and so compose a novel . . . ," can be seen a dissatisfaction with the traditional "realism" of the novelistic form. In both novels then outer reality is seen to dissolve, only now and then to return in partial focus, thereby creating a sense of being beyond time and spatial boundaries. A preoccupation with forms of dual being—centaur, sphinx, hermaphrodite, and angel—is also common to both. Finally, Miss Barney's afterword could stand in itself as an epigraph to *Nightwood:*

> In our human composite, part ape and part angel, is there not scope for an extreme realism and spirituality? And might not an Epicurean be defined as a "Fourth-dimensional Materialist?" In the last sense materiality becomes spiritual, whereas spirits may take human shape. Mystery remains the invisible link between what is outworn by knowledge, and the unborn reality.[46]

All in all, *Nightwood's* imagery, narrative structure, and generic mutability are determined by Djuna Barnes's urge toward centrality The novel intends to be both in the middle of and beyond its contemporary literary period. It succeeds as a novel, but operates beyond traditional novelistic limits. It is from the halt position between uncertainties, from the middle position, that such syntheses of dualities become possible. It remains to be shown how this is equally true of the novel's characters.

In *Nightwood*, character and theme are inseparable, and this is nowhere more apparent than in Doctor O'Connor in his magnified choral role. From his central position in the novel, he operates between the tangible world of daylight and the obscure region of night and dreams, between the concrete and the numinous. Miss Barnes is still a master of surfaces here, but it is a deeper quality that *Nightwood* is after in its descent into the night state of mind, that region anatomized compulsively by Doctor O'Connor once Nora has become trapped in it through Robin. The doctor is the "god of darkness" (*N*, p.126) who aspires toward a Christlike state. " 'Mother of God!' " he cries, " 'I wanted to be your son—the unknown beloved second would have done!' " (*N*, pp.149–50). He is " 'a man with a prehistoric memory' " (*N*, p.164), yet describes himself as his " 'own charlatan' " (*N*, p.96). He is paradox on all levels, an embodiment of the mystery of intermediate being. As such, he is perfectly suited to the choral role he occupies in the drama.

Before further discussion of his character, it should be understood that Miss Barnes fashioned O'Connor after an actual Irish doctor from San Francisco named Dan Mahoney.[47] From the manner in which he comes up now and again in various memoirs of the twenties, such as Robert McAlmon's *Being Geniuses Together,* "Jimmie the Barman's" *"This Must Be the Place,"* and John Glassco's *Memoirs of Montparnasse,* it would seem that Miss Barnes went beyond fact only in the profundity with which she endowed the doctor. Glassco describes him as "the most quoted homosexual in Paris, a man who combined the professions of pathic, abortionist, professional boxer and quasi-confessor to literary women." Quoting the beginning of a typical "astonishing harangue revolving around unmentionable subjects and indescribable practices," Glassco ends by recalling the doctor's self-identification, " 'Dr. God Almighty Maloney [sic], the irrepressible backwoodsman, the original Irish tenor!' "[48] Recently Edouard Roditi remarked in an interview, "He was a remarkable man—it's a great pity that the taperecorder was invented too late. Djuna Barnes did the best she could, and it's brilliant, what she did, but there was more gab, more blarney to him than even appears in *Nightwood.*"[49] Whatever degree of accurate portraiture there is in O'Connor, however, there is no doubt of the importance Miss Barnes intends his role to assume in the total novel. The curious will wish to note that as early as 1915 Miss Barnes wrote a story in which a woman speaks of a former lover named O'Connor: " 'He was the salt of the earth.' "⁵⁰ Slight as the evidence may be, it is entirely possible that the actual Mahoney provided form for a long unrealized conception of a larger-than-life character.

The chief impression that O'Connor makes upon his reappearance in *Nightwood* is that of having somehow become humanized since *Ryder*. Whereas in the earlier novel he had seemed one among many literary devices, in *Nightwood* there are constant reminders of his corporeal reality, of his mortality. And there is drama in his predicament, one that does not simply run parallel to that of the other characters but involves it, in effect contains it. Eliot suggests this when he says that upon successive readings, the doctor, who initially seemed the novel's sole source of vitality, "came to take on a different and more profound importance when seen as a constituent of a whole pattern."⁵¹ In his combined disinterestedness from and profound involvement in universal misery, he becomes a figure who contains multitudes, who takes in " 'a little light laundry known as the Wash of the World' " (*N*, p.126). But in "Go Down, Matthew," with the title sardonically recalling the song "Go Down, Moses," the prophet and lawgiver goes down with his people in the common descent of humanity. " 'The encumbrance of myself I threw away long ago, that breast to breast I might go with my failing friends. And do they love me for it? They do not' " (*N*, p.153). His mortality is finally revealed in his inability to continue to take on the mortal burden. " 'May they all be damned!' " he concludes. " 'The people in my life who have made my life miserable, coming to me to learn of degradation and the night' " (*N*,p.161). In his final, terrible words, the end consists of " *'nothing, but wrath and weeping!'* " in short, ultimate estrangement and universal lamentation. He too belongs to life, which he calls the " 'intermediary vice' " (*N*,p.127).

The reader is never allowed to take Doctor O'Connor at face value, nor is the doctor confined to his oracular role, immense as it may be. At times he becomes physically real in an unexpected way, as in two scenes where he is unaware of being observed. In the first, while in the midst of trying to revive

Robin in her room, he uses the "honesties," the misleading movements of the "dumbfounder," in order to cloak the fact that he is stealing perfume, make-up, and finally a hundred franc note from her table. Felix, observing this, realizes that his acceptance of it would amount to ". . . a long series of convulsions of the spirit, analogous to the displacement in the fluids of the oyster, that must cover its itch with a pearl; so he would have to cover the doctor" (N, p. 36). This "stricture of acceptance (by which what we must love is made into what we can love)" foretells of his relationship (and Nora's) with Robin, and, circularly, of O'Connor's with humanity and with God. Years later, when Felix upon his return first encounters the doctor, he notices that he appears older, sagging with melancholy. However, "The Baron hailed him, and instantly the doctor threw off his unobserved self, as one hides, hastily, a secret life" (N, p.110). In addition, once O'Connor establishes himself as a liar, all that he says becomes affected by it. He declares that it is the anguish of the night that others would beg him to alleviate that has made him a liar. As he tells Nora, " 'There is no truth, and you have set it between you; you have been unwise enough to make a formula; you have dressed the unknowable in the garments of the known' " (N, p.136).

Lying, then, becomes a part of Nightwood's scheme of inversion, whereby the degraded becomes the exalted. It becomes the foundation of discourse revolving around mystery. When O'Connor says that man really desires " 'One of two things: to find someone who is so stupid that he can lie to her, or to love someone so much that she can lie to him' " (N, p.19), there is a religious dimension to his point: " 'Let us put it the other way; the Lutheran or Protestant church versus the Catholic. The Catholic is the girl that you love so much that she can lie to you, and the Protestant is the girl that loves you so much that you can lie to her, and pretend a lot that you do not feel' " (N, p.20). And O'Connor is as much the Catholic as in Ryder, and is so, it is implied, by choice, with no detraction from his multitudinousness. It is a blind appeal[52] that he makes in an empty church, when, following Father Lucas's exhortation to be simple and alone as an animal, and yet think, he exposes himself, crying, with "Tiny O'Toole" in hand in order to embarrass him " 'for the good it might do him,' " " ' "I'm not able to stay permanent unless you help me, O Book of Conceal-ment"!' " (*N*, p.132).

It is as one of the monks bowing down around the " 'Great Enigma' " (*N*, p.83) that the doctor begins with the question from Isaiah, "Watchman, What of the Night?" The tone of his anatomy of night is one of incessantly renewed desperation and humility. It is from this extended choral lamentation in the middle of the narrative that the book takes its title, for the region of night is a kind of black forest.[53]

> "To think of the acorn it is necessary to become the tree. And the tree of night is the hardest tree to mount, the dourest tree to scale, the most difficult of branch, the most febrile to the touch, and sweats a resin and drips a pitch against the palm that computation has not gambled."
> (*N*, pp. 83–84)

His barely interrupted monologue is no less vast than its sub-ject, " 'how the day and night are related by their division,' " and how " 'the very constitution of twilight is a fabulous recon-struction of fear, fear bottom-out and wrong side up' " (*N*,p.80). However wildly illogical it may seem upon initial reading, its essential sense is always maintained. From the doctor's numer-ous digressions there are sharp and abrupt epigrammatical returns:

> "The dead have committed some portion of the evil of the night; sleep and love, the other (*N*,p.86)

> "The sleeper is the proprietor of an unknown land."
> (*N*, p.87)

> "For the lover, it is the night into which his beloved goes . . . that destroys his heart; he wakes her suddenly, only to look the hyena in the face that is her smile, as she leaves that company." (*N*, p.87)

> "Sleep demands of us a guilty immunity. There is not one of us who, given an eternal incognito . . . , would not

commit rape, murder, and all abominations." (*N*, p.88)

"We look to the East for a wisdom that we shall not
use—and to the sleeper for the secret that we shall not
find." (*N*,pp.88–89)

Day and night are not exclusive states, but must be thought of as
one continually. So O'Connor asks Nora " 'to think of the night
the day long, and of the day the night through' " (*N*, p. 84).
Sleep is a middle condition, drawing upon love and death. As
the doctor gradually approaches his concluding assessment of
the particular night of the carriage ride in the *Bois*, it becomes
his point that a refusal to think of sleep and night amounts to a
refusal to think of death: " 'But what of our own death—permit
us to reproach the night, wherein we die manifold alone' " (*N*,
p.97). Digressing, the doctor points this up by contrasting
French nights with American nights. The French alone, he
says, leaves testimony of night and day in the dawn, while the
American destroys one for the sake of the other, " ' . . . separates the two for fear of indignities, so that the mystery is cut in
every cord . . . . ' " (*N*, p.85). The American can only approx-
imate the wisdom of the French through drink. The American
would wash himself clean, yet, " 'The brawl of the Beast leaves
a path for the Beast' " (*N*,p.84). O'Connor goes on:

"We wash away our sense of sin, and what does that bath
secure us? Sin, shining bright and hard. In what does a
Latin bathe? True dust . . . . A European gets out of bed
with a disorder that holds the balance. The lavers of his
deed can be traced back to the last leaf and the good slug
be found creeping. *L'Echo de Paris* and his bed sheets were
run off the same press. One may read in both the travail
life has had with him—he reeks with the essential wit
necessary to the 'sale' of both editions, night edition and
day." (*N*, p. 89)

In his tirade, the doctor gives ample evidence of such "essential
wit," a wit whose play keeps his "narrative" from becoming

unbearably black. Throughout the novel, a comic grotesque vision operates, and is particularly suggestive in the digression on O'Connor's own night wanderings, with his images of public urinals that resemble centipedes and of the pathetic night creatures that frequent them. The doctor speaks of those who turn day into night, and so Nora, as the lover keeping a night watch of anguish and fear, joins the hopeless drunks, prostitutes, addicts:

> "Look for the girls also in the toilets at night, and you will find them kneeling in that great secret confessional crying between tongues, the terrible excommunication:
> 'May you be damned to hell! May you die standing upright! May you be damned upward!' " (*N*,p.95)

The phrase "damned upward" impresses one as a reverse play upon the novel's " 'transcendence downward,' "[54] in Kenneth Burke's term. It is Burke who indicates that *Nightwood* is a lamentation that relies upon religious and moral values which are all exemplified in reverse, effecting a "perverse 'ascent' in terms of decay where corruption and distinction become interchangeable terms."[55] This quality is altogether characteristic of Matthew O'Connor. He vaunts his perversity with the zeal of virtue. There is beauty in the barbarity of his discourse. He is mighty in his persistence; we know he is puny, but his quest for permanence and remedy is of heroic proportions. Finally, the weight of his choral presence, its near complete displacement of the narrative, is yet another reversal of traditional values.

If Matthew O'Connor looms large in this discussion, it is because there is perhaps even more to T.S. Eliot's impression on his first reading than he himself would have granted. Eliot was quite properly preparing the reader to realize the doctor's place in the whole design, and does acknowledge that no subsequent readings diminished him. But the doctor becomes in effect and most indirectly the novel's narrator, telling the story of wracked humanity, of universal misery in which he participates along with the others but which the others are not articulate enough to tell. He is a figure similar to Tiresias in *The Waste Land*. A resemblance that Joseph Frank suggests is probably not accidental. "Like the man-woman Tiresias, symbol of universal experience," he writes, "the doctor has homosexual inclinations; like Tiresias, he has 'fore-suffered all' by apparently being immortal . . . ."[56] In addition, O'Connor, like Tiresias, is "father confessor" to those of the same purgatorial region he inhabits, as well as the prophet of their particular and universal fates. In his role, again, he stands in and for mankind's middle condition.

Wallace Fowlie begins to place the characters in their proper perspective when he states that O'Connor is the most important character, while Nora is actually *Nightwood*'s heroine. This view is possible if one is considering character action, or rather the heroic failure to act. But Joseph Frank's argument that Robin Vote is the central figure, "the figure around which the situation revolves,"[57] is also persuasive, particularly if one looks at the novel from a structural point of view. Robin is the passive center of all of the narrative's events. Indeed, Robin comes to be an "unmoved mover," to take a term Dell Hymes[58] applies to her, for those she meets are drawn to her as toward a magnet. An immediate link between Robin and O'Connor is established by the description of her as "the born somnambule, who lives in two worlds—meet of child and desperado" (*N*,p.35). This is followed only a couple of paragraphs later by the parenthetical information that the doctor is not a licensed practitioner and thus also a desperado. A comparable connection exists in the factor of homosexuality: a lesbian, she dresses as and resembles a boy. The sense of her as a divided creature, suspended between two conditions, is extended by the reference to her as beast turning human, and by her eyes reminding Felix of "the long unqualified range in the iris of wild beasts who have not tamed the focus down to meet the human eye" (*N*,p.37). She is further distanced from humanity by the description of her flesh as of the texture of plant life, which in turn is associated with the jungle aspect of her room. Frank notes that with no knowledge of her prior life, her awakening seems like an act of birth. She embodies a state

of being not beyond but before good and evil: "She is both
innocent and depraved . . . precisely because she has not
reached the human state where moral values become relevant."[59] Her allure is in her unresolved condition. It is the
mystery in Robin that is irresistably fascinating to the others.

It should be observed that the equation of Robin's potential for becoming human, or coming around to life, with
acquiring moral values—Frank calls her "an amorphous mass
of moral possibility"[60]—is the one unconvincing note in Frank's
discussion. If Kenneth Burke is correct in saying that the novel
builds up the sense of Puritan morality, for aesthetic purposes,
by running counter to the puritanical, treating decay as "a
recondite species of distincion,"[61] then Frank is conceptual-
izing according to a framework of values outside the novel. A
reverse morality seems to operate in *Nightwood*, showing " 'purity's black backside' " which Nora comes to love. What becoming human, as against going to the dogs, would involve for
Robin would probably be the full realization of the depths and
pains of love, or the reciprocity that has always been missing
from her loves. In any case, the human state, for Djuna Barnes,
is one where "moral values" are emphatically irrelevant.

Until Robin finally becomes animal, she wanders in perpetual sleep, going to and coming from, in constant "formless
meditation" (*N*,p.59). When she kneels in church, having
abruptly and gratuitously taken the Catholic vow, "her prayer
was monstrous because in it there was no margin left for damnation or forgiveness, for praise or for blame—those who cannot conceive a bargain cannot be saved or damned. She could
not offer herself up; she only told of herself in a preoccupation
that was its own predicament" (*N*,p.47). Her innocence,
similarly, consists in her being utterly unknown to herself, as
the doctor says later, or being unable to do anything in relation
to anyone but herself. Unstable, always in flux, embodying
tendency but never realization, she cannot be saved or
damned, and neither can anyone who tries to give her, or find
through her, form and permanence. But there is salvation in
her ultimate damnation: in becoming one with Nora's dog
there is the finality which fulfills O'Connor's prophesy of her

end. This relates to how a lion had gone down before Robin at the circus where Nora had met her. But many earlier touches had suggested the dog in Robin. Living together, Nora had been afraid to disturb the house: ". . . if she disarranged anything, Robin might become confused—might lose the scent of home" (*N*, p. 56). And Nora had divined Robin's "tragic longing to be kept, knowing herself astray" (*N*, p. 58). When she goes down with the frantic dog in Nora's chapel, she is wholly possessed and the tragic equilibrium of her nature is finally shaken.

In this chthonian rite, there is a return to the primitive that Robin had never been far from:

> Such a woman is the infected carrier of the past: before her the structure of our head and jaws ache—we feel that we could eat her, she who is eaten death returning, for only then do we put our face close to the blood on the lips of our forefathers. (*N*,p.37)

Like the doctor, with his prehistoric memory and semblance of having participated in all periods and recorded times, Robin is detached from the present, always seeming "newly ancient" (*N*,p.42), or "beyond timely changes except in the blood that animated her" (*N*,p.56). Once again, in Robin the tree of time is one that is scaled backward. Her movement ahead amounts to movement backward, as she plays with her toys and dolls or lapses out of time altogether. As is the case with *Nightwood*'s style, the past is everywhere in the present, the present is in effect the past. Into daylight and the historical present rises the "primeval chaos of Robin,"[62] the " 'eternal momentary.' "

Nora too is outside of the historical moment: "The world and its history were to Nora like a ship in a bottle; she herself was outside and unidentified, endlessly embroiled in a preoccupation without a problem" (*N*, p.53). Also, there is a reference to "the equilibrium of her nature, savage and refined" (*N*, p.50), which creates a parallel with the dichotomy in Robin of animal and human. While Robin is described in part with vegetal imagery,

Nora is linked to wood: ". . .there could be seen coming, early in her life, the design that was to be the weather-beaten grain of her face, that wood in the work, the tree coming forward in her, an undocumented record of time" (*N*, p.50). These factors may account for the immediate attraction between Nora and Robin when they meet at the circus, as well as suggest why they are from the beginning " 'haunted' of each other' " (*N*,p.55). Indeed, as Nora later discovers, they are both shadows in each other's dreams. This is because there is a derangement in Nora's equilibrium, as the narrative tells us, which relates to how "Nora had the face of all people who love the people—a face that would be evil when she found out that to love without criticism is to be betrayed" (*N*, p. 51). To love everything is to be despised by everything. In the American salon that, like Sophia Ryder, Nora presides over, she is singular and alone. Like Robin, her life is a wandering. A Westerner who O'Connor himself claims to have delivered at birth, she possesses an estate with a ruined chapel in New England, and when in Europe to do circus publicity, encounters the night circle of the expatriated and dislocated. The striking images of the American West associated with Nora, her "pauper's salon," and the fact that "by temperament Nora was an early Christian; she believed the word" (*N*,p.51): all suggest, as Frank indicates, a spiritual attitude determined by belief in man's innate goodness or capacity for moral improvement, progress, and acceptance of all forms of unconventionality.[63] But Nora as a Protestant also inherits a helplessness in both love and her possessive-redemptive quest. She becomes hopelessly fascinated by the depravity suppressed by the Puritan ethic, and the novel's pattern of reverse values largely evolves out of her "night watch."

Of *Nightwood*'s characters, writes Wallace Fowlie, "Nora is the one who questions and who contains the innocent greatness of the here."[64] She is the heroine in that her total love is incapable of realizing itself, unable to comprehend Robin's apartness, and so her suffering is pure and unrelieved. In Alan Williamson's opinion, "Nora's very attempt to make Robin her protected and saved love-object dooms the relationship . . .

since Robin is unable to respond to or accept Nora Flood's possessive, protective flood of love."[65] Nora who, according to O'Connor, lacks the joy and safety that the Catholic faith provides, is observed by him on her night search for Robin: " 'There goes mother of mischief, running about, trying to get the world home' " (*N*, p.61), in other words back into the bottle. The shock to her Puritanism is, at the same time, however, a penetration of the submerged life within herself. By the time of "Go Down, Matthew," she has become articulate enough to voice her anguish: " 'Love is death, come upon with passion; I know, that is why love is wisdom' " (*N*,p.137). Not that her wisdom is of much good to her; she remains obsessed, turning into herself in the foetus of her thoughts, mad by her own admission. Deprived of the " 'secure torment' " (*N*, p.151) she had known Robin to be, Nora has only the suffering that she calls the decay of the heart.

Nora understands that her love for Robin is incestuous, in the sense that Robin, embodying past time, seems a relative as if found in another generation. Alan Williamson observes that familial or homosexual loves are the important relationships in Djuna Barnes's late works, and that the relationship between Nora and Robin parallels that of Miranda and Augusta in *The Antiphon* in being a union of separated halves of one identity. Love, writes Williamson, "arises from the fragmented individual's craving for Edenic completion; therefore the most perfect love is that in which the lovers are mirror-images, complementary to each other but sharing the same basis of identity in blood and/or sex.[66] But it is a far from perfect love that Nora contemplates when she cries to her confessor, " 'She is myself. What am I to do?' " (*N*, p. 127). Nora is terror-stricken upon encountering a double, thus coming to a dead end: " 'A man is another person—a woman is yourself, caught as you turn in panic; on her mouth you kiss your own. If she is taken you cry that you have been robbed of yourself' " (*N*, p. 143). The doll is the illuminating symbol here. It is obvious that the dolls that Robin plays with signify her childishness. But Nora knows that a doll given to a child is death, an effigy, and that

" ' . . . when a woman gives it to a woman, it is the life they cannot have, it is their child, sacred and profane . . . ' " (*N*, p.142). Matthew O'Connor goes further:

> "The last doll, given to age, is the girl who should have been a boy, and the boy who should have been a girl! . . . The doll and the immature have something right about them, the doll because it resembles but does not contain life, and the third sex because it contains life but resembles the doll. The blessed face! It should be seen only in profile, otherwise it is observed to be the conjunction of the identical cleaved halves of sexless misgiving!" (*N*,p.148)

Nora's love for Robin is hopeless from its inception. In effect, "Robin looks to Nora for a love which can penetrate through her trance, make her capable of antiphonal love, and save her from insanity, while Nora, in loving Robin, is attempting to capture and understand her own subconscious."[67] But their affair involves death in a dual sense. Robin can only finally be possessed in death. And lesbianism is the absorption in the mirror image, which amounts to the forswearing of generation.

Robin's progressive descent toward animality is marked by her virtual abduction by the "squatter," Jenny Petherbridge—who is continually being compared to a bird. With her "beaked head," her "fluttering," her "raven's bill," and, as Nora puts it, her pelvic bones seen flying through her dress, she is a far from noble example of the species. Kenneth Burke, in fact, characterizes the chapter in which she makes her appearance as an example of invective, a term which might more appropriately be reserved for the doctor's grotesquely comic diatribes against her. Her appropriation of Robin removes her further from the human because Jenny is utterly sterile, as unsexed as the doll that Frau Mann is likened to earlier. Jenny is the only character in the novel that could be called bourgeois, according to Frank, and she is certainly the only principal one that could be called one-dimensional. If Hedvig, Felix's mother, personifies a "massive *chic*; (*N*, p. 4), Jenny personifies a total absence of chic, as everything in her possession becomes debased.

Her emotions, her dealings with life, everything about her is described as second hand: "She had a continual rapacity for other people's facts; absorbing time, she held herself respons- ible for historic characters" (*N*, p. 67). O'Connor says that she stands " '. . . between two tortures—the past that she can't share, and the present that she can't copy' " (*N*, p. 124). Her effect upon Robin is implied by the illuminating image of the two in a restaurant, with Jenny leaning over the table and Robin pulling back. There is something absurd about the movement:

> . . . a movement that can divulge neither caution nor daring, for the fundamental condition for completion was in neither of them; they were like Greek runners, with lifted feet but without the relief of the final command that would bring the foot down—eternally angry, eternally separated, in a cataleptic frozen gesture of abandon. (*N*, p. 69)

In Jenny's possession, then, Robin is trapped in the "halt posi- tion of the damned."

Of the principals, there remains Felix Volkbein, with whom the narrative began. Jenny's grasp upon the past is that of a "looter." Felix's is no less tenacious and tenuous, but infinitely more respectful. He has inherited his father's pre- occupation, a "remorseless homage to nobility" (*N*, p.2), that has manufactured a false title, coat of arms, and list of progen- itors. Born of an Italian Jew and an Austrian Gentile, Felix bears the mark of the Wandering Jew, who "seems to be every- where from nowhere" (*N*,p.7). In a summary account of him Miss Barnes writes, "From the mingled passions that made up his past, out of a diversity of bloods . . . Felix had become the accumulated and single—the embarrassed" (*N*, pp.8–9). He too is in an intermediate position in his being, which is to say that his existence is paradoxical. The doctor knows immediately that there is something both missing and whole about the Baron, a man whose sense of correctness prompts him to dress in part for the day and for the evening at all times.

Felix is forever "bowing down" before the "great past" as well as anything in the present, debased or not, that evokes it. Genuinely believing that " 'To pay homage to our past is the only gesture that also includes the future' " (*N*, p. 39), he would have sons who would equally honor, perhaps fulfill, the past. But ironically, as Jack Hirschman notes,[68] the marriage of Felix, the human, with Robin, the timeless, produces a stunted offspring who is the fulfillment of O'Connor's prophesy: " 'The last muscle of aristocracy is madness . . . the last child born to aristocracy is sometimes an idiot, out of respect—we go up—but we come down' " (*N*, p. 40). That the European aristocratic tradition is impotent, Frank points out, is borne out by Robin's flight, which leaves behind only the precociously senile Guido. But Guido is a more ambiguous figure than this in itself implies.

Guido is described as "an addict to death," and as "born to holy decay" (*N*, p. 107), the process, one might suppose, to follow from the collapse of historical tradition as well as terminal generation. Guido is a sophisticated elaboration of Valentine, the autistic child in "Cassation." In his estrangement, the boy, under the guidance that Felix undertakes, enters the church. Once again, the doctor sheds light upon the event. As calamity is what we all seek, he says, Felix need search no longer, for it is in his son:

> "Guido is the shadow of your anxiety, and Guido's shadow is God's."
> Felix said: "Guido also loves women of history."
> "Mary's shadow!" said the doctor. (*N*, p.120)

And, indeed, the boy wears an image in metal of the Virgin from his neck on a red ribbon. Guido is sanctified. The doctor, who says that he never uses the derogatory in the usual sense, states that he is not being derogatory when he calls Guido "maladjusted," Through Guido, Felix understands that " 'The unendurable is the beginning of the curve of joy' " (*N*, p. 117). So it is not through Robin that Felix becomes a votary, but through their son, whose chapping hands he annoints with oil. Guido is outside the historical frame of reference of which Felix is a prisoner. And Felix does finally come to an awareness that it is impossible for a sane mind to discover the secret of time beyond the present condition. In his final words, " 'One has, I am now certain, to be a little mad to see into the past or the future, to be a little abridged of life to know life, the obscure life—darkly seen, the condition my son lives in; it may also be the errand on which the Baronin is going' " (*N*, p.122).

The intricacy and intensity of the relationships between the active characters and the passive but pivotal Robin Vote are heightened by terministic patterns that relate to all of them. From the beginning, the themes that the principal characters embody are reiterated by variation, in musical thematic fashion, of key terms. Kenneth Burke discusses these in his article on *Nightwood* as stylistic devices which go toward carrying to completion the theme of "transcendence downward." The word *turn*, for example, comes forth in the scene where Nora and Robin meet at the circus, suggesting a romantic passion which is analogous to religious passion. Its frequent recurrence in other contexts relates to the process of Robin's "conversion to perversion, or inversion," the course that the inverted passion takes. We might note that the movement of turning also follows from the author's theatricality, calling attention as it does to the spatial relationships within a scene in a manner similar to that of printed stage directions. Also, as turning toward and away from clearly relate to the "going to and coming from" pattern in *Ryder*, they suggest tentative and incessant movement without finality, one aspect of the novel's ambiance. Thus, Burke indicates that the titles "Bow Down" and "Go Down, Matthew" signal the terministic basis of the development of the theme[69] One working title[70] of *Nightwood*, in fact, was "Bow Down," which in the final version was transposed as title to the first section. The title from Ecclesiastes, "Where the Tree Falls," also carries the theme of descent, while incorporating a reference to wood, another pivotal term. In the narrative, the recurrance of "down" bears primarily upon debasement, death, dreaming, decay (like the frequent term *eating*, in the sense of being eaten away), and kneeling in prayer. Burke chooses to quote[71] the passage where the doctor quotes the blasphemies of whores in public toilets: " ' "I'm an angel on all fours, with a child's feet behind me, seeing my people that have never been made, going down face foremost, drinking the waters of night at the water hole of the damned, and I go into the waters, up to my heart, the terrible waters!" ' " (*N*, p. 95). It should be noted that a corresponding pattern of ascent exists and serves a complementary purpose, the upward motif appearing in such terms as *erection*, the more exalted *resurrection* (O'Connor tells Nora that she had died and arisen for love), and the reference to being "damned upward" which just precedes the above quotation. But the downward pattern is finally completed in "The Possessed" when Nora strikes into the jamb of the chapel door and, before her, Robin and the dog go down together to the wood of the floor.

*Blood* is another term subject to contextual variation. Its sense is "folkish," Burke points out,[72] and relates to the theme of the primitive as well as to preconsciousness, a component of Robin's somnambulistic condition, for we read that "Always she seemed to be listening to the echo of some foray in the blood that had no known setting. . . ." (*N*, p. 44). The blood theme also concerns childbirth,[73] and Hedvig Volkbein's desks in "rich and bloody wood" (*N*, pp.5–6) come to mind in turn. The many references to wood and trees ultimately suggest the traditional association of wood with "the feminine principle of matter and mother (*materia, mater*)."[74] In archaic usage, moreover, "wood" carried the meaning of madness, being out of one's mind, a condition which merges with being beyond or out of time. Thus the frequency of reference of trees as a record of undocumented time and the association of "night" and "wood" in the title. As Miss Barnes writes in *The Antiphon*, wood is the substance of the cradle, the cross, and the coffin. The night wood is the medium for recurrence of all lost phenomena. Too numerous to cite here, the recurrence of these terms forms a total pattern which is symmetrical without being rigid, precise and yet rich in ambiguity.

The blood theme, finally, is involved in close association with the heart, one of *Nightwood*'s central symbols. In the secularized religious motifs of the novel, the Bleeding Heart becomes transformed into the tortured human heart as symbolic of the individual and universalized passion. Suffering, by Nora's definition, is " 'the decay of the heart' " (*N*, p. 156), which is the common experience of all four characters in their nights. Felix is not only speaking for himself when he says, " 'We are adhering to life now with our last muscle—the heart' " (*N*, p. 40), nor is O'Connor when he puts it more outrageously: " 'I tell you . . . if one gave birth to a heart on a plate, it would say "Love" and twitch like the lopped leg of a frog' " (*N*, pp. 26–27). It is the agony of the heart that remains when the mind comes up against mystery, and *Nightwood* is one of the rare modern novels to attempt to deal with metaphysical pain and disorder in its full extremity, to go beyond the scope of diagnosis.

In all, *Nightwood* is Djuna Barnes's central work, if not her only achievement of distinction. The book's trans-generic mode enables Miss Barnes to focus the themes and stylistic techniques that had been forming for years into a cohesive whole. It is completely consistent with the earlier work in form and themes, only more concentrated and intricately worked within its selective range. It brings the aims of the novel perhaps as close as possible to those of poetry, particularly with respect to the poetic image. It remains to be seen whether or not *The Antiphon*, a similar attempt in the genre of verse drama, is as successful. But *Nightwood* is a masterful work architecturally and linguistically, comparable to the works of Joyce and Eliot among the moderns, and to those earlier writers quoted or echoed in the novel itself. Like Malcolm Lowry's *Under the Volcano* and William Gaddis's *The Recognitions*, equally neglected works of similar merit, nearly every phrase in it is distinctive and functional, essential to the whole. As one contributor to *A Festschrift for Djuna Barnes on Her 80th Birthday*[75] commented, no novel has been better "languaged" in the twentieth century.

# 6.

## Early Plays and *The Antiphon*

James Joyce was suggested earlier as an influence upon Djuna Barnes in at least one particular phrase of her development. But certain broad parallels between their literary careers seem noteworthy too. It is particularly striking that both became adept in several genres as their writing progressed. This factor was crucial in the shaping of their most representative works. *Ulysses* and *Nightwood* were both instrumental in liberating the novel from two centuries of amassed narrative conventions, an achievement largely resulting from their trans-generic scope. Also both writers produced their masterpieces long before the end of their careers. Miss Barnes's verse drama *The Antiphon,* which did not appear until twenty-two years after *Nightwood,* is comparable to Joyce's late *Finnegans Wake* in being a continuation of formal experimentation with an accompanying increase in complexity and obscurity. While Joyce's *Work-in-Progress* was an ongoing extension of narrative possibilities already introduced in *Ulysses,* however, Miss Barnes's play appeared at a glance to be a sudden and unprecedented departure from her earlier writing.

The reason for this is quite obvious. By 1958, few readers recalled or were even aware of Miss Barnes's beginnings as a playwright, for her early plays, like her poems, were eclipsed in the twenties by her more fully conceived and realized prose fiction. Then, too, although there are indications that Miss Barnes was already beginning work on *The Antiphon* at the time of *Nightwood*'s publication,[1] its slow composition and several manuscript revisions kept her apart from the literary world for so long that she had become generally neglected as a writer of any sort. Yet *The Antiphon* is in truth a fulfillment of one of its author's earliest aspirations. Although it is her only verse play, far outdistancing the early one-act plays in formal and verbal complexity, in a sense it is the culmination of that phase of Miss Barnes's career that had been the most erratic and interrupted in development. It would be a mistake then to discuss *The Antiphon* without some awareness of Miss Barnes's beginnings as a dramatist. For the elaborate rhetorical conception of the verse play rests upon a foundation of which the essential structural and conceptual elements are not unlike those of the early one-act plays.

Djuna Barnes's interest in the theater was apparent from the beginning. During her early years in Greenwich Village, she was constantly involved with theatrical groups in one way or another. Out of her participation in productions of the Washington Square Players, for example, developed some of her earliest theatrical reportage, largely for the *New York Morning Telegraph* in 1916 and 1917. She also appeared on the stage in minor roles in several Theatre Guild productions, an activity she ceased to pursue because of her dislike of public appearance.[2] But she first came to attention as a performed playwright in 1919, when the Provincetown Playhouse produced her one-act play *Three from the Earth*, which was followed in 1920 by *An Irish Triangle* and *Kurzy of the Sea*. The first of this trio was published in 1923 in *A Book*, along with two others, *The Dove*, which had already been staged at Smith College, and *To the Dogs*. Further one-act plays appeared in the twenties in various magazines, but, like so much of Miss Barnes's early work, were never collected or reprinted. Some of these aspired toward the dramatic coherence and scope that are required for staging, but others were intentionally slight, brief trifles which displayed Miss Barnes's fondness for facetiae. In this group belonged several playlets either signed or in the style of Lydia Steptoe, distinguishable from her other sketches of the kind only by their form, and obviously intended solely for reading. Then, during the twenties, Miss Barnes began to write two three-act plays, tentatively titled *Anna Portuguise* and *Biography of Julie von Bartman*.³ These were eventually abandoned, and so apparently were any further intentions of writing for the stage. Her later work as a theatrical columnist for *Theatre Guild Magazine* seemed a postscript to an ambition.

Looking back upon these one-act plays, one becomes aware of how closely they correspond to Miss Barnes's short stories of the same period. A play such as *Three from the Earth* bears out one reviewer's general remark about her style in *A Book:*"She is what might be called a realist of the intangibles in her prose, which must be interpreted to considerable degree inferentially."⁴ One again finds a prose stripped of ornamentation, entirely functional, "naturalistic" in the way it seeks the familiar patterns of common speech, yet continuously elliptical in the context of the developing conflict.

*Three from the Earth* falls immediately after "A Night Among the Horses" in the contents of *A Book*, once again dramatizing a clash between the raffish and the *mondaine*. The play opens with three brothers who seem to be common peasants calling upon Kate Morley, "an adventuress and lady of leisure" (*AB*, p. 15)". A troubled purpose is promptly revealed behind what at first appears to be a social visit, for the Carson brothers have come to retrieve the letters of their father to his onetime mistress. What follows is a "house clearing." Kate is about to go off to marry a supreme court judge, while the brothers are preparing to go abroad in consequence—and this revelation is postponed—of their father's suicide. A history is exposed: the father's marriage to an alleged prostitute, his subsequent promiscuity, and its result. At one point John Carson notices a photograph of Kate with a child. She tells him that her madonna pose was for an amateur theatrical, the "Crown of Thorns," but on the back of the photograph is written, "Little John, God bless him." Then in taking leave, John embraces Kate, kissing her on the mouth. She cries out, "Not that way! Not that way!" to which John answers, "That's the way you bore him" (*AB*, p. 30)!

As later in *The Antiphon*, the "action" of this play is a postmortem, the present determined by a revelation of the past. Its theme, carried through *Ryder* into *The Antiphon*, involves the martyrdom of womankind at the hands of the "mighty righteous and original father" (*AB*, p. 23). When John, taking the photograph, asks, "You have posed for the madonna?" Kate replies that "Every woman has" (*AB*, p. 25). *Three From the Earth* presents Miss Barnes's first portrait of the paradigmatic father-procreator, a type that reemerges in greater detail in Wendell Ryder and Titus Hobbs in *The Antiphon*. This figure dominates the brief play. One reviewer who found it twisted and freakish in plot did admit that "none can deny a real sense of character in the two people who never enter. The Spoon River couple that Miss Barnes sees off-stage through her yellow-hued fin de siècle monocle are decidedly the triumph of the play."[5] The father, who according to Kate had instilled the habit of taciturnity in his sons, was a chemist become gentleman farmer, delicate and eccentric, walking the streets with white rats upon his shoulders. The whore-mother, formerly a dancing girl, seems an early sketch of Kate-Careless in her vulgarity and gross beauty. There is also something in the sons that belies their seeming dumb earthiness, an uneasy intelligence, a restlessness that is manifested in their determination to seek out the great men abroad: Anatole France, de Gourmont, others.

Kate Morley herself is finally seen to be divided in her nature. A critic called her "an intellectual vampire, it may be, or a refined radical who, defying the conventions, is pursued by her materialistic past."[6] Upon first appearance it is Kate who is entirely *fin de siècle*, stylized and as studiously artificial as the boudoir she inhabits. She says in an aside, "Well, there is malice in me—what of it? We've all been a while with the dogs, we don't all learn to bark"(*AB*, p. 19). But her aesthetic malice is no defense against the revelations of the brothers, and Kate's fundamental vulnerability is exposed in her admission, " 'Sometimes I found myself on my knees—' " (*AB*, p. 28).

*Three from the Earth* is one of Miss Barnes's more successful one-act plays, with a crescendo in intensity of emotion that is perfectly suited to the exposition, and a situation that gives issue to a major theme in much of her work. *Kurzy of the Sea*[7] was apparently never published, but seems to have been, like *An Irish Triangle*, a lighter piece.

Appearing in Egmont Arens' magazine *Playboy* in the year following its Provincetown Playhouse production, *An Irish Triangle* was described as "a delightful trifle . . . with touches that are almost Barriesque."[8] Like a number of Miss Barnes's early plays, it begins with two ladies taking tea. In their brief dialogue, a matter of rumor is aired.

Kathleen O'Rune, through the course of a long winter, has visibly risen above her station. Her neighbor Shiela O'Hare, however, is the "usual poor," middle-aged, thin and sad. When Shiela observes that Kathleen's sorrow has gone from her eyes and that her smile is no longer twisted with sadness, Kathleen announces that she has learned of the nobilities of literature and the subtleties of life, of taste in dress and all matters of elegance. Her transformation, it so happens, is by way of her fine husband's having gone up the hill to the Manor House to learn the ways of its mistress in the course of an affair with her. John, Kathleen affirms, has transgressed "for the good that's in it," and she does not hesitate to generalize that "It's in need of education is Ireland, and the refinement that comes down out of the hills, from behind grand doors, in the early dawn with red eyes."[9] Shiela, ostensibly prudent and severe but secretly thrilled, becomes Kathleen's object of pity along with all of ignorant and lamenting Ireland. In a final ironic revelation, Kathleen informs her that, lest the women begin to outstrip their  men, she herself will begin to climb the hill so as to instruct her husband in the matters of which he remains ignorant, permitting him also to learn "in how many styles one may lead a good life, though a hearty."[10]

The play's irony, of course, is in the means by which the manners and morals of the nobility come down upon the poor. This amounts to a comment upon the fragility of aristocracy, the vulnerability of its forms and values. In plays such as this and *Three from the Earth,* and stories like "A Night Among the Horses," are found the beginnings of an effort to come to terms with the dichotomies between social classes as the historical consequence of the opposition of nature and civilization. In *Ryder* and *The Antiphon*, aristocracy is dramatized in its late phase of decline as an institution that has been undermined through the ages by natural forces, particularly the procreative act. Much as Robin's elusive course in *Nightwood* ended in her ascent-descent to the level of beast, Kate Morley, Sophia Ryder, and Augusta in *The Antiphon* are brought around from the civilized state to their essential condition, that of "Mother."

*She Tells Her Daughter*, published in *Smart Set* in 1923, is yet another one-act play that looks behind the facade of culture. Seated in her elegant drawing room, Madame Deerfont interrupts her daughter of sixteen in her reading in order to make a revelation. Ellen Louise Theresa puts down the chapbook, "The Book of Beautiful Women," and her mother begins the "true" account of her life, of her career as a repulsive woman. Her story, randomly involving acts of tormenting animals and pasting Poison labels on her father's pharmaceutical bottles, winds around to her affair with a man with something "terrible and excessive" in his manner. Recalling a meeting in the hay of his livery stable during which she suddenly took possession of his knife, Madame Deerfont suddently breaks off her narrative. The remainder of her account is designed either to cover or evade the ultimate truth for the benefit of her enthralled daughter. Unable to reveal one truly awful and savage moment in her past, the mother resumes the same blasé pose with which she began.

Only four pages in length, *She Tells Her Daughter* intends to convey a sense of terror and enigma by means of the economy that has been noted in numerous short stories. Its dramatic effectiveness is necessarily limited by its brevity, which suggests that its appropriate mode of presentation would be as a curtain raiser. The fact that the initial stage directions dwell in much detail upon the odors in the room, however, would suggest that Miss Barnes had intended it as no more than a play to be read. In addition, there is nothing in what follows that directly involves staging techniques, a characteristic of many of her plays of the twenties. Just as her short stories of the period ignore the rules of standard narrative, her one-act plays make no effort to conform to the principles of the well-made play. The intent in both genres seems to be to get to the essence of a situation as quickly and directly as possible. Miss Barnes's plays consequently become less playable as they gradually cease to appear.

In addition, *She Tells Her Daughter* illustrates what should already be apparent, that her plays are without exception plays about women. As such, they anticipate Miss Barnes's first large statement in *Ryder* on the nature and role of women. Ellen Louise Theresa, rather than recoiling from the truth about to be sprung, becomes eager, perhaps sexually aroused, and unashamedly involved. Her blasé retreat from the ultimate revelation copies her mother's. Their identification with each other is total yet brittle. It is the eternal opposition of the sexes that again and again forces women into an uneasy conspiracy against men. In all of Miss Barnes's work, the male is reducible to his sexual drive. In forcing childbirth upon the woman, he causes her pain and enforces the principle of otherness. But the female impulse is toward oneness, and this becomes attainable when women come together on their own terms and momentarily identify on the grounds of their universal plight, the fact that all women have posed for the madonna. The male becomes compassionate only when his being is seen as composite of male and female, recalling the original Adamic unity, as is the case with Doctor O'Connor and at moments with Wendell Ryder. Likewise, there is always a trace of almost masculine resilience and assertiveness in Miss Barnes's sturdiest women. Helena Hucksteppe, in *To the Dogs*, is typical.

At first sight, Helena appears diminutive against the frail beauty of decor in her room, while Gheid Storm on entering her room is "decidedly masculine." In the verbal duel that ensues, however, it is Helena who rises to heights over her would-be suitor. Proclaiming herself a woman who is emphatically *not* in need, she responds to Storm's need by saying, "Nor do I participate in liberations—" (*AB*, p. 51). Although he claims that he has never "gone to the dogs" for the sake of love, he came to Helena like a dog when he "scented a great lover." Helena declares respect for her own dogs, but says that

"Mongrels may not dig up buried treasure" (*AB*, p. 52). In short, Storm is undeveloped, while Helena began "beyond bitterness." He cannot touch her, and the only action of the play is her protracted contemptuous rejection of him as a lover and as a man.

Helena is another of Miss Barnes's overdrawn women, given to remarks like "Only those who have helped to make such death as mine may go a little way toward the ardors of that decay" (*AB*, pp. 55–56). Such a character begins as a finished portrait. Nothing remains to be revealed, for there is no development possible beyond accentuation of details that are extreme from the beginning. In *To the Dogs* there is really no contest because Helena is the victor in sexual supremacy at the outset. The male, Gheid Storm, is rendered impotent, reduced to abject passivity with every advance he attempts to make. Dramatic tension seems to evaporate as the play continues in spasms of antagonism.

Despite a desire to shortcut the steps of dramatic exposition by concentrating only upon the brief and conclusive confrontation of Helena and Storm, Miss Barnes is finally unable to sustain much interest in its outcome. One riposte simply follows another, the level of intensity remaining unvaried. The work's form thus becomes unnecessary, and it finds its proper place in a collection consisting mostly of short stories. In *A Book*, *Three from the Earth* is unique in being a fully crafted piece for the stage. The remaining one-act play, *The Dove*, can only be judged to be flaccid by dramatic standards.

The enigmatic young girl called The Dove might be speaking for the author in saying, "I'm impatient of necessary continuity . . . I want the beautiful thing to be, how can logic have anything to do with it, or probable sequence?" (*AB*, pp. 157–58) The Dove is another familiar figure in Miss Barnes's work: the dangerous child with overtones of the vampire. Barely out of her teens, she might be a younger Helena Hucksteppe who, upon being asked why she does nothing, answers "A person who is capable of anything needs no practice" (*AB*, p. 155). The Dove has come somehow to live with the Burgson sisters, Vera and Amelia, in their luxuriously sensual but rather outlandish apartment. As later in *The Antiphon*, Miss Barnes's attention to decor is close and functional. Besides the obligatory frills, the room contains abundant firearms and two suggestive pictures, one of an early English tandem race, the other of a madonna and child.

*The Dove* is a study of ennui in the parlor. Vera Burgson succinctly sums up the situation at the beginning:

> We say this little thing in French and that little thing in Spanish, and we collect knives and pistols, but we only shoot our buttons off with the guns and cut our darning cotton with the knives, and we'll never, never be perverse . . . , and we keep a few animals—very badly—hoping to see something first hand. . . . (*AB*, p. 149)

As the play develops, however, the author has little to do except to sustain an atmosphere of understated perversity and suppressed violence. Vera tells The Dove at one point that her terrible quality is "not one of action, but just the opposite, as if you wanted to prevent nothing" (*AB*, p. 154). Since the sisters can only live a life of imagination, and since The Dove's passivity is its axis, it is fitting that the tension finally explodes absurdly. Amelia's ranting brings her craving to destroy almost to the surface, whereupon The Dove silences her by sinking her teeth into Amelia's breast, the bite of the vampire. Then, abruptly moving offstage, The Dove shoots a bullet through a symbolic portrait of two Venetian courtesans, prompting Amelia's ironic curtain line, "*This* is obscene!" (*AB*, p.163)

Its successful operations in the short stories notwithstanding, dispensing with "necessary continuity" in the course of stretching out a stagnant situation that is best summed up in a few phrases does not result in a work that is distinctively theatrical. Certain details in the play are of interest all the same, such as a recurrent motif of militarism which is present in the women's obsession with weapons and in their deportment, touches suggestive of a more developed theme in *Nightwood*. Also the young girl, at once sensitive and cold, passive and dangerous, simple and enigmatic, is still another early sketch toward the finished portrait of Robin Vote. Intrinsically, however, *The Dove* is *hors de genre* only in a negative sense. Like *To the Dogs*, it appears to fall short of meeting the requirements of the genre rather than to transcend them. In addition to aforementioned flaws, these plays fail to measure up to their probable models. The influence of Strindberg behind "A Night Among the Horses" is again apparent in *To the Dogs*, but Miss Barnes's play seems a rhetorical exercise alongside *Miss Julie*. And *The Dove* is all *fin de siècle* filtered through Village bohemianism.

The majority of these one-act plays share a static quality that is still present in *The Antiphon*, where it becomes an integral factor in the whole time sense of the play. And the greater life or élan of Miss Barnes's verse play is largely in its language, while the early works avoid poetic expression as rigorously as do her stories of the period. It appears that her involvement with the one-act play became an attempt to perfect a dialogue that would be terse and concrete while conveying the elusiveness of experience. In this sense the experiment was inseparable from her achievement of economy in her prose fiction, which was as tightly edited as a silent film of the period. Ironically, however, many of the stories, most notably "Aller et Retour" and "Spillway," were more theatrical than the plays, employing elements of dramatic structure to create and intensify their situations. The impression is confirmed by a playlet like *Little Drops of Rain*.

This belongs to a group of brief plays that might all be categorized as "Ten-Minute Plays," as those examples that appeared in *Shadowland* were captioned. Lydia Steptoe's *Little Drops of Rain* resembles her nondramatic contributions to *Vanity Fair* in its unseriousness and tone of purposeful pointlessness. It has no action as such, but is rather a dialogue between youth and age counterpointing the temperaments of two centuries. An aged Lady Lookover confronts young Mitzi Ting in an old garden, and what follows is a lighter version of the garden scene between mother and daughter in "Aller et Retour." Lady Lookover's witty denunciation of the present along with the past is similar in spirit to Madame von

Bartmann's: ". . .under the frills of the nineteenth century beats the heart of an indefatigable cynicism, made still sharper by a romantic twinge." And she continues, "My life was lived without punctuation. . . . Your life is riddled with colons and full stops." The dowager mocks the younger generation's urge to "go to the dogs," for with her accumulated sense of the past she knows the meaning of that phrase. Lady Lookover is Miss Barnes's recurrent terrible woman, gifted with an authority distilled from unlimited experience: "I made it my business to be a little more than ugly; it is that little extra that has made the world bow down since the first dawn."[11] Her prediction that Mitzi must expect nothing from the future except respectable marriage finally anticipates the ironic conclusion of Madame von Bartmann's journey. A measure of the wit in this play carries over into "Aller et Retour." But the story moves in carefully planned stages toward Madame von Bartmann's agonized monologue, thereby achieving a dramatic climax that is beyond the scope of this aphoristic sketch.

Other "Ten-Minute Plays," trifles clearly unintended for performance, incline a bit more toward a rudimentary plot and thus begin to resemble those short stories of aristocratic intrigues that tried to work a comedy of manners into their rather mechanical arrangements of ironies. *Water-Ice*, for instance, concerns a Lady Fiora Silvertree, a "recluse of celibate mind"[12] who has deliberately renounced a life of passion and emotion. Only once a year she requests news from the outside world, always in expectation of hearing that her lover still waits for her. The news that she has been totally forgotten finally thaws her, and she exits in search of her Lucien and of warmer weather. *Two Ladies Take Tea* is an equally slight sketch, like the others worth noticing primarily for the details, turns of phrase, or thematic motifs that are later incorporated into more important work. In this play, for example, the madonna image reappears in the setting, the tall windows "representing the Nativity at that moment when the Mother is most poignantly convalescent." The play is a verbal contest, at moments heated, between Countess Nicoletti Lupa and the young American Fanny Blaze who has come to announce her amorous conquest of the Count. The girl backs down when the Countess convinces her that her husband is headed toward death, that he possesses "one of those debauched skulls that come to a family only when the blood can feel no more terror, the heart no more anguish and the mind no further philosophy."[13] This, of course, is the condition of being "beyond the end" at which so many of Miss Barnes's characters arrive: Katrina Silverstaff, Nora Flood, and finally Augusta in *The Antiphon*. In *Two Ladies Take Tea* the offstage Count becomes a central presence in much the same way as the parents in *Three from the Earth* and, in the late verse play, Titus Hobbs. In effect these plays, like most of the author's early writing, become a testing ground for nearly all of the symbols, images, turns of phrase, and configurations of characters that go into *Nightwood* and *The Antiphon*.

There are other "Ten-Minute Plays," all similar in intent and execution. As in *The Beauty*, wherein a strong woman without illusions rejects a series of suitors in search of one who will refuse to worship her, women stand supreme, capable beyond the aspirations of men. As the last suitor tells Katrina Malevolitch about women generally, "They tear a man down from the high position in which God placed him."[14] And in *Five Thousand Miles*, when two former lovers reunite on a desert island, it is "She" who rejects "He" at the sight of a washed up eggbeater, a sign of returning civilization, and she does so with an air of "congealed hauteur."[15] There is simply no room or even need for men in these plays.

As a group, the early theatrical pieces of Djuna Barnes anticipate *The Antiphon* in three primary respects. Most of them are plays which achieve their full effect on the printed page, and in many cases dramatic production would simply be out of the question. All of them utilize the verbal duel, effecting what Marie Ponsot calls a "monologued counterpoint" which "affords the quick pleasures and panache of a first-class fencing match."[16] And, most important, they all have as a central theme the nature of women. *A Passion Play* of 1918 is no exception, but is notable as the only early play by Miss Barnes that is, like *The Antiphon*, allegorical in conception.

*A Passion Play* recounts the meeting of two prostitutes and two thieves by the dark wood bordering Calvary on the eve of the Crucifixion. Two crosses are visible in the distance, and the thieves are fully aware of what they portend: ". . . there's evil in the air when a tree or a cross rears up. For one there's the nest to hatch out crows, and for the other the nails to hatch out death." No plot as such develops from this, but much time is spent reflecting upon the potency and cleansing force of evil. As in *Nightwood*, whores and thieves acknowledge a common bond of humanity beneath what is claimed as the public good. One thief puts it this way: "We are the common pools in which the refuse is flung. . . . The amazing gutter in which the world casts its wash and then cries 'Tis muddy.'" And the second thief later affirms, "Yet there's something healthy about a man who has the malady of sin upon him." Before the night is over, the four enter the woods together.

By dawn the thieves have departed, and Sarah and Theocleia behold three figures hanging upon three crosses. The third they fail to recognize and, at the curtain, they begin to dice for the thieves' silver pieces. Thus ends this ironic *Passion Play*, which, instead of again dealing with antagonism between the sexes, establishes their union on a level of degradation. Nonetheless, the second thief does state, "Truly women are wonderful. A man commits a little thing and dies therefore; a woman all things and lives not till then. They are the tables on which we write, 'We have been.'" The point is underscored by Sarah's inclusion of the loin cloth of Theocleia's thief into their final bargain. "It will make a pretty hanging," she says "and there's that on it they say a man draws when he dies a violent death. And later we can say: 'Thus our children would have looked.'"[17] The final impression is that women, whether in the role of whore or of mother, hold the destiny of their men in their hands.

With its symbolic setting and its poetic dialogue, Djuna Barnes's *Passion Play* abandons the surface naturalism characteristic of most of her early work in the genre. This play is an exception to the rule in much the same way that "The Perfect Murder" stands apart from the other short stories by possessing abstract and allegorical properties. Like *The Antiphon*, which is allegorical at the broadest level of interpretation, *A*

*Passion Play* presents characters which possess an archetypal reality. The fundamental principle that they represent is, once again, an inversion of the traditional concept in Judeo-Christian thought of good as the antithesis of evil. But in *The Antiphon*, this is only one among many reversals and paradoxes that are worked into a highly complex and frequently obscure pattern.

A great deal has been said about the obscurity of this play since it appeared in 1958. One might have supposed that in revising it for inclusion in the 1962 volume of *The Selected Works*, Miss Barnes would have intended to clarify a number of passages for bewildered readers. Except for a few points at which the interruption or abridgement of dramatic monologues seems to alter meaning or to facilitate both readability and playability, this was not the case. Besides correcting printer's errors, she seems to have been trying to gain an even tighter compactness of blank verse with no reduction of its eccentric punctuation or abundant archaisms. Despite the diversity of critical opinion on either published version of *The Antiphon*, no one denies that the play presents formidable difficulties for its readers. There is a story that Janet Flanner tells of how, when admitting to Miss Barnes her concordance with T. S. Eliot's admiration of its archaic language but inability to "make head or tail of its drama," Miss Barnes replied, " 'I never expected to find that you were as stupid as Tom Eliot.' "[18] The language surely stands as a barrier to ready comprehension of much of the play's action and motives. One does not have to read far into the first act to discover a nearly forbidding richness of invention. Take, for instance, these early lines of Miranda's addressed to Jack Blow:

> It's true the webbed commune
> Trawls up a wrack one term was absolute;
> Yet corruption in its deft deploy
> Unbolts the caution, and the vesper mole
> Trots down the wintry pavement of the prophet's head.[19]

As often elsewhere, the context in which this is placed provides no direct illumination of its meaning, which is already concealed in archaisms, cramped syntax, and compound metaphors. Considering the abundance of such passages, John Wain reached a conclusion similar to that of many reviewers: that Miss Barnes had developed the "clotted" quality of Jacobean verse to such a degree that her language became too opaque for either stage performance or solitary reading.[20]

In language as well as form, *The Antiphon* is a reaction against the state of the contemporary theater. As a theatrical columnist, it will be recalled, Miss Barnes discovered that what was missing in modern drama was a sense of contemplation, the " 'will-to-see-things-through with the mind' " that had been eventually sacrificed for action that was too often mere fumbling. " 'If some character in the play of a hundred years ago was irresolute . . .,' " she wrote, " 'he probed that sickness with his wit, and came forth with a soliloquy or an argument that made of him, no matter how ludicrous his situation, a figure of ponderable value.' "[21] Although the theatrical "Almanack" columns cite numerous instances of the past recaptured in this respect, such moments are seldom found to be sustained and are usually the result of some particular actor's contribution to his role beyond the written play. Without mind, Miss Barnes perceived, the stage becomes an arena of noise and clatter, and the spectator is driven to the silence of the cinema for the experience of reflection that language once provided in the theater.

So *The Antiphon* is first of all an effort to recapture the oral grandeur that had once engaged the mind in dramatic spectacle. Its blank verse at once elevates its language above common speech. In addition, the play's action is so minimal, with so much of its length given to excavation into the pasts of the principal characters, that a static situation is created in which attention is drawn largely toward the language itself. It seems that Miss Barnes's early difficulty in creating and sustaining dramatic tension is transformed here into an asset. Disdain for traditional plot and structure again enables the author to create space in which to pursue the elusive aspects of human relationships. And it is precisely this factor which most disturbs critics, who time and time again raise doubts as to the play's suitability for stage performance.

It would be unwise to proceed to discuss this issue without first pausing to consider the plot of *The Antiphon* itself. For if the language becomes the main thing, and if that language is compact or opaque in a way that produces frequent obscurity, the coherence of the dramatic action as a whole is threatened. The reader or spectator is repeatedly brought to a *cul-de-sac* from which he must set out again toward some point of illumination or recognition, and the rise and fall of the action are thus radically affected. There is a "breaking-up of surfaces," according to Howard Nemerov, an abandonment of traditional plot sequence and coherence: ". . . allegory, moral and anagoge are made to emerge as if by a kind of Cubist handling from the shattered reflections of 'story.'"[22] This, he argues, is the direct result of the play's almost total lack of literal level of action. To be sure, Miss Barnes's "Cautionary Note" to the 1962 version of *The Antiphon* warns that "this play is more than merely literal,"[23] and the ironic jab of her remark is worthy of her aristocratic Augusta at her more imperious moments. When attempting to describe the concrete events of the play, one becomes aware of the author's extreme distrust of literal experience itself, of the reality of the present moment.

As in *Nightwood*, time and place are abruptly and specifically indicated at the beginning. The play opens in England during the war of 1939, as the stage directions state. Miranda, daughter of Augusta Burley Hobbs, returns to Burley Hall, a former "college of chantry priests" (*A*, p. 80) and the ancestral Beewick township home of the Burleys since the late seventeenth century. The manor is a ruin, open for refuge to travellers but still presided over by Miranda's Uncle Jonathan as surviving steward and custodian. Miranda, caught up in the flight of war refugees from the Continent, has been accompanied from Paris by Jack Blow. Although he appears in the dress and assumed role of coachman, he is in fact Miranda's brother Jeremy. This information is not disclosed until the final curtain, but one senses that Miranda has become aware of the disguise. At what point she actualy perceives Jack's identity is a matter of ambiguity.[24] But it is clear, as the family past begins to unfold in act 1, that Jack Blow knows and presumes too much. "You talk too much, too much leave out,"[25] observes Miranda.

It is Jeremy himself, who had fled his American home some twenty years earlier, who has summoned Augusta as well as her daughter to her childhood home, fully aware that she would be accompained by her mercenary sons Dudley and Elisha. These are the "merchants" that Miranda recurrently and apprehensively fears and, as they enter a momentarily empty stage while Augusta is still asleep in her car, it is clear that the daughter's vague terror is justified. In the presumed absence of the lost loved brother, Dudley and Elisha intend their mother and sister no good: "The ground they stand on, let's uncover it, / Let us pull their shadows out from under them!"[26] But the principals remain ignorant of their presence in this act. As Jack whispers in an aside, "I'm not too sure what's brewing hereabouts!"(A, p. 111).

This first act serves as a prologue to the lengthy second, which resumes the exposition and is continuous in time with the first. Miranda, with Jack's encouragement, had already begun to visualize her mother's past by recalling the coming of her polygamous and freethinking American father, Titus Hobbs, to Beewick, and his own mother's engineering of the meeting with Augusta. Also, Jack had related at length to Burely his meeting with Miranda in Paris and their subsequent flight. Act 2 opens with Augusta's emphatic entrance. She does not recognize her brother at first, and Jeremy is of course disguised. Augusta's speculations on his whereabouts as well as on an altered Burley Hall lead to prolonged reflections upon past events: Augusta's departure for America with her husband, his subsequent treachery by adultery again with the connivance of Titus's mother Victoria, who "could cluck in anyone for daughter" (A, p. 154), and the childhood of Miranda, unprotected among "Procuress, procured, and bastard!" (A, p. 166). Mounting along with this is Augusta's profound sense of ambivalence toward her daughter, heightened by an intense identification with her. As Augusta says, "In short, I can't afford her / She's only me" (A, p. 162). Presently, with Jack and Uncle Jonathan offstage, Dudley and Elisha don animal masks and proceed to taunt and torment the women viciously. Their abuse is interrupted with Jack enters bearing a doll house. "Hobb's Ark, beast-box, doll's house," which reveals in miniature through its tiny windows the scene of ultimate betrayal by the father; the rape of Miranda by a travelling Cockney that had been arranged by Titus "for experiment."[27] This climactic revelation of Miranda's sacrifice—" 'Do not let him—but if it will atone—' " (*A*, p. 186) she had cried—brings out her will to vindicate not only Augusta as woman and as victim, but also her father, raised as she had been to trust innocently in his faith.[28] At this point, with all "shaken by diminutive," the act closes.

The third act is a lamentation and Augusta's final agony, involving the specific antiphon of the title. Mother and daughter are alone onstage, the others having retired for the night. It is clear by this point that something has happened to the play's sense of time. With the intense absorption in the past that has come about, the present has become diffuse. The dread of the war of 1939 has become generalized, transformed into a timeless sense of holocaust, of the imminent collapse of civilization. The shift to an allegorical dimension has taken place. Now, upon the reunited halves of a gryphon, "once a car in a roundabout," Augusta and Miranda confront one another. As the play's "Cautionary Note" has forewarned, ". . . their familiarity is their estrangement, their duel is in hiatus, their weapons tempered" (*A*, p. 79). Augusta, failing to get Miranda to tell her of her life, loves, and adventures, turns to play. Exchanging shoes and hats, they begin an imaginary voyage together which becomes a quest for identity. Augusta, however, is torn and divided. "I think it's time I saw me as Augusta," she says, but she cannot resist for long her need to merge with, to become her daughter. In Miranda, however, she has "a daughter for inquisitor!" (*A*, p.195). Miranda recalls her love for her mother in its Edenic phase:

Before the tree was in the cross, the cradle, and the coffin,
The tragic head-board, and the victim door,
The weeper's bannister, the cunning pannel. (*A*, p. 194)

But, she accuses, "Titus Adam/Had at you with his raping hook," whereupon "A door slammed on Eden, and the Second Gate, / And I walked down your leg" (A, p.195).

The antiphonal duel thus proceeds in phases of empathy and antagonism, oneness and duality. At one poignant moment, Miranda urges,

> Rebuke me less, for we are face to face
> With the fadged up ends of discontent:
> But tie and hold us in that dear estrangement
> That we may like before we too much lose us. (A, p. 213)

The crass world intrudes, however, and Augusta yields. As she hears Dudley and Elisha preparing to depart, she simultaneously senses that her longed-for Jeremy is near. Miranda attempts to hold her, to block her  way as she tries to mount the stairs. Augusta brings a curfew bell down upon her daughter, and both collapse upon the gryphon. At the abrupt final curtain, Jack speaks of " . . . the hour of the uncreate; /The season of the sorrowless lamenting" (A, p. 223), and exits "with what appears to be indifference."

The movement of *The Antiphon* involves a gradual tapering off of plot momentum, a cessation of action. Its carefully timed *ralenti* accompanies the shift of the work to a more purely allegorical level. Correspondingly, there is an increasing absorption in its language and even its visual or scenic element. In the hush of act 3, there is a notable change in the quality of the verse, of which Miranda's key lines offer evidence:

> Where the martyr'd wild fowl fly the portal
> High in the honey of cathedral walls,
> There is the purchase, governance and mercy.
> Where careful sorrow and observed compline
> Sweat their gums and mastics to the hive
> Of whatsoever stall the head's heaved in—
> There is the amber. As the high plucked banks
> Of the viola rend out the unplucked strings below—
> There is the antiphon.
> I've seen loves so eat each other's mouth

Till that the common clamour, co-intwined,
Wrung out the hidden singing in the tongue
Its chaste economy—there is the adoration.
So the day, day fit for dying in
Is the plucked accord. (*A*, p. 214)

It is a "hidden singing" that is brought out here by means of
chaste economy in the cathedral silence of the night. The tone
of liturgical gravity of this passage had been introduced earlier
by Miranda's admonition,

Be not your own pathetic fallacy, but be
Your own dark measure in the vein,
For we're about a tragic business, mother. (*A*, p. 205)

And the singing quality is sustained throughout the act by lyric
passages in which Augusta tries to approach her daughter by
pretending, by turning their encounter into fairy tale and
imaginary journey. But the chant is fated to end in discord, the
women being too world-weary and old to undo the curse of the
father. Their absurd death fulfills Miranda's warning, "He,
who for fear, denies the called response / Denies the singing,
and damns the congregation!" (*A*, p.209).

It is here in the final act that a musical motif is brought out
in full degree in verse and supportive image. As in *Nightwood*,
high and low themes have been in interplay throughout. On
the one hand, bandstand instruments onstage reinforce
Augusta's recollection of Kapellmeister Stack with his baton,
conducting a trumpet voluntary to the approach of a major-
general, "Miranda's first cadet" (*A*, p.135). And there is a
refrain that Jack Blow frequently hums: "Hey then,
'Who / Passes by this road so late,' Always gay?" (*A*, p.89), a line
from the opening of "Compagnons de la Marjolaine," the song
of the Chevalier du Guet Royal, which had been organized in
the eighteenth century for night patrol of the streets of Paris.
Besides its simple effectiveness in arousing apprehension, the
refrain also extends the dimension of time beyond the present
military threat on the Continent. But musical themes play

upon a higher level in the final antiphon, where the sustained image of the viola in Miranda's lines quoted above lends an overtone of chamber music to the liturgical chant. Finally the hidden singing that is plucked out in the formal and resonant verse of the last agony is terminated by the cacophony of panic that precipitates the death blow, followed by Jack's flat coda at his exit.

Visual conception and design are functional too in *The Antiphon*. The set is an extremely important element. Superbly visualized down to the last prop—the brass curfew bell which becomes the death instrument that rings the antiphon to a close—the scene, the Great Hall of Burley, is so suggestive of the play's main themes that it stands as its symbolic core. The first cluster of objects introduced in the stage directions, the "flags, gonfalons, bonnets, ribbons and all manner of stage costumes" (*A*, p.81) which hang over the balustrade, immediately relates to Miranda, to her associations with the theatrical world, her international past, and her fondness for pageantry. A dressmaker's dummy in "regimentals," placed before a Gothic window, sustains the hint of pageant or military processional (while serving as a coy reminder that Miss Barnes's world is one in which fashion counts). Haphazardly arranged about this dummy are "music stands, horns, fiddles, guncases, bandboxes, masks, toys and broken statues, man and beast" (*A*, p.81). These evoke not only the father with his love of the hunt and of music-making, but also time past, childhood and the nursery,[29] elements to be echoed in numerous snatches from nursery rhymes. The masks of pig and ass are to be donned by the sons, bringing the recurrent man-beast dichotomy into focus in a crucial agon in act 2. And the broken statues, of course, suggest the wear of time as well as the fractured mother-daughter entity, Miranda and Augusta perceiving themselves in their intense empathy as a divided whole.

Little by little it becomes clear that the set incorporates things in the concrete present that represent occurance in the historical past or altogether outside of chronological time. In the moment which brings present and past together, there is captured an explicit and ominous sense of ruin. The Gothic

window is paneless, a ruined colonnade is visible through a
crumbled wall, and Miranda's theatrical costume is "elegant
but rusty" (*A*, p. 82). The decline of Western civilization which
is one allegorical motif in the play is thus visualized before ever
articulated. In effect, the compression or condensation notice-
able in the play's language becomes evident in its visual scheme
too. The set could bear strong comparison to the shadow boxes
of Joseph Cornell, which evoke a past beyond chronology by
juxtaposition of "found" objects: perhaps a clay soap bubble
pipe, a fragment of an old map, a child's alphabet block or toy
tin sun, all enclosed within a twilight blue box decked with
astrological symbols on the interior walls. Similarly, individual
concrete objects instantaneously assume universal and timeless
dimension in Miss Barnes's set. The Great Hall of Burley is in
line with the earlier visual collages in *Nightwood*: the rococo halls
of Hedvig Volkbein, the jungle room of Robin, the American
salon of Nora, and the squalid lodgings of the doctor, all
memorable settings which suggest the accumulation of time.

Miss Barnes's principal themes of divided being and the
receding present thus begin to emerge in *The Antiphon*. They
are embodied together in one of the play's two key stage
properties. At the end of a central table with an apt formal
setting are the two halves of the gryphon which once had been
a car in a carousel and thus once a part of childhood. But it is
not the antiquity or the fantasticality of the piece alone that is
significant. It was the father who once halved the gryphon with
a saw. In act 3, it is upon the reunited halves that the mother
and daughter "voyage" and become one being. It has been
suggested that this mythic figure, half eagle, half lion, relates to
Dante's encounter with the gryphon in canto 31 of the
*Purgatorio*, "that beast/Which in two natures one sole person
is,"[30] symbol of "incarnation, duality resolved, divine and
human nature made one."[31] The allusion possibly extends to
the car that the gryphon fastens to the barren tree in the
subsequent canto, causing it to come to flower—which, in turn,
might be taken to illuminate Augusta's frequent plea to
Miranda to put her to a tree at her death.[32] Paradoxically, however, it is finally upon the gryphon that the two women fall to

death after having become momentarily whole and again divided, a fulfillment of Augusta's utterance, "Love is death . . ." (*A*, p.196).

Equally important is the sinister toy, the doll's house called "beast-box" which Jack brings onstage in act 2, his motive being "to medecine contumely / With a doll's hutch—that catches villains!" (*A*, p.224). This bizarre object seems the equivalent of the supernatural machinery, the macabre masquerade often employed in Jacobean tragedy.[33] The device conforms to Aristotle's rule that "the supernatural should be used only in connection with events that lie outside the play itself, things that have happened long ago beyond the knowledge of men, or future events which need to be foretold and revealed . . . ."[34] But there are no gods to intervene in 1939. There is only Jack-Jeremy who has engineered the revelation, apparently hoping that his conjuring will have the purgative effect of bringing the family past into focus. In effect, the miniaturization of the manor with its doll inhabitants is the objective correlative of the act of memory which reduces the complexity of experience to manageable proportions. The trick evokes what Doctor O'Connor called " 'the almost fossilized state of our recollection,' " making the doll house " 'an accumulation, a way to lay hands on the shudder of a past that is still vibrating' " (*N*, pp. 118–19). So Augusta bawdily asks upon seeing Titus's effigy, "Was this the stick that leapt me, gentlemen?" (*A*, p. 182). But something undeniable appears before her through tiny windows. As Jack accuses,

> The crystal, like a pregnant girl, has hour
> When it delivers up its oracle,
> Leaving the chamber to the adversary.
> The eye-baby now you're pregnant with
> You'll carry in your iris to the grave.
> You made yourself a *madam* by submission . . . .(*A*, p. 185)

It may be true that in *The Antiphon* "the tragic flaw is neither more or less than life itself,"[35] considering that the play ultimately functions on an allegorical level. But in its specific past action it was Augusta's *hamartia* or error of judgement, followed by her moral weakness and submission, that was the source of the present tragedy of estrangement. The doll house indicts Augusta, its rape scene making it an *"abattoir."*[36] As she can neither finally confront nor effectively deny its truth, it traps her in the halt position of the dammed.

All in all, the ornate and complex visual plan of *The Antiphon* is so highly developed that, beyond its symbolic significance, it nearly becomes something independent of the play itself. In other words, it exceeds the limits of basic dramatic necessity to such a degree that it almost seems a separate element. In addition, it has occurred to a number of critics that the language also detaches itself from the drama, taking on a life of its own extrinsic to the events of the play and the lives of its characters. It should be clear, however, that what is involved here is the trans-generic mode that has been noted as operative in all of Djuna Barnes's major work. The overall failure of her early one-act plays betrayed a restlessness, an impatience with the delimiting forms of modern theater and the deadening effect of so much activity without reflection. The consequence of all this was to look backward and create for this late and mature play a hybrid form evocative of major phases of historical drama. Thus *The Antiphon* taps the origin of modern drama in rituals of the medieval Christain church, suggests variations upon the forms of Greek tragedy and early closet drama, and most directly revives the tone and grandeur of Elizabethan drama with a nod at the Jacobean tradition as well. Also with the prominence of the set as a work of art and the multiple-level musicality of the verse, the play attempts to broaden the scope of dramatic form, to present new possibilities for modern theater.

As suggested earlier, this departure has aroused a widespread anxiety on the part of readers which has to do with the question of the work's performability. Lionel Abel is not alone in wondering how the most intelligent audience could possibly understand the play when hearing its difficult lines for the first time spoken on stage. The sheer difficulty of its verse, he suggests, renders the play, doubtfully readable in the first place, virtually unplayable as well. The reviewer for the *Times Literary Supplement* concurs in the opinion that only an audience willing to devote much time to study of the text could get the gist of it from its performance. But the audience alienating difficulty of the language, he suggests, completes the author's "rejection of the normal experiential world which she begins by obliterating most conventional manifestations of character." So the real reason for Miss Barnes's use of dramatic form is "to create a formal complexity beyond the range of other verse forms, and complexity is integral to her vision.[37] This amounts to saying that *The Antiphon* is in no sense a conventional drama, that its deviation from the genre is deliberate, and that it has no business being subjected to the common standards of dramatic criticism.

Apart from a reading of *The Antiphon* given in Cambridge, Massachusetts, in 1958 by the Poet's Theatre as a result of Edwin Muir's admiration of the play, it has been put to the actual test of staging only once. In February 1961, the Royal Dramatic Theatre of Stockholm presented *The Antiphon* in a translation by Dag Hammarskjold and Karl Ragnar Gierow. The reviews that followed in the Swedish press seem to have been on the whole affirmative in response to Olaf Melander's ability to convey the nuances of such an "exclusive" drama in his production. While one reviewer claimed that the play was ultimately unfit for staging because " 'it is as a lyrist rather than a dramatist that Djuna Barnes has created her mysterious world,' "[38] the response of Dr. Ivar Harrie was more typical:

> Yes, the audience really caught on—gradually. After the first act people were very awed—and a little afraid of showing how lost they felt. The second act has a bewildering—but unescapably exciting—effect. The third act . . . broke down all resistance: there was no alternative but to surrender to the dramatic poem.[39]

Although *The Antiphon* has yet to be presented in its own language on the stage, the overall success of the Stockholm effort casts doubt upon the pronouncements concerning its staging potential that greeted its publication in 1958.

The appropriateness of language to genre, however, comes into more serious question on another level. Kathleen Raine, although convinced that she is discussing a work of great distinction, feels that its speeches are not shaped by the active emotions of the characters: ". . . they are aggregates of fancy, not imaginative expressions proceeding from an inner unity of condition or thought."[40] Thus the play loses dramatic immediacy. Another critic, Donna Gerstenberger, comes to a similar conclusion but from the observation that "the passion and feeling of the play are lost in the intensity and difficulty of the verse, and what external action there is always carries with it the sense that it is an afterthought."[41] So beyond the problem of comprehension that the language presents to the reader, it is argued that the verse is essentially antidramatic, divorced from the feelings of its characters and the events that arouse them. Lionel Abel states the problem even more cogently. The reader as well as the presumed spectator, he argues, confronts characters who, rather than speaking from emotion, are writing poems onstage:

> . . . the characters scarcely talk to each other. Each one is intent on subtilizing and distilling his own thought and feeling into a verse expression adequate to the author's norms of rhetoric, and these are not at all dramatic norms. The result: there is no dialogue in any proper sense of the term . . . and the words spoken by any one character have scarcely any effect on the others.[42]

Most readers would allow that there is a certain justice in Abel's remarks. The characters do at times seem to be speaking in a kind of vacuum; the speech of one character frequently seems undifferentiated from that of another. If all voices are finally one and the same voice, the result is that the play indeed becomes static despite the aptness of overall effect for the author's theme of identity. Abel finally throws up his hands: "But I am judging *The Antiphon* as a play—I don't know if there are any categories for judging a closet-drama."[43]

*The Antiphon* exhibits Miss Barnes's characteristic impatience with familiar categories. Richard Eberhardt was prompt to call it "a poem, a verse play for reading"[44] rather than a play for acting. "This is Senecan drama, not for the public stage but the closet," wrote another reviewer. "Its chief effect is to reveal to us Djuna Barnes' romantic image of herself, and that is no small thing."[45] And Miss Barnes herself asserted that *The Antiphon* was written not for acting but primarily for the writer.[46] All in all, it would seem that it is as a closet drama that the work must finally be judged, even if this category has become an elusive one in the present age. True to its form, like Milton's *Samson Agonistes* and Browning's "Pippa Passes," it applies "the standards of one day to the art of a later day."[47] This fact in itself, of course, does not determine its category. The fact is that it is literary to such a degree that to read it as a poetic drama rather than as a dramatic poem is to create confusion.

Aside from the question of playability, it remains to determine what position *The Antiphon* takes in Djuna Barnes's collective work. Seemingly isolated in time from the main body of her writing and problematic in genre, it actually relates back to the concerns of the young playwright of the twenties whose work at that time had begun to take a turn more literary than dramatic. *The Antiphon* gives evidence of a mature awareness of dramatic form and of classical theater, while either ignoring inherited conventions or adapting them to its own purposes. Like *Nightwood* it is at once experimental and traditional: experimental in its radical departure from the standard generic modes, traditional in its use of past forms to delineate a modern landscape. That the author and her major works still remain difficult to classify late in a century of literary experimentation, is one indication of the success of her method.

*The Antiphon* is traditional in still another respect. It invites comparison with two other verse plays of the twentieth century that revive the ancient theme of a curse upon a house. A parallel with W.B. Yeats's *Purgatory* has been described as follows:

As in *Purgatory*, the scene . . . is a compelled if somewhat unwilling return to the ancestral home, the place where many of the difficulties of the present were begot. And as in Yeats' play, much of the present action seems to be defined by a sexual conflict in the past arising from the indignation suffered by an aristocratic mother from a pleasure-loving father . . . . The past in both plays provides the source of a neurotic hatred in the present, and both end with death that falls short of resolution.[48]

Striking similarities also exist between *The Antiphon* and T.S. Eliot's *The Family Reunion*. The return in each becomes a drama of sin and attempted expiation that reaches into the ancestral past. From each conflict emerges an overbearing sense of time. The past dominates Burley Hall as much as it does Wishwood, as in Eliot's choral passage:

In an old house there is always listening, and more is
     heard than is spoken.
And what is spoken remains in the room, waiting for
     the future to hear it.
And whatever happens began in the past, and presses
     hard on the future.
The agony in the curtained bedroom, whether of birth
     or of dying,
Gathers in to itself all the voices of the past, and pro-
     jects them into the future.[49]

For Harry, Lord Monchensey, the present is a "loop in time,"[50] while in *The Antiphon* it exists as a dial without hours, allowing the hidden to be revealed, mystery to be manifest.

With such corresponding thematic overtones in mind, one might suppose that these two plays were directly influential upon *The Antiphon*. Both appeared in 1939, a time when Miss Barnes was involved in the initial phases of composition, and could have played a part in the formative process. Of course neither Yeats's one-act play nor Eliot's work fall into the category of closet drama. Yeats's devotion to a public theater remained constant in his later years, and his free verse possessed colloquial ease and flow. Eliot, moreover, sought to bridge the gap between everyday speech and rhetorical eloquence so that the one would merge into the other without impediment. For this reason *The Family Reunion* demanded to be staged, to become public. The difficulties of Miss Barnes's verse, for reasons mentioned earlier, create an immediate barrier to stage transition. The dramatic poem's full effects, if available at all, are at hand on the printed page.

What is clear, however, is the continuity between *The Antiphon* and Miss Barnes's earlier works, notably *Ryder*. As Marie Ponsot observes, *The Antiphon* continues, clarifies, and concludes the earlier story. In the later work, Wendell Ryder becomes Titus Hobbs and Amelia reappears as Augusta. Sophia is again present in Victoria, Augusta's mother-in-law, while Kate-Careless appears in passing as an ugly mistress of the father. Also, Miss Ponsot notes, "Julie of *Ryder*, Nora of *Nightwood* and Miranda are essentially one person, grown from girlhood into death."[51] Finally Miss Barnes's play provides "a clearer and wider view of the ancestral figures who stalk her work."[52] Along with the characters who are transfigured to greater or lesser degree evolve the themes which are prominent in *Ryder*, *Ladies Almanack*, and the short stories, and which accumulate in *Nightwood*: the post-Edenic condition of women, the middle condition as the measure of humanity, and the paradox of time which reveals the modern age as a shambles.

*The Antiphon* offers what is perhaps Djuna Barnes's strongest image of "the horror of what men do to women in making them mothers, and women to men in giving birth to them."[53] Again the cycle of procreation is seen to be unending, ceaselessly repeating the loss of Eden and terror of schism or division. Even more than before, the figure of father and procreator is presented as a suprahuman agressive force. Like Ryder, Titus Hobbs is recalled as pliant, "an eager, timorous, faulty man" (*A*, p.144). But the feminine component, maternally affectionate and receptive to all nature as in O'Connor, has all but vanished in the new patriarch, "Titus! Self-appointed Holy Ghost and Father. / Prophet, Savior, out of Salem—brag of heaven; / Wived in righteous plenty—Solomon."[54] Wendell the freethinker has become Titus the anarchist, bent upon principled destruction of social and familial order. Miranda's conception is rape, and it is rape that the father in turn eventually brings upon the daughter. Miranda and Augusta become co-sufferers, sacrifices to the Old Testament force of Original Sin. The sons all the while become either blind like the time-bound merchants Dudley and Elisha, or confused like Jack-Jeremy, ambivalent and unsure in his motives, and not at all unlike young Wendell. The women in turn become the victims of the next generation of men, of Dudley and Elisha's overt malice as well as Jack's uncertain intentions and machinations. For mother and daughter love is death. "Perambulator rolling to the tomb; / Death with a baby in its mouth" (*A*, p.219).

Djuna Barnes's universe is one in which women find their very strength in submission. If the masculine principle of domination and imposition is indomitable, as generation after generation after the fall of Adam and Eve have demonstrated, then what recourse is left to women in the end? To rebel against or to try to destroy the male is to subvert the order of civilization and invite self-destruction, as shown by Julie Anspacher and Katrina Silverstaff in *Spillway*. To allow that all women have posed for the madonna, however, and to embrace the archetypal role of mother like Sophia can be a sort of victory. Alternately, there is the recourse of standing apart, of existing within the limits of a separate universe which excludes men or moves beyond the range of the masculine psyche. In *Ladies Almanack* and those one-act plays in which ladies take tea, men are ruled out altogether. The union of women draws a line at the threshold of masculine dominion.

Hence the bond between Augusta and Miranda. Alone in the third act in the night where waking distinctions dissolve and merge, the two reach the plane of metaphor where Augusta is Miranda and Miranda is Augusta, familiarity in estrangement. As women they are estranged from the universe as a totality. As mother and daughter, they are at the same time one and separate. As mother, Augusta perceives that "Miranda's all Augusta laid up in Miranda."[55] Yet when Miranda finally will not let Augusta know her, their oneness becomes torment. "In what pocket have you my identity?" asks Augusta. "I so disoccur in every quarter of myself / I cannot

find me" (A, p.213). As the two stare upon each other "with
unbuttoned eyes." the essential paradox of the middle
condition is revealed.

To transcend the literal and mundane world of facts (that
of the merchants) and confusion (that of Jack-Jeremy) is to
attain the level of poetic vision or metaphor where dualisms
vanish and everything is interrelated and significant. Augusta
and Miranda share the suffered understanding, the tragic all-
knowingness of Miss Barnes's superior women, from Madame
von Bartmann to Nora Flood. Their distinction lies in their
attainment of the middle vision which abolishes duality by
making new connections: the plucked accord, the reunited
gryphon, the rendered antiphonal response. But this is a tragic
business. To be divided is to go down unknowing, while to be
united is to suffer the loss of identity. The middle plane is the
halt position of both total coherence and dissolution. The duel
between Augusta and Miranda is one between "two beasts in
chancery" (A, p.188). There can be no victory or resolution
short of death, for mother and daughter are suspended,
"Caught in the utmost meridian and parallel" (A, p. 222). They
are "the damned," Jack Blow says, "who won't capitulate!" (A,
p. 86).

A condition of suspension dominates the entire play, and
is in fact integral to its sense of time. Miranda first sees in
Burley Hall "a rip in nature," a premonition seconded by Jack's
opening lines: "There's no circulation in the theme, / The very
fad of being's stopped" (A, p.82). The dial without hours
measures the time of the play. Yet at the same time, the women
are trapped in a "clocked encounter" (A, p.189) that cannot be
stopped. The literal action advances by clock time, but its
solidity or reality gradually diminishes. The antiphon of the
third act is out of time. When Miranda says "Mother, there's no
more time. All's done" (A, p.199), she announces that chronological time has been abolished, that the present is finished.
The abrupt instrusion of clock time that the departure of the
sons heralds promptly precipitates destruction as well.

The exhaustion of Augusta and Miranda sums up the
world-weariness of a shopworn age. As in her earlier work,

Miss Barnes sees history as recorded devaluation. The year 1939 is the age of the barbarian, of the merchant who tauntingly boasts, "We're timely" (*A*, p.150). Augusta is all too aware that in her time "Glory used to be the aim—now it's possessions" (*A*, p.172). Since "nothing now is wrought by hand / To give into the hand particular, / Nor pride of execution" (*A*, p.108), the apocalypic moment is at hand. If, however, time has run out, there is the recurrence of the past to fill the gap. What the clock cannot measure of history cannot be abolished, nor can it be falsified or cheapened. "They say a snail from Caesar's grave / Crawled into Napoleon's snuff box" (*A*, p. 91), reflects Jack Blow, possibly hinting at a continuity beneath the broken surface of historical record. The stopped watch will then leave a void to be filled by the past rushing in, and the given present moment will be one of historical recession.

It is this sense of time that is a dominant subject of Djuna Barnes's later poems, from "Transfiguration" of 1938 to "The Walking-Mort" of 1971. These are so few in number to date, however, that *The Antiphon* stands out as Miss Barnes's major act of poetic expression so far. Its position in modern poetry is probably unique. It is anachronistic in its turn against the present, against its literary practices as well as its aesthetic standards. Up to a point it resembles the long poems of David Jones, *In Parenthesis* and *The Anathémata*, with their complex patterns of recondite allusions reaching back to the remotest areas of history. But its shape is that of a dramatic poem out of the tradition of closet drama, a conspicuous departure from a period where a verse play stands or falls as performed before the public. Furthermore, as a poet Miss Barnes would seem to hold with James Joyce on at least one point. Poetry, wrote Joyce, "speaks of that which seems unreal and fantastic to those who have lost the simple intuitions which are the test of reality. Poetry considers many of the idols of the market place unimportant—the succession of the ages, the spirit of the age, the mission of the race."[56] *The Antiphon* speaks out against the standards of the marketplace, the dominance of clock time, and the illusion of recorded history. Its effort to get back to a lost reality is intense enough to risk obscurity and ambiguity. A reader might in the end wish indeed to direct Jack Blow's words to Miranda back against their author: "What a ferocious travel is your mind!" (*A*, p. 87). Yet upon successive readings *The Antiphon* becomes a quarry from which precious ore may be extracted. It is finally Djuna Barnes's most compact and definitive work.

# Postscript

Since *The Antiphon*, Djuna Barnes has been writing only poetry. This brings her career full circle, for it was as an aspiring poet that she started out. Most of her late poems, however, have yet to appear in print. It is astonishing that only five have been published from 1938 to date, but it has always been Miss Barnes's nature to astonish. Unpredictability still marks her career, and it would be foolish at this time to come to any conclusions about the latest stage of it. But patterns do at least begin to take shape in the few available examples, and these poems may be given some consideration alongside *The Antiphon* insofar as they tend to echo its central themes.

If a handful of late poems is any indication of the nature of what may be forthcoming, then it is remarkable how long ago Miss Barnes predicted the direction her late poetic work would take. Around the time when she was writing mournful love poems and pastoral lyrics which were ambivalent about nature and the poet's relationship to it, she was able to conceive of a different type of poem and give a suggestive nod in the direction of her work to come. This occured in the story "The Grande Malade," first titled "The Little Girl Continues." In the midst of her narrative, the girl speaks of a poem she remembers:

> Ah, that poem, that small piece of a poem! a very touching thing, heavy, sweet—a fragment of language. It makes you feel pity in your whole body, because it is complete

161

but mutilated, like a Greek statue, yet whole, like a life, Madame.[1]

Mutilated yet whole: the paradox is by now familiar. One recalls the broken statues and fragments of antique sculpture that were a part of *Nightwood*'s landscape and tied in with the themes of disassociation and the persistence of the past. The concept also summons up the recurrent problem of fractured being, of the divided whole, most recently encountered in the Augusta-Miranda relationship, the symbol of the gryphon, and so on. But the paradox most immediately announces a shift in poetic form. The poems that Miss Barnes stopped writing after the twenties were more or less traditional in versification, symmetrical and self-contained, undistinguished. They often gave the impression that the poet was becoming restless and impatient, restrained by conventional poetics yet hesitant to abandon formal unities for the possible undiscipline of free verse. To conceive of a poem as "a fragment of language" at this point was to begin to deal with a dilemma familiar to most modern poets.

The process of departing from tradition in order to find a voice in the modern age was apparent in the step from the early stories to *Spillway* and from *Ryder* to *Nightwood*. It is also visible in the contrast between "Transfiguration" and a later version of the same poem. Appearing in the *London Bulletin* in 1938, "Transfiguration" already indicates that the poet is moving on to new ground:

The prophet digs with iron claws
Into the desert's sinking floors.

The insect back to larva goes,
Struck to seed the climbing rose.

To Moses' empty gorge like smoke
Rush inward all the words he spoke.

The knife of Cain lifts from the thrust;
Abel rises from the dust.

Pilate cannot find his tongue:
Judas climbs the tree he hung.

Lucifer roars up from the earth;
Down falls Christ into his death.

To Adam back the rib is plied,
A woman weeps within his side.

Eden's reach is thick and green,
The forest blows, no beast is seen.

The unchanged sun in raging thirst
Feeds the last day to the first.[2]

There is no formal innovation here. The conventional
closed couplets and evenness of rhyme and meter are well
chosen to impart the poem's phases of time recession and historical reversal. It is rather the approach to subject that is new
in Miss Barnes's poetry. In contrast to the earlier lamentations
over the passage of time and the loss it entails, this poem shows
total formal detachment. The poem's images, superficially
illogical, derive from a trick of the silent cinema, that of
running the film backwards so as to produce an effect of comic
impossibility. But it is not a comic effect that the poet is after;
rather the shock that is produced by tampering with traditional
imagery. The poem thus found its proper place in a review
oriented largely toward surrealism.

"Transfiguration" anticipates *The Antiphon* by condensing
one of its central themes. The initial couplet is prophetic of the
violation of nature in the age of the machine, although its
second line suggests the natural cycle of sinking or recession
which continues despite the impact of modern weaponry or
machinery. The imagery of the second couplet extends the
impression of nature turning back upon itself, while the third
begins the reversal of scriptural motifs, a step by step erasure
of the Western spiritual heritage. The images are consistently
forceful and violent through the sixth couplet, but the seventh,
with Adam's rib restored, brings the movement to a point of

rest. With the return to Eden, to the state of the natural world in the beginning, the cycle is nearly complete, leaving only the final lines to summon up the universe before creation and the inauguration of calendar time. The last day is "fed" to the first, the present moment in history possessing the force to destroy civilization and terminate the regenerative processes of the natural world: the ultimate "loop in time."

"Fall-out Over Heaven" is a reworking of "Transfiguration" for inclusion in 1958 in a *festschrift* for T.S. Eliot's seventieth birthday. The new poem is foreshortened and framed by carefully chosen epigraphs:

### Fall-out Over Heaven

'I'll show you fear in a handful of dust.'
            (*The Waste Land*)
'And dust shall be the serpent's meat.'
            (Isaiah: lxv. 25)

The atom, broken in the shell
Licks up Eden's reach, and Hell.

To Adam back his rib is thrown;
A mole of woman quakes, undone.

From the ground the knife of Cain
Slays the brother it has slain.

To Moses' empty gorge, like smoke
Rush backward all the words he spoke.

Lucifer roars up from earth.
Down falls Christ into his death . . .

'She, supposing him to be the gardener . . .'
            (John: xx. 15)[3]

The changes are determined by the fractured sense of

existence and anomie heightened by the atomic age, the broken poem the consequence of the broken atom. Not only the brief epigraphs but also the terminal ellipsis fragment the poem. The line from *The Waste Land*, which expresses a modern anxiety, is linked to its source to the Holy Scriptures, establishing the juxtaposition of the contemporary with the biblical that follows in the subsequent couplets. In their new order, these sustain paradox. The forward movement from Eden to the Christ-Lucifer up-down inversion of the last couplet underlies the backwind effect retained from "Transfiguration" (which is made more explicit by the revision of the fourth couplet). Finally, the new reading heightens the overall concept at crucial points. The metaphor of the woman within Adam as a quaking mole is much stronger than the weeping woman, while the end-rhymed words *thrown* and *undone* sum up the active direction of the poem as a whole. "Fall-out Over Heaven" is, in short, both more compact and more fragmented than its earlier version.

In this manner, Miss Barnes creates what her "little girl" had envisioned: a poem "mutilated" yet entire. The end ellipsis leaves the poem open, and the suspension is in turn sustained by the ambiguity of the fragment from the Gospel According to Saint John. The opening epigraphs imply a contrast between Isaiah's prophecy of Christ and the peaceable kingdom, and the warring kingdom of the modern age. The movement of the poem itself is the return of all to dust. Is the phrase from John then meant to offer hope of resurrection? If so, the poem would assume a final circularity of framework. But Miss Barnes's attention is upon the moment when Mary mistakes Christ for the gardener. With such a conclusive note of non-recognition or faulty vision, the poem remains opaque.

The subject of Christ's resurrection recurs behind Djuna Barnes's Easter poem, "Galerie Religieuse":

The blood of the Lamb and the oriflamme
Wax and wane in the racked heart's core.
Hell flowers lightly; an angel slain
And cropped of earth twines with the twain.

Above the arc of the icy laces,
The long sheaved wings of the heavenly choir,
With lambent, forefold, impending faces,
Shout upward through the motes of prayer,
Shaking the ranks of stately lilies
In *Saint Dennis*, where His love is spent,
Dwindling on the mouth of Time,
Spiked on the votive thorn of Lent.[4]

The irony of the title hovers over the altar imagery presented here. The familiar opening image of the "racked heart" is given some urgency by association with the blood of the lamb and the oriflame, the ancient red banner of Saint Dennis. The poetic detachment that the title implies is soon established, however, by the shift of attention to an arc of "icy laces." The vision next ascends above the arc and the "motes of prayer." But the concluding image of Christ, re-crucified "on the votive thorn of Lent," is one of a dwindled Christ. The poem finally conveys the waxing and waning of faith in the course of time, the dwindling of the symbolism of the altar to the merely aesthetic, and a Christ fixed on the verge of resurrection.

"Galerie Religieuse" reads quite differently from Miss Barnes's early verses, which usually were set in perfectly measured quatrains with very minor internal variations. This poem of 1962 reflects certain discoveries that had taken place in the interim in *The Antiphon*. Partly because of its length, Miss Barnes needed to break up the blank verse of the long dramatic poem. To avoid tedium and manage the many sudden shifts of emotion and image, she found a number of devices at her disposal: unexpected variations of meter, displaced punctuation, foreshortened lines, and frequent broken sequences of verses. "Galerie Religieuse" is as compact a poem as any of the longer passages of *The Antiphon*. As, for instance, in Miranda's poem of the antiphon quoted in the last chapter, multiple disparate images are interconnected to transmit one complex impression with rapid force. The poet no longer has the leisure for the orderly development of individual images in quatrains. The irregular stresses, and internal and end rhymes of the altar poem, are suited to its changes and contrasts. Predictable sequence is broken, and the poet arranges rhyme and meter to meet her needs as she proceeds.

Miss Barnes's two remaining late poems, "Quarry" of 1969 and "The Walking-Mort" of 1971, exhibit similar characteristics. The later of these is the less irregular in its prosody:

## The Walking-Mort

Call her walking-mort; say where she goes
She squalls her bush with blood. I slam a gate.
Report her axis bone it gigs the rose.
What say of mine? It turns a grinning grate.
Impugn her that she baits time with an awl.
What do my sessions then? They task a grave.
So, shall we stand, or shall we tread and wait
The mantled lumber of the buzzard's fall
(That maiden resurrection and the freight),
Or shall we freeze and wrangle by the wall?[5]

The poem hovers on being a sonnet, a form which Miss Barnes employed on occasion in her early career. The imperative of the opening line calls for trochaic emphasis, but then the poem settles down to strict iambic pentameter. Its affinity to the sonnet is ironically reinforced by the play in line seven on the concluding line of Milton's Sonnet 16, "They also serve who only stand and wait."[6] This touch of parody also sets up a parallel between Milton in his blindness and the poet in her old age. And it is probably not accidental that the rhyme sequence, regular up to the sixth line, is thrown awry upon the word *grave*.

This late poem circles back to *The Book of Repulsive Women* in its concentration upon age and death. The title, typically juxtaposing the modern and archaic in diction, also sums up the middle condition of death in life. A dilemma is posed to which, in the uncompleted sonnet, there is no resolution. The identity of "she" and "I" remains ambiguous. The poet's images seem a detached observation of the painful effects of age in another, but the speaker could be describing a mirror image as well. The question of split identity carries over from *The Antiphon*, until the unifying "we" takes over in the last four lines and the poet's distance is abandoned for the universal question. "The Walking-Mort" is a grim poem, wherein old age is seen to be a state of terrible restless suspension. Even though the somewhat cryptic parenthetical line, "That maiden resurrection and the freight," seems to envision a release, the last line sustains the physical and spiritual pall of frozen existence before the grave.

"Quarry," which is said to be Miss Barnes's epitaph,[7] is closely related in theme to "The Walking-Mort":

### Quarry

While I unwind duration from the tongue-tied tree,
Send carbon fourteen down for time's address.
The old revengeful without memory
Stand by—
I come, I come that path and there look in
And see the capsized eye of sleep and wrath
And hear the beaters' "Gone to earth!"
Then do I sowl the soul and strike its face
That it fetch breath.[8]

Here the poet struggles for release from the tongue-tied state in which she is frozen. Her obsession with time is recurrent: she who "baits time with an awl" now seeks "time's address." The phrase "unwind duration" recalls the phases of "Transfiguration" of going backward beyond time and memory. But in this poem the movement is downward, as signaled by the double metaphor of the mine and the hunt implicit in the title (and reinforced by the downward thrust toward lines four and nine, which carry syllables of uniform stress). Time is a quarry that the poet would mine, while at the same time she is being pursued underground. The cry of the beaters announcing that the quarry has been holed is also a cry of death. Looking into "the capsized eye of sleep and wrath," the poet re-enters the middle realm in which Robin and O'Connor wandered in *Nightwood*. She is able to wake, to revive herself only by an assault upon the soul.

Whatever poems Miss Barnes may choose to publish in the future, it may be assumed that "Quarry," as an epitaph, must sound her final note. It is a fragment of language; like "The Walking-Mort," it could be thought of as a splinter of *The Antiphon* which compresses its major theme. It is the poet's final confrontation with oblivion and paradox. The pursuit of the "old revengeful without memory" is the pursuit of the poet by oblivion, but in seeking "time's address" she becomes the pursuer as well. "Quarry" thus turns back to Augusta's lines in *The Antiphon:*

> Fie! this striving, fancying, believing!
> I have, I say, small patience with the mind
> That dares oblivion and peoples it
> With such cranks of heart. I would be Helen,
> Forgotten for forever and forever
> By each several recalling generation
> Throughout eternal times succeeding.[9]

The passage recalls in turn a parenthetical observation in *Nightwood*: "those long remembered can alone claim to be long forgotten" (*N*, p. 9). This is the credo of a poet who would suppress autobiography and thus subordinate life to art, who once responded enthusiastically to the observation of a German critic, "Her work has not fallen into oblivion, it was predestined for it."[10] *Nightwood* has already weathered the fluctuations of memory in its life in print, *The Antiphon* is hardly known, and in time their author may indeed disappear into her work and the work become the recalled forgotten in literary history. But it is to be hoped that, by deciding to publish her considerable number of poems now in manuscript, Djuna Barnes will see fit to "sowl the soul" once again in this last phase of her career.

# Notes

## INTRODUCTION

1. Hilton Kramer, review of *The Selected Works of Djuna Barnes, Reporter*, 5 July 1962, p.40.

2. Sylvia Beach, *Shakespeare and Company* (New York: Harcourt, Brace & Co., 1959), p. 112.

3. George Steiner, "The Cruellest Months," *New Yorker*, 22 April 1972, p. 134.

4. Melvin Friedman, *Stream of Consciousness: A Study in Literary Method* (New Haven: Yale University Press, 1955), p.261.

5. Lowry's admiration of Djuna Barnes is evident from remarks in his letters and from several accounts of his career. Durrell's is warmly expressed in his contribution to *A Festschrift for Djuna Barnes on Her 80th Birthday*, and it may be significant that Scobie, in *Justine*, is mentioned as having given an oral rendering of "Watchman, What of the Night" from *Nightwood*.

6. Sharon Spencer, *Space, Time and Structure in the Modern Novel*, pp. 39–43.

7. John Hawkes, "Notes on the Wild Goose Chase," *Massachusetts Review* 3, no. 4 (Summer 1962): 787.

8. Barnes, "Questionnaire," *Little Review, May 1929, p. 17*.

9. *Henry Raymont*, "From the Avant-Garde of the Thirties, Djuna Barnes," *New York Times*, 24 May 1971, p. 24.

10. W.H. Scarborough, review of *The Selected Works of Djuna Barnes, Chapel Hill Weekly*, 9 September 1962, p. 5B.

11. Barnes, *Nightwood*, p. 4.

12. Ibid., p. 121.

13. Barnes, *Spillway*, p. 46.

14. Barnes, *Nightwood*, p. 101.

15. Ibid., p. 111.

16. Barnes, *The Antiphon*, in *Selected Works*, p. 85.
17. Roger Shattuck, " 'Nightwood' Resurrected," *Village Voice*, 24 May 1962, p. 10.

## CHAPTER 1

1. Guido Bruno, "My Four Years with Frank Harris," *Bruno's Review of Two Worlds*, December 1920, p. 44.
2. Bruno, "In Our Village," *Bruno's Weekly* 1, no. 2 (7 October 1915): 104.
3. Ibid., no. 4 (21 October 1915): 142-43.
4. Djuna Barnes, "Vagaries Malicieux," *Double Dealer* 3, no. 17 (May 1922): 253.
5. "The Barnes Among Women," *Time*, 18 January 1943, p. 55.
6. Natalie Clifford Barney, "Djuna Barnes," in *Aventures de l'esprit*, p.228.
7. Jack A. Hirschman, "The Orchestrated Novel," p. 54.
8. Djuna Barnes, "Jess Willard Says Girls Will Be Boxing for a Living Soon," *New York Press*, 25 April 1915, part 5, p. 9.
9. Barnes, " 'I'm Plain Mary Jones of U.S.A.' Insists 'Mother' Jones," p. 2.
10. Barnes, "Djuna Barnes Pays a Visit to the Favored Haunt of the I.W.W.'s," p. 7.
11. Barnes, "Djuna Barnes Probes the Souls of the Jungle Folk at the Hippodrome Circus," p. 2.
12. Barnes, "Futuristic Impressions of the Picadilly Chorus Girls in 'To-Night's the Night,' " p. 2.
13. Barnes, "Vagaries Malicieux," pp. 249–60.
14. Ibid., p. 256. Or, as Miss Barnes writes later, "Now it is no longer the Village that will get a girl by her back hair and sling her into damnation, it is Paris." See Barnes, "The Days of Jig Cook," p. 31.
15. Barnes [Lydia Steptoe], *Little Drops of Rain*, *Vanity Fair*, September 1922, p. 50.
16. Ibid., "The Diary of a Dangerous Child." p. 56.
17. Barnes, *Little Drops of Rain*, p. 50.
18. Barnes, "Dangerous Child," p. 56.
19. Barnes, "Fashion Show Makes Girl Regret Life Isn't All Redfern and Skittles," *New York Press*, 25 April 1915, part 4, p. 4.
20. Barnes, "The Woman Who Goes Abroad to Forget," *New Yorker*, 8 December 1928, p. 28.
21. Susan Sontag, "Notes on 'Camp,' " *Against Interpretation and*

*Other Essays* (New York: Dell Publishing Co., Laurel Editions, 1970), p.280.

22. Ibid., p. 281.
23. Ibid., p. 279.
24. Barnes, "Dangerous Child," p. 56.
25. Barnes, "Vagaries Malicieux," pp. 256–57.
26. Barnes [Lydia Steptoe], "What Is Good Form in Dying?" p. 73.
27. Ibid., p. 102.
28. Raymont, p. 24.
29. Barnes [A Lady of Fashion] *Ladies Almanack*, p. 34.
30. Barnes [Lady Lydia Steptoe] "Hamlet's Custard Pie," p. 34.
31. Barnes, "The Dear Dead Days," p. 42.
32. Barnes, "Playgoer's Almanack," July 1930, p. 26.
33. This was briefly continued as the "Knickerbocker Almanack" in the *New York World*, but the column proved to be short-lived.
34. Barnes, "The Wanton Playgoer," *Theatre Guild Magazine*, April 1931, p. 31.
35. Ibid., June 1931, p. 37.
36. Ibid., May 1931, p. 33.
37. Ibid., September 1931, p. 21.
38. Barnes, "Why Actors?" p. 43.
39. Barnes, "The Wanton Playgoer," June 1931, p. 37.
40. Barnes, "Playgoer's Almanack," January 1931, p. 35.
41. Barnes, "The Wanton Playgoer," September 1931, p. 21.

## CHAPTER 2

1. Frederick L. Gwynn and Joseph L. Blotner, eds., *Faulkner in the University: Class Conferences at the University of Virginia, 1957–1958* (New York: Random House, Vintage Books, 1959), p. 201.
2. Djuna Barnes, "The Book of Repulsive Women," p. 91.
3. Frederick J. Hoffman, *The Twenties: American Writing in the Postwar Decade*, rev. ed. (New York: Free Press, 1966), p. 38.
4. Barnes, "How the Villagers Amuse Themeselves," *New York Morning Telegraph*, 26 November 1916, sec. 2, p. 1.
5. Edward Engleberg, ed., *The Symbolist Poem* (New York: E. P. Dutton, 1967), p. 251.
6. Ibid., p. 235.
7. Guido Bruno, "Books and Magazines of the Week," *Bruno's Weekly* 1, no. 15 (30 October 1915): 161.
8. Hirschman, pp. 52–53.
9. Guido Bruno, "In Our Village," *Bruno's Weekly* 1, no. 14 (21 October 1915): 143.
10. When republished in *Bruno's Weekly*, 23 September 1916, p. 1005, this drawing bore the title, "The Vampire: A Nocturn in Black."

See also "Djuna Barnes' Vampire Baby," *Vanity Fair*, July 1915, p. 33.

11. Guido Bruno, "My Four Years With Frank Harris," *Bruno's Review of Two Worlds*, December 1920, p. 44.

12. Barnes, "What Does 291 Mean?," *Greenwich Village*, 22 February 1915, p. 23.

13. *Atlantic Journal*, 6 January 1924, The Djuna Barnes Papers.

14. At least some of these were drawn from life. The portrait facing page 30 is of the actress Helen Westley in the play *John Ferguson*. One drawing appeared in March, 1920 in the *Dial* as "Head of a Polish Girl." And Charles Norman says that one drawing is of Mary Pyne. See *Poets & People* (New York: Bobbs-Merrill, 1972), p. 18.

15. Djuna Barnes, *A Book*, p. 103.

16. Wylie Sypher, *Rococo to Cubism in Art and Literature* (New York: Random House, Vintage Books, 1960). p. 242.

17. Barnes, "Call of the Night," *Harper's Weekly*, 23 December 1911, p. 22.

18. Barnes, "Shadows," *Munsey's Magazine* 59, no. 2 (November 1916): 272.

19. Barnes, "To One Feeling Differently," *Playboy* 2, no. 1 (1923): 36.

20. Barnes, "The Lament of Women: Ah My God!" *Little Review* 5, no. 8 (1918): 37.

21. Barnes, "To the Dead Favourite of Liu Ch'e," p. 444.

22. Barnes, "The Yellow Jar," *Munsey's Magazine* 58, no. 4 (September 1916): 605.

23. Barnes, "Vaudeville," p. 67.

## CHAPTER 3

1. Howard Nemerov, "A Response to *The Antiphon*," p. 88.

2. Certain autobiographical elements in *Ryder* are worth noting. Although Djuna Barnes refuses to write publicly in this vein, certain of her notes taken down for various biographical sketches, along with the published summaries themselves, bring to light material that may have gone into the novel.

"Storm-King-on-Hudson" could be taken to refer to Cornwall-on Hudson where Miss Barnes was born in 1892, the only girl among five children. Her father, Wald Barnes of Springfield, Massachusetts, wrote poems, novels, composed operas, and painted rural water-colors. Along with Miss Barnes's paternal grandmother, he educated his children privately. Wendell shares a parallel diversity of skills and, late in *Ryder*, is in constant trouble with the authorities for taking his children's education into his own hands.

The grandmother, Zadel Barnes, was a suffragist, abolitionist, and prohibitionist, also inclined to spiritualism. With her second husband, Alex Gustafson, she stumped in Hyde Park and wrote on the liquor question. Like Sophia, she held a literary salon in Grosvenor Square in London around the time of the Pre-Raphaelites. Among the diverse group she entertained was Oscar Wilde, who is mentioned occasionally in *Ryder*.

Miss Barnes's mother, Elizabeth Chappell, was born in 1862 in Oakham, Rutland, England, of a family of cabinet makers and builders, and, like Amelia, in her youth studied violin at London's Conservatory of Music. Amelia is seven years old at her father's death in 1869. By trade he had been a builder, "by heart a cabinet-maker."

It would be rash, of course, to proceed on the assumption that *Ryder* is an "autobiographical novel." Correspondance of details is rough or nonexistent beyond the above particulars, and Miss Barnes may simply be using familiar material to get her bearings in beginning a diffficult novel.

It is striking that a similar familial configuration is also present in *The Antiphon*.

3. Djuna Barnes, *Ryder*, p. 10.

4. Vincent McHugh, *New York Evening Post*, 29 September 1928, section 3, p. 9. The original drawings, now in the Djuna Barnes Papers at the University of Maryland, were not so minute. As they were reduced to about one-tenth of their size in reproduction and deprived of the bold color they possess, the unique tapestry effect they actually possess can only be imagined.

5. Review in *Newark Evening News Magazine*, 11 August 1928, p. 3x.

6. Ernest Sutherland Bates, "A Robust Tale," *Saturday Review*, 17 November 1928, p. 376.

7. Eugene Jolas, *transition*, June 1929, p. 326.

8. Review in the *Nation*, 5 December 1928, p. 639.

9. Review in the *New Republic*, 24 October 1928, p. 282.

10. *New Republic*, p. 282.

11. Review by Vincent McHugh in the *New York Evening Post*, 29 September, 1928, p. 9.

12. Jolas, p. 326.

13. Suzanne C. Ferguson. "Djuna Barnes's Short Stories," p. 32.

14. Barnes, "James Joyce," p. 65.

15. Barnes, "Lament for the Left Bank," p. 138.

16. Burton Rascoe, *A Bookman's Daybook*, edited with an introduction by C. Hartley Grattan (New York: Horace Liveright, 1929), p. 27.

17. Barnes, "James Joyce," p. 104.

18. Ibid., p. 65.

19. Hirschman, pp. 63–67.

20. Bates, "A Robust Tale," p. 376.

21. Barnes, "Lament for the Left Bank," p. 136.
22. Larry McMurtry, "A Piece of Fluff, a Fine Woman's Novel," *Washington Sunday Star*, 26 November 1972, sec. F. p. 2.


## CHAPTER 4

1. Neville Braybrooke, review of *Spillway* by Djuna Barnes, *Time & Tide*, 24 May 1962, p. 30.
2. Djuna Barnes, "The Letter That Was Never Mailed," p. 69.
3. Djuna Barnes, "The Perfect Murder," pp. 249–55.
4. In an interview for the Swedish press at the time of the stage presentation of *The Antiphon* in Stockholm, Miss Barnes freely admitted that she wrote "A Night Among the Horses" with *Miss Julie* in mind. See Sven Ahman, "Controversial Genius: Exclusive U.S. Authoress in World Premiere at Dramatic Theatre: 'I Wrote Because I Was to Die,'" The Djuna Barnes Papers.
5. Barney, *Aventures de l'esprit*, p. 230.
6. Djuna Barnes, *A Night Among the Horses*, p. 174.
7. Graham Greene, "Fiction Chronicle," p. 678.
8. Gertrude Stein, *How to Write* (Paris: Plain Edition, 1931), p. 23. But perhaps in confirmation of the following: "The difference between a short story and a paragraph. There is none."
9. Barnes, *Spillway*, p. 9.
10. Greene, "Fiction Chronicle," p. 678.
11. Hirschman, p. 57.
12. Barnes, "The Dear Dead Days," p. 42.
13. Ibid.
14. Ferguson, p. 34.
15. In the Charles Henri Ford Archive at the University of Texas Humanities Research Library, there is an unpublished manuscript of a story called "Behind the Heart," apparently written in the early 1930s and employing the same first person narrator.
16. Barnes, "The Models Have Come to Town," *Charm*, Nov. 1924, p. 86.
17. Stanley Edgar Hyman, "The Wash of the World," p. 58.
18. This technique imparts a nearly musical flow to the narrative, without which it might seem altogether too stark. Often in these stories, elements of musical composition or the very presence of music are important. Prior to Madame von Bartmann's speech, for instance, she plays a waltz of Schubert on the piano, ending in a Grand Opera manner. After speaking to Richter, she has her daughter play from Beethoven. Also to be noted are the references to music in "The Passion," as appear later in quotation.
19. Ferguson, p. 27.

20. Ibid., p. 41.

21. Robert McAlmon gives an account of the two girls, calling them "Toni" and "Sari," and particularly of the latter's affair with Radiguet. See *Being Geniuses Together*, pp. 81–85. Kay Boyle identifies "The Little Girl Continues" as a description of Radiguet's death in her revised edition, with supplementary chapters of *Being Geniuses Together* (Garden City, New York: Doubleday & Co., 1968), p. 126.

22. Barnes, "The Days of Jig Cook," p. 32.

23. Barnes, *Selected Works*, p. 53.

24. Ferguson, p. 32.

25. Ibid., p. 40.

26. Ibid., p. 39.

27. Ibid., p. 36.

28. In the first version, they speak at this point of Handel and go on to discuss chamber music versus the concert hall, perhaps a tongue-in-cheek reference to the scope and style Miss Barnes employs here.

29. In a letter to Solita Solano of 22 October 1961, Miss Barnes refers to a favorite quotation of hers which she says is taken from the Catholic writer, Josef Pieper: "A man who dared to walk straight up to fearfulness." The Djuna Barnes Papers.

*CHAPTER 5*

1. T.S. Eliot, Introduction to *Nightwood*, by Djuna Barnes, p. xiv.

2. Jacques Maritain, *Creative Intuition in Art and Poetry* (New York: Pantheon Books, Bollingen Series, vol. 35, no. 1, 1953), p. 329.

3. William Pratt, ed., *The Imagist Poem* (New York: E.P. Dutton, 1963), p. 18.

4. From the dust jacket advertisement written by Eliot for the 1936 British edition of *Nightwood*.

5. Eliot, Introduction to *Nightwood*, p. xii.

6. Joseph Frank, *The Widening Gyre*, pp. 31–32.

7. Spencer, p. 41.

8. Frank, p. 32.

9. Ibid., p. 49.

10. Walter Sutton, "Literary Image and the Reader," *Journal of Aesthetics* 16 (September 1957): 118.

11. Spencer, p. 42.

12. Kimon Friar and Malcolm Brinnin, eds., *Modern Poetry* (New York: Appleton-Century, Crofts, 1951).

13. Greene, p. 679.

14. Eliot, p. xii.

15. Hirschman, p. 119. According to Hirschman, the first chapter introduces the characters, and the following three follow their entanglements to a crucial point. The central "act" is the fifth chapter,

but "action is transposed to the dramatic discourse between Nora Flood and Dr. O'Connor." The next two chapters represent the fates of the principal characters except for Robin, and the final part serves as a dramatic epilogue. Hirschman's scheme begins by ignoring the fact that the central character, Robin Vote, does not appear until the second chapter, and further discrepancies should be apparent without further comment.

16. A. Desmond Hawkins, "Views and Reviews," *New English Weekly*, 29 April 1937, p. 51.

17. Hirschman, p. 77. Again, Hirschman's handling of the time factor is unconvincing. Miss Barnes's depiction of the Paris of the 1930s expatriates is concrete enough to maintain a sense of temporal specificity for as long as is necessary to the drama of character involved.

18. Wallace Fowlie, *Love in Literature*, p. 139.

19. Fowlie, p. 143.

20. Hirschman, p. 121.

21. Ibid., p. 124.

22. Clifton Fadiman, review of *Nightwood*, by Djuna Barnes, *New Yorker*, 13 March 1937, p. 103.

23. Only a few pages later, Felix's monocle is described as "a round blind eye in the sun" (*N*, p.8).

24. A suite of ten lithographs by Chirico accompanying a poem by Jean Cocteau, *Mythologie* (Paris: 4 Chemins, 1934), less monumental than his paintings, comes to mind in particular. In them, businessmen shed their suits to cavort in public baths with garlanded figures out of Roman mythology, centaurs, sea monsters, etc. The effect is what Wolfgang Kayser, in *The Grotesque in Art and Literature*, trans. Ulrich Weisstein (New York: McGraw-Hill, 1966), refers to in discussing Chirico's juxtaposition of the ancient and modern, blending the historically incompatible, in order to challenge modern man's claim to his heritage (p. 170). Kayser's evocation of a series of paintings by Max Ernst bears striking similarity to Robin's first appearance and its thematic and imagistic content: "Growing profusely and enormously, plants shoot up and produce blossoms which end in animal faces. For their part, the animals which are creeping about are of a plant-like nature. Even the human and demonic creatures mingle with this profuse vegitation of malignant jungle" (p.172). The work of Magritte comes to mind apart from Kayser, for it has in common with Djuna Barnes the capacity to translate commonplace detail into metaphorical surprise, as in one painting where a vase of flowers on a table is cut out in silhouette to reveal a full, unspoiled landscape.

25. Sypher, p. 27.

26. Ibid., p. 26.

27. Ibid., p. 47.

28. Ibid., p. 52.

29. Scarborough, p. 5B.

30. Ulrich Weisstein, "Beast, Doll, and Woman: Djuna Barnes' Human Bestiary," *Renascence* 15 (1962): 4.

31. Eliot, p. xvi.

32. Janet Flanner [Genet], "Letter From London," *New Yorker*, 20 February 1937, p. 36.

33. Olivia Manning, review of *Spillway*, by Djuna Barnes, *Spectator*, 25 May 1962, p. 690.

34. Theodore Purdy, Jr., review of *Nightwood* by Djuna Barnes, *Saturday Review*, 27 March 1937, p. 11.

35. Hilton Kramer, p. 38.

36. Ibid., p. 39.

37. Friedman, p. 262.

38. Ibid., p. 261.

39. Kramer, p. 39.

40. There are strong resemblance to *Nightwood* in one German romantic work in particular, the pseudonymous *Night Watches of Bonaventura* of 1804, attributed sometimes to Jean Paul, sometimes to Friedrich Schelling. See Gerald Gillespie's introduction to his edition of *Die Nachtwachen des Bonaventura* (Austin: University of Texas Press, 1971), pp. 1–26.

As Wolfgang Kayser indicates, Bonaventura was the first to employ the sequential, spatial, mosaic novel for the grotesque (Kayser, p. 72). Divided into sixteen fragments called "Night Watches," it is a loose, grotesquely satanic novel, moving from satire to despair and tragedy (Gillespie, p. 2), and conceiving the world as a madhouse. Like O'Connor, its narrator, a multitudinous spirit in the flesh, would defy the misery of fate with laughter. One of his concerns is with the distinction between poetic night and prosaic day, and he ultimately affirms the triumph of darkness, hate, and madness (Gillespie, p. 15). And the final note of the book, not unlike O'Connor's final exclamation, is nothingness: "And the echo in the channel-house cries for the last time NOTHING!" (Gerald Gillespie, ed. *Die Nachtwachen des Bonaventura*, p. 247).

Although it could be related to *Nightwood* in other particulars, its influence upon Miss Barnes is at this point a matter of conjecture. Finally, it is noteworthy that in Bonaventura's novel, "Events are often related through projection into other art forms, such as woodcuts, paintings, sculpture, or drama" (Gillespie, p. 6).

41. Frederick J. Hoffman, Charles Allen, and Carolyn Ulrich, *The Little Magazine: A History and A Bibliography*, 2nd ed. (Princeton, New Jersey: Princeton University Press, 1947), p. 177.

42. Eugene Jolas, *The Language of Night* (The Hague [Holland]: Servire Press, 1932), p. 47.

43. Hoffman, p. 178.

44. In biographical notes among The Djuna Barnes Papers, Miss Barnes mentions having gone to Freiburg-im-Bresgau to do a story on twilight sleep, and one might wonder if it had been intended for publication in *transition*.

45. Lawrence Durrell includes Miss Barnes with Virgina Woolf and Anaïs Nin in this tradition in a dust jacket note for Anna Kavan, *Julia and the Bazooka* (London: Peter Owen, 1970).

46. Natalie Clifford Barney, *The One Who Is Legion or A.D.'s After-Life* (London: Eric Partridge, 1930), pp. 154–60.

47. Possibly related to Dan Mahoney is an as yet unpublished typescript of a group of poems called "The Book of Dan or Laughing Lamentations." See the Djuna Barnes Papers.

48. John Glassco, *Memoirs of Montparnasse* (New York: Oxford University Press, 1970), pp 24–25.

49. Daniel Halpern, "Interview With Edouard Roditi," *Antaeus* 2 (Spring 1971): 106.

50. Djuna Barnes, "And After Death—Two," *Trend*, February 1915, p. 529.

51. Eliot, p. xiii.

52. Alan Williamson, "The Divided Image: The Quest for Identity in the Works of Djuna Barnes," *Critique: Studies in Modern Fiction*, 7 (1964), p. 72.

53. In a letter to a translator of *Nightwood*, Miss Barnes states that she had had the Black Forest in mind. The Djuna Barnes papers.

54. Kenneth Burke, "Version, Con-, Per-, and In-," p. 335. For a more extensive treatment of terministic inversions and other verbal patterns in *Nightwood*, see Paula Kellner Nelson, "The Function of Figures of Speech in Selected Anti-Realistic Novels" (Ph. D. dissertation, New York University, 1972).

55. Burke, p. 336.

56. Frank, p. 43.

57. Frank, p. 32.

58. Quoted in Burke, p. 333. See Dell Hymes, "Journey to the End of Night," *Folio* 18 (February 1953): 43–62.
This would complement A. Desmond Hawkins's designation of O'Connor as the "omniscient passive."

59. Frank, p. 33.

60. Ibid., p. 34.

61. Burke, p. 346.

62. Frank, p. 37.

63. Frank, p. 38.

64. Fowlie, p. 142.

65. Williamson, p. 70.

66. Ibid., p. 62.

67. Ibid., p. 63.

68. Hirschman, pp. 92–93.
69. Burke, pp. 333–35.
70. Another, to judge by one of several typescript versions of the novel in the Djuna Barnes Papers, seems to have been *Anatomy of Night*.
71. Burke, p. 340.

Burke errs here, for the doctor is speaking, not Nora. The analysis seems to go even beyond error at a point where the critic attempts syllabic correlations between the author's name and the names of characters.

72. Ibid., p. 337.
73. Burke, p. 338.
74. Burke, p. 339.
75. Coburn Britton in *A Festschrift for Djuna Barnes on Her 80th Birthday*, n.p.

## CHAPTER 6

1. In a letter to Charles Henri Ford of 4 August 1936, Djuna Barnes states that she has begun to write a verse drama. Also, a letter of 2 July 1936 mentions her visit to an ancestral home in England which had been a fourteenth-century monastery. The Charles Henri Ford Papers, Humanities Research Center, University of Texas.
2. From a sheet of autobiographical notes. The Djuna Barnes Papers.
3. The Djuna Barnes Papers.
4. Warren Wilmer Brown, review of *A Book* by Djuna Barnes, *Baltimore News*, 22 October 1923, Section 2, p. 32.
5. Kenneth Macgowan, "The New Plays," *New York Globe*, 3 November 1919, p. 14.
6. Burns Mantle, review of *Three From the Earth* by Djuna Barnes, *New York Evening Mail*, 5 November, 1919, p. 15.
7. This play, according to one account of its production, "dealt with a fisherman's son who fished up a mermaid who was yellow-haired, naked, and loved him. Norma Millay, in a tennis net and long Godiva hair, played the mermaid who eventually was revealed as a sportive barmaid . . . ." See Helen Deutsch and Stella Hannau, *The Provincetown: A Story of the Theatre* (New York: Farrar & Rinehart, 1931), p. 53.
8. Heywood Broun, review of *An Irish Triangle* by Djuna Barnes, *New York Tribune*, 15 January 1920, p. 12.
9. Barnes, *An Irish Triangle*, p. 5.
10. Ibid., p. 3.
11. Barnes [Lydia Steptoe], *Little Drops of Rain*, p. 50.
12. Barnes, *Water-Ice*, *Vanity Fair*, July 1923, p. 59.

13. Barnes, *Two Ladies Take Tea*, p. 70.

14. Barnes [Lydia Steptoe], *The Beauty, Shadowland,* October 1923, p. 74.

15. Barnes, *Five Thousand Miles, Vanity Fair,* March 1923, p. 50.

16. Marie Ponsot, "Careful Sorrow and Observed Compline," p. 47.

17. Barnes, *A Passion Play,* pp. 5–17.

18. Janet Flanner, *Paris Was Yesterday: 1925–1939,* ed. Irving Drutman (New York: Viking Press, 1972), pp. xvii–xviii.

19. Barnes *The Antiphon* (1958), p. 8.

20. John Wain, review of *The Antiphon* by Djuna Barnes, *Observer,* 2 February 1958. The Djuna Barnes Papers.

21. Barnes, "Hamlet's Custard Pie," p. 34.

22. Nemerov, p. 90.

23. Barnes, *The Antiphon* in *Selected Works,* p. 79.

24. In a four-page summary of the action of *The Antiphon,* evidently prepared for the assistance of translators of the work, Miss Barnes makes it clear that the ambiguity here is intentional. See "Notes Toward a Definition of *The Antiphon*" in the Djuna Barnes Papers.

25. Barnes, *The Antiphon* (1958), p. 13.

26. Ibid., p. 24.

27. Ibid., p. 95.

28. In view of frequent misreadings of this scene, Miss Barnes is particularly emphatic on this point in her "Notes Toward a Definition of *The Antiphon.*" Stanley Edgar Hyman, for example, erroneously states that the father himself raped Miranda. See Hyman, p. 60.

29. Barnes, "Notes Toward a Definition of *The Antiphon,*" p. 1.

30. Paola Milano, ed., *The Portable Dante* (New York: Viking Press, 1947), p. 352.

31. Nemerov, p. 90.

32. There is a note of martyrdom in the request which is unmistakable. But Miss Barnes may also have in mind the primitive belief that the souls of the dead animate trees, or that a tree planted upon a grave will revive the spirit and protect the body from corruption. See chapter 9 of Sir James George Frazer, *The Golden Bough: A Study in Magic and Religion,* 1-vol., abridged ed. (New York: Macmillan, 1958), pp. 132–33.

33. Kathleen Raine, "Lutes and Lobsters," *New Statesman,* 8 February 1958, p. 174.

34. Aristotle, *On Poetry and Style,* trans. with an introduction by G. M. A. Grube (New York: Liberal Arts Press, 1958), p. 31.

35. Nemerov, p. 89.

36. Barnes, *The Antiphon* (1958), p. 95.

37. "A Daughter for Inquisitor," review of *The Antiphon* by Djuna

Barnes, *Times Literary Supplement*, 4 April 1958, p. 182.

38. Nils Beyer in *Stockholms Tidingen*, 18 February 1961. From a sheet of excerpts of reviews of the Swedish production of *The Antiphon*. The Djuna Barnes Papers.

39. Dr. Ivar Harrie in *Expressen*, 18 February 1961.

40. Raine, p. 175.

41. Donna Gerstenberger, "Three Verse Playwrights and the American Fifties," in *Modern America Drama: Essays in Criticism*, ed. William E. Taylor (De Land, Florida: Everett, Edwards, 1968), p. 122.

42. Lionel Abel, "Bad by North and South," *Partisan Review* 25 (Summer 1958): 462.

43. Ibid., p. 465.

44. Richard Eberhardt, "Outer and Inner Verse Drama," *Virginia Quarterly Review* 34 (1958): 620.

45. Rudd Fleming, review of *The Antiphon* by Djuna Barnes, *Washington Post and Times Herald*, 16 March 1958. The Djuna Barnes Papers.

46. Letter to Willa Muir, 20 August 1962. The Djuna Barnes Papers.

47. T.H. Dickinson, quoted in William Flint Thrall and Addison Hibbard, *A Handbook to Literature* (New York: Odyssey Press, 1960), p. 92.

48. Gerstenberger, p. 120.

49. T. S. Eliot, *The Family Reunion* (New York: Harcourt, Brace & World, Harvest Books, 1967). p. 93.

50. Ibid., p. 18.

51. Ponsot, p. 48.

52. Ibid., p. 47.

53. Abel, p. 465.

54. Barnes, *The Antiphon* (1958), p. 114.

55. Ibid., p. 62.

56. James Joyce, "James Clarence Mangan," *Critical Writings*, ed. Ellsworth Mason and Richard Ellmann (New York, The Viking Press, 1959), p. 185.

*POSTSCRIPT*

1. Barnes, *Spillway*, p. 32. In *Selected Works of Djuna Barnes*, "a fragment of language" is changed to "part of a language." The alteration, of course, does not greatly alter the sense of the passage as a whole.

2. Barnes, "Transfiguration," *London Bulletin*, First Series, no. 3 (June 1938): 2.

3. Barnes, "Fall-out Over Heaven," p. 27.

4. Barnes, "Galerie Religieuse," p. 266.

5. Barnes, "The Walking-Mort," p. 34.

6. John Milton, "Sonnet 16," in *Seventeenth-Century Prose and Poetry*, 2nd ed., ed. Alexander M. Witherspoon and Frank J. Warnke (New York: Harcourt, Brace & World, 1963), p. 897.

7. Barnes, *Ladies Almanack*, p. 88. Mentioned in postscript, "About the Author."

8. Barnes, "Quarry," p. 53.

9. Barnes, *The Antiphon* (1958), p. 113.

10. Quoted by Miss Barnes in a letter to Wolfgang Hildesheimer of 10 April 1968. The Djuna Barnes Papers.

# Bibliography

The following bibliography is selective. It should be supplemented by Douglas Messerli's *Djuna Barnes: A Bibliography*. The reader is also referred to the Djuna Barnes Papers at the McKeldin Library at The University of Maryland at College Park, Maryland.

An asterisk precedes items accompanied by illustrations by Djuna Barnes.

## ABBREVIATIONS

| | |
|---|---|
| *The Antiphon* (1962 version in *Selected Works of Djuna Barnes*) | *A* |
| *A Book* | *AB* |
| *The Book of Repulsive Women* | *BRW* |
| *Ladies Almanack* | *LA* |
| *Nightwood* | *N* |
| *A Night Among the Horses* | *NAH* |
| *Ryder* | *R* |
| *Spillway* | *S* |

## I. WORKS OF DJUNA BARNES

### Books

*The Antiphon*. New York: Farrar, Straus & Cudahy, 1958.
*\*A Book*. New York: Boni & Liveright, 1923.
\*"The Book of Repulsive Women: 8 Rhythms and 5 Drawings." *Bruno Chap Books* 2, no. 6 (November 1915): 89–111.
*\*The Book of Repulsive Women: 8 Rhythms and 5 Drawings*. The Outcast Chapbooks, no. 14. Yonkers, New York: Alicat Bookshop Press, 1948.
\*[A Lady of Fashion] *Ladies Almanack*. Paris: the Author, 1928.

184

*[A Lady of Fashion] *Ladies Almanack*. New York: Harper & Row, 1972.
*A Night Among the Horses*. New York: Horace Liveright, 1929.
*Nightwood*. London: Faber & Faber, 1936.
*Nightwood*. Introduction by T. S. Eliot. New York: Harcourt, Brace & Co., 1937
*Nightwood*. Introduction by T. S. Eliot. New York: New Directions, New Directions Paperbooks, 1961.
*Ryder*. New York: Horace Liveright, 1928.
*Selected Works of Djuna Barnes*: *Spillway, The Antiphon, Nightwood*. New York: Farrar, Straus & Cudahy, 1962.
*Spillway*. London: Faber & Faber, 1962.

### One-Act Plays

*An Irish Triangle. Playboy*, May 1921, pp. 3–5.
[Steptoe, Lydia] *Little Drops of Rain. Vanity Fair*, September 1922, p. 50.
*A Passion Play. Others: A Play Number*. Edited by William Saphier. February 1918, pp. 5–17.
*She Tells Her Daughter. Smart Set*, November 1923, pp. 77–80.
*Two Ladies Take Tea. Shadowland*, April 1923, p. 17.

### Poems

"Fall-out Over Heaven." In *T. S. Eliot: A Symposium for His Seventieth Birthday*. Edited by Neville Braybrooke. New York: Farrar, Straus & Cudahy, 1958.
"Galerie Religieuse." In *The Wind and the Rain: An Easter Book for 1962*. Edited by Neville Braybrooke. London: Secker & Warburg, 1962.
"The Lament of Women: Ah, My God!" *Little Review* 5, no. 8 (December 1918): 37.
"Quarry." *New Yorker*, 27 December 1969, p. 53.
"To the Dead Favourite of Liu Ch'e." *Dial* 68, no. 4 (April 1920): 444.
"Transfiguration." *London Bulletin*, First Series, no. 3 (June 1938): 2.
"Vaudeville." *Vanity Fair*, May 1923, p. 67.
"The Walking-Mort." *New Yorker*, 15 May 1971, p. 34.
"The Yellow Jar." *Munsey's Magazine* 58, no. 4 (September 1916): 605.

### Short Stories, Literary Essays and Sketches, etc.

[Steptoe, Lydia] "The Diary of a Dangerous Child." *Vanity Fair*, July 1922, p. 56.
"A Duel Without Seconds." *Vanity Fair*, November 1929, p. 84.
"Dusie." In *Americana Esoterica*. Edited by Carl Van Doren. New York: Macy-Masius Publishers, 1927.

"James Joyce." *Vanity Fair*, April 1922, p. 65.
"Lament for the Left Bank." *Town and Country*, December 1941, pp. 92, 136–138, 148.
"The Letter That Was Never Mailed." *Vanity Fair*, December 1929, pp. 68–69.
"The Perfect Murder." In *Harvard Advocate Centennial Anthology*. Edited by Jonathan D. Culler. Cambridge, Mass.: Schenkman Publishing Co., 1966, pp. 249–255.
"Renunciation." *Smart Set* 57, no. 2 (October 1918): 65–69.
"Vagaries Malicieux." *Double Dealer* 3, no. 17 (May 1922): 249–60. Or *Vagaries Malicieux: Two Stories by Djuna Barnes*. New York: Frank Hallman, 1974.
[Steptoe, Lydia] "What Is Good Form in Dying?" *Vanity Fair*, June 1923, p. 73.
*"The Woman Who Goes Abroad to Forget." *New Yorker*, 8 December 1928, p. 28–29.

**Newspaper and Magazine Articles**

"Arab-Morocco." *Hearst's International-Cosmopolitan*, July 1934, pp. 175–76.
"The Days of Jig Cook." *Theatre Guild Magazine*, January 1929, pp. 31–32.
*"The Dear Dead Days." *Theatre Guild Magazine*, February 1929, pp. 41–43.
*"Djuna Barnes Pays a Visit to the Favored Haunt of the I.W.W.'s." *New York Press*, 11 April 1915, Pt. 4, p. 7.
*"Djuna Barnes Probes the Souls of the Jungle Folk at the Hippodrome Circus." *New York Press*, 14 February 1915, Pt. 4, p. 2.
*"Futuristic Impressions of the Picadilly Chorus Girls in 'To-Night's the Night.' " *New York Press*, 31 January 1915, Pt. 4, p. 2.
*[Steptoe, Lydia] "Hamlet's Custard Pie." *Theatre Guild Magazine*, July 1930, pp. 34–35.
*" 'I'm Plain Mary Jones of U.S.A.' Insists 'Mother' Jones." *New York Press*, 7 February 1915, Pt. 7, p. 2.
"Lou-Tellegen on Morals and Things." *New York Press*, 16 May 1915, Pt. 4, p. 5.
"May Vokes in an Unguarded Hour." *New York Press*, 23 May 1915, p. 19.
"The Models Have Come to Town." *Charm*, November 1924, p. 16.
*"Playgoer's Almanack." *Theatre Guild Magazine*, July 1930. pp. 26–27.
*"Playgoer's Almanack." *Theatre Guild Magazine*, January 1931, pp. 34–35.
"Profiles: Lady of Fourteenth Street." *New Yorker*, 6 April 1929, pp. 29–32.

"The Stage Sets the Style." *Theatre Guild Magazine*, October 1930, pp. 38-39.
*"The Wanton Playgoer." *Theatre Guild Magazine*, June 1931, pp. 36–37.
*"The Wanton Playgoer." *Theatre Guild Magazine*, September 1931, pp. 20–21.
*"Why Actors?" *Theatre Guild Magazine*, December 1929, pp. 42–43.

## II. WORKS ABOUT DJUNA BARNES

### Bibliography

Messerli, Douglas. *Djuna Barnes: A Bibliography*. New York: David Lewis, 1975.

### Books

Anderson, Margaret. *My Thirty Years' War: The Autobiography, Beginnings and Battles to 1930*. New York: Horizon Press, 1969.
Barney, Natalie Clifford. *Aventures de l'esprit*. Paris: Editions Emile-Paul Frères, 1929.
*A Festschrift for Djuna Barnes on Her 80th Birthday*. Edited by Alex Gildzen. Kent, Ohio: Kent State University Libraries, 1972.
Fowlie, Wallace. *Love in Literature: Studies in Symbolic Expression*. Bloomington: Indiana University Press, Midland Books, 1965.
Frank, Joseph. *The Widening Gyre: Crisis and Mastery in Modern Literature*. New Brunswick, New Jersey: Rutgers University Press, 1963.
Gerstenberger, Donna. "Three Verse Playwrights and the American Fifties." In *Modern American Drama: Essays in Criticism*. Edited by William E. Taylor. De Land, Florida: Everett, Edwards, 1968, pp. 117–28.
Guggenheim, Peggy. *Out of This Century*. New York: Dial Press, 1946.
Hirschman, Jack A. "The Orchestrated Novel: A Study of Poetic Devices in the Novels of Djuna Barnes and Herman Broch and the Influences of the Works of James Joyce upon Them." Ph.D. dissertation, Indiana University, 1962.
Hyman, Stanley Edgar. "The Wash of the World." In *Standards: A Chronicle of Books for Our Time*. New York: Horizon Press, 1966.
McAlmon, Robert. *Being Geniuses Together: An Autobiography*. London: Secker & Warburg, 1938.
Nin, Anaïs. *The Novel of the Future*. New York: Collier Books, 1970.
Scott, James B. *Djuna Barnes*. Boston: Twayne Publishers, 1976.

188    The Art of Djuna Barnes

Spencer, Sharon. *Space, Time and Structure in the Modern Novel*. New York: New York University Press, 1971.

## Periodicals

Abel, Lionel. "Bad by North and South." *Partisan Review* 25 (Summer 1958): 461–66.
[Anonymous] "A Daughter for Inquisitor." *Times Literary Supplement*, 4 April 1958, p. 182.
Burke, Kenneth. "Version, Con-, Per-, and In-: Thoughts on Djuna Barnes' Novel, *Nightwood*." *Southern Review* 2 (1966–67): 329–46.
Eberhardt, Richard. "Outer and Inner Verse Drama." *Virginia Quarterly Review*, 34 (1958): 618–23.
Ferguson, Suzanne C. "Djuna Barnes's Short Stories: An Estrangement of the Heart." *Southern Review* 5, no. 1 (January 1969): 26–41.
Greene, Graham. "Fiction Chronicle." [The Catholic] *Tablet*, 14 November 1936, pp. 678–79.
Hawkes, John. "Notes on the Wild Goose Chase." *Massachusetts Review* 3, no. 4 (Summer 1962): 784–88.
Nemerov, Howard. "A Response to *The Antiphon*." *Northwest Review*, Summer 1958, pp. 88–91.
Ponsot, Marie. "Careful Sorrow and Observed Compline." *Poetry*, October 1959, pp. 47–50.
Raine, Kathleen. "Lutes and Lobsters." *New Statesman*, 8 February 1958, pp. 174–75.
Shattuck, Roger. " 'Nightwood' Resurrected." *Village Voice*, 24 May 1962, p. 10.
Sutton, Walter. "Literary Image and the Reader." *Journal of Aesthetics* 16 (September 1957): 112–23.
Weisstein, Ulrich. "Beast, Doll, and Woman: Djuna Barnes' Human Bestiary." *Renascence* 15 (1962): 3–11.
Williamson, Alan. "The Divided Image: The Quest for Identity in the Works of Djuna Barnes." *Critique: Studies in Modern Fiction* 7 (Spring 1964): 58–74.

# Index

189

*80th Birthday, A*, 127, 170n
Fielding, Henry, 37, 39
*Finnegans Wake*, (Joyce), 128
Fitzgerald, F. Scott, 8
Flanner, Janet, 104-05, 141
Ford, Charles Henri, 180n
Ford, Ford Madox, 58
Fowlie, Wallace, xii, 97, 116, 119
Frank, Joseph, xi, xii, 91, 94, 95, 116, 117, 119, 123
Frazer, Sir James George, 181n
Friar, Kimon, 96
Friedman, Melvin, x–xi, 105
Frost, Robert, 2
"Function of Figures of Speech in Selected Anti-Realistic Novels, The" (Nelson), 179n

Gaddis, William, 126
Gerstenberger, Donna, 153
Gierow, Karl Ragnar, 152
Gillespie, Gerald, 178
*Girl From the Reeperbahn, The*, 15
Glassco, John, 110
*Golden Bough: A Study in 'Magic and Religion* (Frazer), 181n
Gorelik, Mordecai, 12
Greene, Graham, 64, 96, 104
Griffith, D.W., 4
*Grotesque in Art and Literature, The* (Kayser), 177n
Gustafson, Alex, 174n
Gustafson, Zadel (Barnes) Budington, 27, 173–174n

Hall, Radcliffe, 50
Hammarskjold, Dag, 152
"Harlot's House, The" (Wilde), 20
Harrie, Ivar, 152
Harris, Frank, 20, 24
Hartley, Marsden, 2
*Harvard Advocate*, 60
Hawkes, John, xi
Hawkins, A. Desmond, 96, 179n
*Heart of Darkness* (Conrad), 68
Herbert, George, 104
Hirschman, Jack, 3, 7, 23, 48–49, 66,

96, 97–98, 123, 176–77n
Hoffman, Frederick J., 19
Hyman, Stanley Edgar, 181n
Hymes, Dell, 116

*In Parenthesis* (Jones), 159
*Intruder in the Dust* (Faulkner), 17

Jimmie the Barman. *See* Charters, James
Jolas Eugene, x, 39, 41, 107–108
Jones, David, 159
Joyce, James, x, 2, 7, 39, 47–49, 56, 57, 105, 106, 107, 126, 128, 159
*Julia and the Bazooka* (Kavan), 179n
Jung, Carl, x, 107
*Justine* (Durrell), 170n

Kavan, Anna, 179n
Kayser, Wolfgang, 177n, 178n
Kramer, Hilton, ix, 105–106

Lamb, Mary, 39
"Language of Night, The" (Jolas), 107–108
Lautréamont. *See* Ducasse, Isidore
Le Galliene, Eva, 12
*Lie Down in Darkness* (Styron), xi
*Little Review*, xi, 17, 47, 58
*London Bulletin*, 162
*Long Day's Dying, A* (Buechner), xi
Lou-Tellegen, 4
"Love Song of J. Alfred Prufrock" (Eliot), 95
Lowry, Malcolm, xi, 126, 170n
Loy, Mina, 2
Lyly, John, 37, 39

McAlmon, Robert, 50, 110, 176n
*McCall's, 3, 4*
McMurtry, Larry, 52
*Madame Bovary*, 64
Margritte, René, 100, 107, 177n
Mahoney, Dan, 110–111, 179n
Mallarmé, Stéphane, 105, 107
Maritain, Jacques, 89
Marprelate, Martin, 39